THE
Southern Living®
COMPLETE
Do•Ahead
COOKBOOK

THE
Southern Living®
COMPLETE
Do•Ahead
COOKBOOK

Oxmoor House®

Copyright 1991 by Oxmoor House, Inc.
Book Division of Southern Progress Corporation
P.O. Box 2463, Birmingham, Alabama 35201

Library of Congress Catalog Number: 91-60996
Hardcover ISBN: 0-8487-1056-8
Softcover ISBN: 0-8487-1165-3

Manufactured in the United States of America
Fourth Printing 1993

Executive Editor: Ann H. Harvey
Director of Manufacturing: Jerry R. Higdon
Art Director: Bob Nance

The Southern Living® Complete Do-Ahead Cookbook
from *Today's Gourmet* series

Senior Foods Editor: Margaret Chason Agnew
Editor: Lisa A. Hooper
Copy Chief: Mary Ann Laurens
Editorial Assistant: Carole Cain
Director, Test Kitchen: Vanessa Taylor Johnson
Assistant Director, Test Kitchen: Gayle Hays Sadler
Test Kitchen Home Economists: Caroline Alford, R.D., Telia Johnson,
    Angie C. Neskaug, Christina A. Pieroni, Kathleen Royal, Jan A. Smith
Senior Photographer: Jim Bathie
Photographer: Ralph Anderson
Senior Photo Stylist: Kay E. Clarke
Photo Stylist: Virginia R. Cravens
Designer: Barbara Ball
Production Manager: Rick Litton
Associate Production Manager: Theresa L. Beste
Production Assistant: Pam Beasley Bullock

Concept/Text by Nao Hauser
Recipe Development by Nao Hauser (pages 20-29, 60-87); OTT
    Communications, Inc.
Cover photograph by Ralph Anderson

Cover: *Elegant Raspberry Tart (page 158).*
Back cover: *Overnight French Toast (page 35), Shrimp and Vegetable Kabobs
    (page 121), Quick Spaghetti Sauce (page 29), and Lemon-Orange
    Tarts (page 156).*
Page 2: *Chicken and Sausage Stew and Cottage Cheese-Dill Bread (page 185).*

To subscribe to *Southern Living* magazine, write to *Southern Living*®, P.O. Box 830119, Birmingham, AL 35283.

Contents

Cooking Ahead

*C*ooking ahead is neither a technique nor a style of preparation, but a way of life. It frees you to cook the dishes you want to when time is available.

The keys to cooking ahead are knowing which foods keep well, how long they will keep, and how to store and serve them. You'll find this critical information in over 300 recipes and 27 menus in *The Southern Living Complete Do-Ahead Cookbook*. Following these recipes and menus will bring many rewards. You will have a hearty main dish on hand when your family is hungry, a cake in the freezer when company drops by, a surprise to pack in your child's lunchbox, enough hors d'oeuvres to feed the small army of guests you invited to a party—foods that ensure good meals and good times. And depending on your schedule, many of the recipes offer refrigerating instructions and freezing instructions. Just choose the storage method that best suits your preparation schedule.

Cooking ahead is as old-fashioned as freezing your family's favorite casserole or simmering enough soup to last two or three days. And it's as up-to-date as the latest kitchen gadget that will help you whiz through preparing a second batch of your favorite recipe. Cooking ahead has always promised the economy and good nutrition of saving what's abundant for another day, and for today's household, the savings may be multiplied by having good food at home instead of dining out.

There's nothing very technical in this book—no laborious canning instructions or split-second microwave timing. There is just enough flexibility in choosing the time you will cook to make preparing and sharing wonderful food an enjoyable part of your busy life.

Come home from work and take made-ahead Spaghetti and Meatballs and Italian Vegetable Salad from the refrigerator for a family treat. Menu begins on page 176.

Finding the Time _____

Freezing and refrigeration have expanded the possibilities of make-ahead cooking to include at least part of almost any recipe. What you will find in *The Southern Living Complete Do-Ahead Cookbook* are those foods that can be refrigerated, frozen, or kept at room temperature for periods of time ranging from overnight to 1 year without loss of flavor or texture, and with minimal reduction of nutrients. This means that you don't have to find time to cook just before mealtime. If a recipe indicates that a dish can be frozen up to one month, then you can prepare it anytime up to one month before serving.

But finding time to clean and cook vegetables for a soup or to measure and mix the ingredients for a cake can be difficult for many cooks. To resolve this problem, you can break down procedures into smaller time spans. You can clean the vegetables one day, and cook the soup the next. You can measure ingredients for a cake several days before baking the cake as long as you refrigerate the perishables and store the dry ingredients in airtight containers.

Cooking time does not have to be continuous. If you are making a spaghetti sauce, you can start the sauce, cook it for an hour, cool it slightly, and refrigerate it in a tightly covered container. Later that day or the next, reheat the sauce to simmering and complete the cooking. This holds true for any simmered food, such as a soup or stew, that requires more than an hour on the stove. Just be sure that any meat or poultry in the dish is cooked thoroughly before you remove the pot from the heat—there shouldn't be any pinkness.

If you're chopping onions, green pepper, or parsley, you can just as easily chop enough for two recipes; divide the chopped vegetables, and refrigerate or freeze part of them for use in another dish. (Chopped onion should be used within a month.)

Doubling a recipe can be the most straightforward time-saver. In many recipes you can double the ingredients and divide them into two batches. If you decide to put twice the amount of food into one pot, as with a soup or stew, you'll need a pot large enough so that foods will brown quickly and liquids can simmer without boiling over. The larger quantity of food will probably take longer to cook, so you will have to rely on signs of doneness rather than timing.

While the food processor is out, chop an extra batch of peppers and onions to keep on hand in the freezer.

Chopped Green
Pepper
August 12

Helpful Equipment

Be prepared to cook ahead by planning your shopping ahead. Failing to do this may result in your "found" time being spent in the supermarket instead of in the kitchen.

A separate chest-type or upright freezer may encourage make-ahead cooking, but the freezer attached to your refrigerator can hold many meals. Temperature, however, is critical. Maximum storage times, according to the Freezer Guide on page 230, are for foods kept at 0°F or lower. If the temperature in your freezer is 10°F, count on only half the storage time. A separate freezer will generally stay colder because it is opened less frequently than one attached to a refrigerator. In either, a freezer thermometer will let you know whether prolonged storage is feasible in your freezer.

Some more puzzling questions most cooks face are what's in the freezer and how long has it been there. The value of the freezer is limited if the food in it has not been labeled and dated. And the value of even a small refrigerator/freezer will be greatly enhanced if you keep a list of its contents and the date the foods were placed in the freezer. For maximum convenience, include a list of any ingredients that are needed to complete, garnish, or accompany each prepared dish so that you can have these items on hand before you defrost the frozen item. If the recipe is in this cookbook, include the page number on the label so that you can quickly turn to the instructions for reheating and serving.

The microwave oven, when used in conjunction with the freezer, is often mentioned as a cook's greatest convenience. You can freeze a whole dish or single portions and defrost and reheat the food in minutes in the microwave oven. Cookware designed to go from freezer to microwave to table minimizes clean-up time. The microwave oven makes it possible to defrost and reheat meals when needed. And it gives you greater cook-ahead flexibility for defrosting and heating ingredients kept in the freezer.

Be sure to note on the label the number of servings as well as any ingredients that need to be added to the frozen item once it is thawed.

Entire meals frozen in labeled individual microwave-safe trays make it easy for family members to help themselves to dinner.

A blender, automatic rice cooker, food processor, salad spinner, mini-chopper, or ice cream freezer can add convenience to daily kitchen routines.

Any appliance that offers a shortcut will make cooking ahead more convenient. Some equipment you may want to consider:

Food Processor   The larger food processors make it possible to process a double batch of ingredients without emptying the processor bowl. It can be especially useful for making large batches of chopped meat mixtures and bread dough. Whatever size food processor you may have, an extra processor bowl or two can make the work go much faster. You can switch bowls instead of emptying and cleaning the bowl between steps, or you can prepare ingredients for more than one recipe at a time.

Mini-Chopper   A pint-size chopper makes quick work of mincing a single clove of garlic or a few fresh herbs. It also provides you with a second chopping tool so that you can be preparing one ingredient in the food processor and another in the mini-chopper. And most mini-choppers are easier to clean.

Salad Spinner   Washing lettuce and parsley when you bring them home from the store or whenever you have a spare moment is an uncomplicated do-ahead task. Wrap the freshly washed and dried greens in paper towels and place in a zip-top plastic bag. They will keep in the vegetable bin of the refrigerator about a week.

Electric or Hand-Turned Ice Cream Freezer   This piece of equipment isn't essential, of course. But homemade ice cream, sorbet, and frozen yogurt keep well, and they can turn ripe seasonal fruits into a make-ahead bounty.

Automatic Cookers   Some cooks swear by slow cookers, especially for stews and pot roasts, because you can prepare food in the morning and come home to a cooked main dish at night. Cherished in Oriental kitchens, automatic rice cookers not only cook rice perfectly every time but also halt the cooking and keep the rice warm, making the timing flexible. In addition, they make it possible to cook large quantities of rice at one time so that you will have some left over for use in another recipe.

Storing Prepared Foods

Each recipe in this book has specific instructions for proper storage. The key to keeping foods fresh is to seal out air, so use containers with tight-fitting lids and heavy-duty zip-top plastic bags, plastic wrap, or aluminum foil.

Foods to be frozen, except baked goods that must cool to room temperature, should be refrigerated first, so that they are cooler when you put them in the freezer. Foods will freeze faster if they start out at a lower temperature, and the faster the food freezes, the fresher it will taste when reheated and served. Food also freezes faster in smaller quantities, but the smaller amounts leave more surface area exposed to the slow oxidation that causes frozen food to deteriorate. So consider your own convenience; you'll probably want to freeze some items in individual portions and others in family-size amounts. Do not refreeze cooked dishes that have been frozen and reheated once before; flavor and nutrients will suffer, and there is increased danger of bacterial growth.

Glass or rigid plastic containers with tight-fitting lids are perfect for freezing casseroles, soups, and baked items.

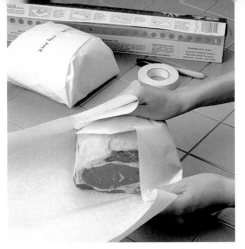

For the butcher wrap, place food diagonally in one corner of freezer wrap. Fold the corner over the food. Then fold sides in tightly, and roll up. Seal and label the package.

For the drugstore wrap, place food in center of freezer wrap. Bring the short ends together and fold down. Then fold sides to form points; press points under package. Seal and label the package.

Wrap all foods to minimize exposure to air and moisture. Do not use ordinary plastic wrap and aluminum foil, thin plastic bags, and dairy cartons in the freezer. Safeguard your investment of time and money by storing foods in containers and wrappings designed for the freezer. These will be labeled as such when you buy them. They fall into three general categories:

Rigid Containers   These may be plastic, plastic-coated cardboard, or glass. They are excellent for liquids and may be used for all but irregularly shaped foods, such as a whole chicken or a roll of cookie dough. Their own lids, used with freezer tape, if directed, provide an adequate seal. Choose a container not much larger than the food it will hold, but do leave about one inch of space between the level of the food and the top of the container, because liquids and the moisture in solid foods will expand as they freeze. Choose microwave-safe containers for convenient microwave defrosting and reheating.

Freezer Wraps   Use heavy-duty aluminum foil and plastic-coated freezer paper for wrapping odd-shaped items. Some plastic wraps are sturdy enough for freezer use; check the label to be sure. You'll need freezer tape to secure wrappings; ordinary tape will loosen in the freezer. If you are stacking several items in one package, such as meat patties, chops, or cutlets, separate them with double layers of wax paper, plastic wrap, or freezer paper. To wrap food effectively, use either the butcher wrap, or the drugstore wrap method for wrapping food with freezer paper.

Freezer Bags   Use only those plastic bags labeled for freezer use. After you have put the food in the bag, press out as much air as possible before sealing and labeling. If you freeze large quantities of food as well as prepared dishes, you may want to invest in a vacuum-seal appliance that cuts bags from a roll to fit foods and provides an airtight seal. An advantage of this system is that you can

Line a baking dish with heavy-duty aluminum foil, leaving a generous overhang. Add food and freeze until firm enough to remove from the dish.

When frozen, remove food from the dish. Fold overhangs to seal; label food and return to the freezer. This allows the dish to be used for other recipes.

boil the food in the bag to reheat—a time-saver if you don't have a microwave oven.

Good freezer packaging should protect the food as well as give you easy access to the items in desired quantities. Here are some ways to package prepared dishes for convenient reheating and serving:

Aluminum Foil Pans   Baked foods such as lasagna and meat loaf can be baked, frozen, and reheated in the same heavy-duty aluminum foil pan. Freeze the dish, cooked or uncooked, and wrap it tightly with heavy-duty aluminum foil or freezer paper. Aluminum foil pans can be washed and reused if they haven't been damaged.

Lined Baking Dishes   If you don't want to leave a dish in the freezer, line the dish with heavy-duty aluminum foil or plastic wrap, leaving a generous overhang on all four sides of the dish. Add the food, and freeze until solid. Remove the foil liner, and wrap the food, using the foil or plastic wrap overhangs, or seal it in a freezer bag. Label the food package, and return it to the freezer. When ready to serve, remove all wrapping, and replace the food in the dish to reheat.

Single Servings   Freeze single servings of soup, stew, chili, and spaghetti sauce in individual microwave-safe containers or freezer bags for fast help-yourself convenience. If you don't have a lot of small containers or don't want them cluttering your freezer, freeze portions of food in bowls, mugs, or giant-size muffin tins lined with plastic wrap. Place the containers on a baking sheet to hold them steady in the freezer. After the food is frozen, wrap the single portions with plastic wrap, and toss them into a freezer bag. Remove the plastic wrap before microwaving.

Tray Meals   Making complete meals for reheating in a conventional oven is tricky, because cooking times must be coordinated so that one food doesn't overcook before another is heated through. Commercial frozen food packagers address this problem by pre-cooking the parts of a dinner to varying degrees of doneness. You will achieve better results with tray dinners if you include only meats and grains; cook vegetables separately just before serving time for best flavor, texture, and nutrient retention.

Tray combinations are easier to coordinate if using microwave ovens because everything heats quickly and will stay moist if covered with plastic wrap or the plastic lid that comes with the dish. To prepare for freezing, arrange the meal's main course and accompaniments on divided microwave-safe plastic or heavy paper plates. Freeze plates on baking sheets; remove from freezer, and wrap tightly in freezer plastic wrap, or wrap in regular plastic wrap, and place in large freezer bags. Do not include bread or desserts with the meal because they reheat much faster than meats, grains, and vegetables.

From Storage to Table _____

Most cooked foods do not have to be defrosted before baking or reheating. You can take most foods out of the freezer and put them in the refrigerator about eight hours before you plan to serve them. Do not defrost at room temperature dishes that contain meat, fish, eggs, or poultry. You will find specific instructions for reheating and serving with each recipe in this book. Below are general procedures for reheating.

Stovetop Reheating   Frozen soups, sauces, and stews can be reheated on the stovetop without defrosting. To prevent scorching, start cooking over low heat, and add just enough water to cover the bottom of the pan, or use a double boiler. Stir often to break up the food and distribute heat evenly.

When the food has defrosted, you can increase the heat to medium. Cook and stir until soups just reach the boiling point; cover stews, sauces, and other semi-liquid foods, and simmer about five minutes or until thoroughly heated. If the food has thickened or lost some of its moisture, stir in some water while reheating. Ingredients such as lemon juice, vinegar, and fresh herbs lose some of their strength during storage and reheating. However, more seasonings can be added as desired during reheating.

Oven Reheating   A casserole will reheat faster and with less risk of dryness if it has been defrosted in the refrigerator. If there was no chance to defrost it, bake it in a moderate oven, allowing extra baking time. Use bubbling edges, brownness, and other signs of doneness as your guide to timing. Cover the dish if the food seems to be getting too dry. Add toppings after the food has defrosted, or the topping may burn before the food is done. Unbaked pies, pastries, and other crisp or crusty treats should not be defrosted before reheating. Follow specific recipe directions.

Microwave Reheating Follow the directions in your microwave oven owner's manual. Small quantities of food heat more evenly in the microwave oven, so it makes sense to reheat individual portions on serving plates. Small quantities needn't be defrosted, but they should be stirred, if possible, to distribute heat evenly, and the plate should be covered unless the food has a crisp topping. Larger quantities of food should be defrosted on LOW (30% power) before reheating. Be careful not to reheat foods too long in the microwave oven. Check individual portions every minute and stir, if possible. Check larger quantities every two minutes, stirring, if possible. This will prevent overcooking and dryness.

Many of the recipes in this book include directions for adding a topping or a garnish when reheating or before serving. These quickly prepared items add a fresh taste and appearance to the dish. You can add a garnish to the recipes with sprinklings of chopped fresh parsley or other fresh herbs, extra grated Parmesan cheese, citrus slices, chopped tomatoes or sweet pepper, shredded carrot or radish, croutons, toasted almond slices, or chopped nuts or olives.

Make-Ahead Fare on the Menu _____

The natural choices to complement made-ahead dishes are those foods that should be prepared close to serving time for best nutrient retention, flavor, and texture. Most important among foods to prepare just before serving are fruits and vegetables; some of their precious vitamin content begins to diminish as soon as they are cut, and this process is hastened by cooking and storage. Among the four to six servings of fruits and vegetables that everyone should consume daily, it is wise to include at least one serving of raw fruit and a small green salad, because the uncooked produce provides nutrients and fiber that may be lost in cooking.

If you have a made-ahead entrée ready to reheat, then your cooking time before a meal should be spent preparing fresh produce — perhaps baking potatoes and cutting up crudités, steaming broccoli and arranging salads of lettuce and tomato, or boiling green beans and slicing a melon for dessert. None of this needs to be elaborate; the less you do to fresh foods apart from basic cooking, the more nutritious the dish is likely to be. The important place of grains on everyday menus can often be filled with good bakery breads, but pasta practically cooks itself, couscous can be done in five minutes, and you can steam rice, bulgur, or barley "automatically" with a rice cooker or with predictably good results in the microwave oven.

If you have a soup, stew, or casserole ready to reheat, you can set up a salad bar while the entrée is heating. Or, if you wish, you can bake potatoes and set up a "potato bar" with a selection of cheeses, bacon bits, chives, and other toppings. The same concept will work with cooked green vegetables, which can be matched with a choice of toasted nuts, breadcrumbs, chopped egg, pimiento, Parmesan cheese, or various seasoned butters, or salad dressings.

Impromptu Entertaining _____

Many cooks don't get too systematic about cooking ahead until they face a big party countdown. The only calm way to anticipate the arrival of 40 people for cocktails is to fill the refrigerator and freezer well in advance with plenty of appetizers and snacks. The only way to share a multi-course sit-down dinner—and enjoy the conversation with the six or eight friends you've invited—is to do most of the cooking ahead. You'll find several specific party menus in the chapter Ready for Entertaining. But every recipe in this book is well suited to some kind of party plan, whether a brunch, a picnic, a covered-dish supper, an open house, or a romantic dinner for two.

When you are composing a party menu, do keep in mind what kind of reheating or last-minute finishing touches each dish will need and in what kind of pan, pot, or dish. Try to coordinate recipes so that you won't have to bake more dishes at the last minute than your oven can hold—or need more baking sheets than you own or can borrow. Think about creating some "breathing time" for yourself at a sit-down dinner by including a cold or room temperature first course and dessert—perhaps ones that can be placed on the plates before guests are seated. And don't overlook recipes for beverages, breads, pickles, and relishes in any do-ahead menu; these foods can add distinction to a simple meal with the greatest of serving ease.

When your guest list is long or your dinner plan fancy, you'll want to select recipes that allow for a comfortable sequence of preparations and a viable storage plan. For greatest flexibility in time and space, choose some party fare that can be tucked into the freezer weeks ahead, some items that will hold in the refrigerator up to a week, and at least one item that will keep well for up to a week at room temperature, such as a snack mix.

Remember also that the invitation to share make-ahead fare needn't come from you. It can be a neighbor's suggestion that you drop by for coffee, a relative's expectation that you'll spend the weekend, your office holiday party, or any situation where a food gift would be appropriate. Many of the recipes in this book not only keep well but also wrap and travel well—and it is as wonderful to have them ready for giving as it is to have them ready to serve at home.

When You Have Time

*T*ake just a few minutes to prepare seasoned butters and you can freeze taste treasures that will last for months. Devote half an hour to making a pie crust, and you'll be able to serve an impromptu dessert whenever unexpected guests arrive. Turn pick-of-the-crop produce into roasted peppers or freezer jam, and you'll enjoy a bountiful harvest year-round.

The recipes in this chapter are culinary building blocks that can be stored from one to 12 months. Prepare them when you have time, and they will be ready to incorporate into, or serve with, other foods. Not only are these foods more economical to make than they are to buy, but more important, you can't buy prepared foods as delicious as these. For everyday convenience try the easily made barbecue and spaghetti sauces, salad dressings, or herb vinegars in this chapter.

Discovering the versatility of these foods is part of the joy of having them on hand. Make three or four kinds of seasoned butters, and you will have instant enhancers for pasta, grilled fish and meats, baked potatoes, and steamed vegetables, or sweet toppings for toast, pancakes, and muffins. Roast garlic to blend with mayonnaise, and use it as a sauce for a cold chicken lunch or a dip for tomorrow night's party. Match roasted red, green, and yellow peppers with goat cheese or hard salami to create appetizers that will set an elegant tone for a special dinner—or heap the roasted peppers on a hero sandwich for a satisfying supper. Try the caramelized onions, and you won't believe how flavorful they can be when served over broiled or roasted meats or stirred into a rich French onion soup.

Toss a fresh salad anytime with delicious made-ahead toppings such as crisp Herbed Croutons (page 27) and Fresh French Dressing or Creamy Buttermilk Dressing (page 26).

Strawberry Freezer Jam

2 cups crushed fresh
  strawberries
4 cups sugar
1 (1¾-ounce) package powdered
  pectin
¾ cup water

Combine strawberries and sugar, stirring well. Let stand 20 minutes, stirring occasionally.

Combine pectin and water in a small saucepan. Bring to a boil; boil 1 minute, stirring constantly. Pour pectin mixture over strawberry mixture; stir 3 minutes. Immediately pour jam into jelly jars or frozen food containers, leaving ½-inch headspace. Cover at once with lids. Cool to room temperature.

TO STORE: Refrigerate jam up to 3 weeks. Freeze up to 1 year.

TO SERVE: Thaw at room temperature. Serve with biscuits, pancakes, or French toast or over ice cream or pound cake. Yield: 6 cups.

Strawberry Puree

2 cups fresh strawberries
¼ cup sugar
2 teaspoons amaretto or other
  almond-flavored liqueur

Combine all ingredients in container of an electric blender; process until smooth.

TO STORE: Refrigerate puree in a tightly covered container up to 2 weeks. Freeze puree in a labeled airtight container up to 3 months.

TO SERVE: Thaw puree in refrigerator, or defrost on MEDIUM LOW (30% power) in microwave oven. Serve puree over ice cream, angel food cake, or pound cake. Yield: 1½ cups.

Pineapple Puree: Substitute 2 cups fresh pineapple chunks for strawberries and 1 tablespoon dark rum and 1 teaspoon lime juice for amaretto. Serve over ice cream, angel food cake, or pound cake. Yield: 1½ cups.

Fresh Strawberry-Orange Butter

1 cup sliced fresh strawberries
1 cup unsalted butter or
  margarine, softened
¼ cup honey
1 tablespoon grated orange rind

Position knife blade in food processor bowl; add all ingredients. Process 1 minute or until fluffy, scraping sides of processor bowl once.

TO STORE: Refrigerate butter in a tightly covered container up to 2 weeks. Freeze butter in a labeled airtight container up to 6 months.

TO SERVE: Thaw in refrigerator. Serve with pancakes, French toast, biscuits, or muffins. Yield: 1¾ cups.

Cinnamon-Honey Butter

½ cup unsalted butter or
   margarine, softened
2 tablespoons honey
1 teaspoon ground cinnamon

Cream butter until light and fluffy. Add honey and cinnamon, beating until well blended. Place butter on wax paper, and shape into two 2½-inch sticks.

TO STORE: Cover tightly, and freeze up to 6 months.

TO SERVE: Thaw sticks in refrigerator; cut off pats as needed. Serve with pancakes, waffles, muffins, or toast. Yield: ½ cup.

Nut Butter: Add ¼ cup ground toasted pecans to creamed butter, beating well. Serve with rice or other cooked grains. Yield: ½ cup.

Orange Butter: Add ¼ cup sifted powdered sugar and 1 tablespoon grated orange rind to creamed butter, beating well. Serve with cooked vegetables such as carrots or sweet potatoes. Yield: ½ cup.

Chive Butter: Add ¼ cup minced fresh chives to creamed butter, beating well. Serve with broiled chicken, fish, pasta, or potatoes. Yield: ½ cup.

Garlic Butter: Add 2 tablespoons minced fresh parsley and 1 tablespoon crushed garlic to creamed butter, beating well. Serve with bread, broiled seafood, or cooked vegetables. Yield: ½ cup.

Chicken Broth

6 pounds chicken pieces
2½ quarts water
3 stalks celery with leaves, cut
   into 1-inch pieces
2 medium onions, quartered
1 bay leaf
1½ teaspoons salt
¾ teaspoon pepper
½ teaspoon dried whole thyme

Combine all ingredients in a large Dutch oven. Bring to a boil; cover, reduce heat, and simmer 1½ hours. Strain broth through a cheesecloth- or paper towel-lined sieve, reserving chicken pieces and vegetables for other uses. Cover broth, and chill thoroughly. Skim and discard solidified fat from top of broth.

TO STORE: Refrigerate broth in a tightly covered container up to 3 days. Freeze in a labeled airtight container up to 3 months.

TO SERVE: Thaw and use as directed in recipes that call for chicken broth. Yield: 10 cups.

Easy Barbecue Sauce is quick to make. When grilling or baking, brush it on beef, chicken, or pork for an extra touch of flavor.

Easy Barbecue Sauce _____

1 (16-ounce) can tomato sauce
1 cup chopped onion
½ cup Worcestershire sauce
¼ cup butter or margarine
¼ cup vegetable oil
2 tablespoons sugar
2 tablespoons dark brown sugar
2 teaspoons instant coffee
   granules
1 teaspoon salt
1 teaspoon garlic powder
1 teaspoon pepper
½ teaspoon ground ginger
½ teaspoon ground allspice

Combine all ingredients in a medium saucepan. Bring mixture to a boil; reduce heat, and simmer 10 minutes, stirring occasionally. Cool completely.

TO STORE: Refrigerate in a tightly covered container up to 1 month.

TO SERVE: Stir well. Brush on beef, pork, or chicken during grilling, broiling, or baking. Yield: 3½ cups.

Roasted Garlic Mayonnaise

12 cloves garlic
1 tablespoon vegetable oil
1 tablespoon fresh lemon juice
1 teaspoon Worcestershire sauce
1 cup mayonnaise
¼ cup chopped fresh parsley
¼ cup chopped fresh basil
Salt and pepper to taste

Place garlic and oil in a small baking dish; stir well. Bake at 300° for 30 minutes or until garlic is soft and golden. Cool to room temperature.

Place garlic mixture, lemon juice, and Worcestershire sauce in container of an electric blender; process until smooth. Add mayonnaise and remaining ingredients; process until smooth.

TO STORE: Refrigerate in a tightly covered container up to 1 month.

TO SERVE: Serve mayonnaise with grilled poultry, fish, or vegetables, or use as a dip for cold seafood or crudités. Yield: 1 cup.

Caramelized Onions

3 pounds onions (about 8 medium), thinly sliced
¼ cup plus 2 tablespoons butter, melted

Separate onions into rings; cook in butter in a large Dutch oven over low heat 3 hours or until onion is lightly browned, stirring once each hour for the first 2 hours, and every 15 minutes the last hour.

TO STORE: Refrigerate onions in a tightly covered container up to 1 week. Freeze in a labeled airtight container up to 6 months.

TO SERVE: Cook over low heat until hot, stirring occasionally. Serve with broiled or roasted meats or poultry, or use to prepare Easy French Onion Soup. Yield: about 2½ cups.

Easy French Onion Soup

2½ cups Caramelized Onions
2 (10½-ounce) cans condensed beef broth, undiluted
7 (¾-inch-thick) slices French bread
1 cup (4 ounces) shredded Gruyère cheese

Cook onions over low heat until hot, stirring occasionally. Add water to beef broth to equal 5 cups. Stir broth mixture into onions; cook over medium heat until thoroughly heated.

Place bread slices on a baking sheet; sprinkle evenly with cheese. Broil 6 inches from heat 2 to 3 minutes or until lightly browned.

Ladle soup into individual soup bowls; top each with a slice of French bread, cheese side up. Yield: 7 cups.

Roasted Peppers

12 medium-size sweet red,
   green, or yellow peppers
Olive or vegetable oil

Wash and dry peppers. Cut peppers in half lengthwise; remove seeds. Place half of peppers, skin side up, on a lightly greased baking sheet. Broil 6 inches from heat 5 to 10 minutes or until skins are charred. Place peppers in a plastic bag; close tightly, and let stand 10 minutes to loosen skins. Peel peppers, and cut into ½-inch strips. Repeat procedure with remaining peppers. Place peppers in an airtight container; add just enough oil to cover peppers.

TO STORE: Refrigerate up to 1 month, adding oil, if needed, to keep peppers covered.

TO SERVE: Remove peppers from oil; drain off excess oil. Serve peppers with sautéed sausage, veal, or chicken or as an accompaniment to fresh mozzarella or goat cheese. Roasted Peppers may also be used to prepare Tomato Pepper Sauce. Yield: 4 cups.

Note: Roasted Peppers may be pureed and frozen in airtight containers without oil up to 3 months.

Tomato Pepper Sauce

⅔ cup Roasted Peppers
2 tablespoons olive oil
1 cup peeled, seeded, and
   chopped tomato
1 tablespoon capers
1 tablespoon chopped fresh
   parsley
1 tablespoon chopped fresh
   cilantro
¼ teaspoon salt

Place peppers in container of an electric blender; process until smooth.

Heat oil in a medium saucepan. Stir in pureed peppers, tomato, and remaining ingredients; reduce heat, and simmer 5 minutes. Serve with grilled chicken or fish. Yield: 1¾ cups.

Strawberry Vinegar

2 cups sliced fresh strawberries
2 cups white wine vinegar
¼ cup sugar

Place strawberries in a 1-quart jar. Press strawberries with a wooden spoon to release juice; set aside. Combine vinegar and sugar in a medium saucepan. Bring to a boil; reduce heat, and simmer until sugar dissolves. Pour vinegar mixture over strawberries; cover with airtight lid. Let stand at room temperature 48 hours. Strain vinegar through a cheesecloth- or paper towel-lined sieve; discard strawberries.

Place vinegar in a medium saucepan. Bring to a boil; boil 2 minutes. Cool; pour into 2 half-pint jars.

TO STORE: Store at room temperature indefinitely.

TO SERVE: Use in salad dressings or vinaigrettes. Yield: 2 cups.

Basil Vinegar

1 cup packed fresh basil leaves
1 quart red or white wine
  vinegar
Fresh basil sprigs
2 cloves garlic, halved

Slightly bruise 1 cup basil leaves; place in a 1-quart jar. Bring vinegar to a boil in a medium saucepan; pour over basil leaves. Cover with airtight lid, and store in a dark place 2 to 4 weeks.

Strain vinegar into decorative jars, discarding basil leaves. Add basil sprigs and garlic. Seal jars with cork or other airtight lid.

TO STORE: Store at room temperature indefinitely.

TO SERVE: Use in salad dressings, vinaigrettes, or basting sauces. Yield: 3¾ cups.

Tarragon-Lemon Vinegar: Substitute fresh tarragon for basil leaves. After straining, add fresh tarragon sprigs and lemon rind spirals. Yield: 3¾ cups.

Turn ordinary salad dressings and vinaigrettes into something special with Basil or Tarragon-Lemon Vinegar. Store the vinegars in decorative bottles.

Creamy Buttermilk Dressing

1 cup mayonnaise
1 cup buttermilk
¼ cup minced fresh chives
2 tablespoons minced fresh
   parsley
1 clove garlic, crushed
¼ teaspoon salt
⅛ teaspoon ground white
   pepper

Combine all ingredients in a small bowl; stir well.

TO STORE: Refrigerate in a tightly covered container at least 2 hours and up to 2 weeks.

TO SERVE: Stir well before serving. Serve over salad, or use to prepare Bacon-Buttermilk Dressing. Yield: 2 cups.

Bacon-Buttermilk Dressing: Stir 7 slices of cooked and crumbled bacon into Creamy Buttermilk Dressing. Yield: 2¼ cups.

Fresh French Dressing

1 cup vegetable oil
⅓ cup catsup
¼ cup sugar
¼ cup finely chopped onion
¼ cup cider vinegar
1 teaspoon celery seeds
Salt to taste

Combine all ingredients in container of an electric blender; process until smooth.

TO STORE: Refrigerate in a tightly covered container at least 2 hours and up to 2 weeks.

TO SERVE: Stir well before serving. Serve over salad, or use to prepare Russian Dressing. Yield: 1½ cups.

Russian Dressing

1 cup mayonnaise
½ cup Fresh French Dressing
2 tablespoons minced onion
2 tablespoons minced green
   pepper
2 tablespoons minced pimiento
2 teaspoons prepared
   horseradish

Combine all ingredients in a small bowl, stirring well. Yield: 1¾ cups.

Vinaigrette Dressing

¾ cup vegetable oil
¼ cup red wine vinegar
1 clove garlic, crushed
¼ teaspoon salt
¼ teaspoon freshly ground
   pepper

Combine all ingredients in a jar. Cover tightly, and shake vigorously.

TO STORE: Refrigerate up to 1 month.

TO SERVE: Shake dressing well. Serve as a salad dressing, or use as a marinade for meats, seafood, or vegetables. Yield: 1 cup.

Croutons

6 slices French bread, crust
  removed
¼ cup butter or margarine

Cut bread slices into ½-inch cubes. Melt butter in a large skillet; add bread cubes, and toss to coat. Spread bread cubes on an ungreased baking sheet. Bake at 300° for 30 minutes or until very crisp, stirring every 5 minutes. Cool completely.

TO STORE: Store croutons in an airtight container at room temperature up to 1 week. Freeze in a labeled airtight container up to 1 month.

TO SERVE: Serve croutons with soups or salads. Yield: about 2 cups.

Herbed Croutons: Add 1 teaspoon dried whole oregano, 1 teaspoon dried whole basil, and ½ teaspoon garlic powder to melted butter; toss with bread cubes. Yield: about 2 cups.

Pastry Shell

1 cup all-purpose flour
¼ teaspoon salt
3 tablespoons shortening
2 tablespoons cold butter
2 to 3 tablespoons cold water

Combine flour and salt; cut in shortening and butter with a pastry blender until mixture resembles coarse meal. Sprinkle cold water (1 tablespoon at a time) evenly over surface; stir with a fork until dry ingredients are moistened. Shape pastry into a ball; chill.
Roll pastry to ⅛-inch thickness on a lightly floured surface. Place in a 9-inch pieplate; trim off excess pastry along edges. Fold edges under and flute.

TO STORE: Cover tightly, and freeze up to 6 months.

TO SERVE: For baked pastry shell, thaw slightly, and prick bottom and sides of pastry shell generously with a fork. Bake at 450° for 12 to 14 minutes or until pastry shell is golden brown. For filled pies, thaw pastry shell, and follow directions in specific recipes. Yield: one 9-inch pastry shell.

Chocolate Crumb Crust

1½ cups chocolate wafer
  crumbs
⅓ cup butter or margarine,
  melted

Combine crumbs and butter in a small bowl; stir well. Firmly press crumb mixture evenly over bottom and up the sides of a 9-inch pieplate. Bake at 350° for 8 minutes. Cool completely.

TO STORE: Cover tightly, and freeze up to 6 months.

TO SERVE: Fill frozen crust with desired filling. Yield: one 9-inch crust.

Ground Beef Mix

3 pounds ground beef
1 large green pepper, finely chopped
3 cloves garlic, minced
1 cup water
1 tablespoon plus 1 teaspoon beef-flavored bouillon granules
2 medium onions, finely chopped
¼ teaspoon pepper

Combine beef, green pepper, and garlic in a large skillet. Cook over medium-high heat until meat is browned, stirring to crumble meat; drain well. Remove meat from skillet. Add water and bouillon granules to skillet. Bring to a boil, stirring to dissolve granules. Add onion; cover, reduce heat to medium, and cook 15 minutes. Uncover and cook 5 to 10 minutes or until liquid evaporates. Stir onion mixture and pepper into beef mixture.

TO STORE: Spread beef mixture in a 15- x 10- x 1-inch jellyroll pan; cool. Cover tightly, and freeze at least 4 hours. Crumble frozen mixture into small pieces. Freeze in a labeled airtight container up to 2 months.

TO SERVE: Use in Quick Chili or Quick Meaty Spaghetti Sauce. Yield: 10 cups.

Quick Chili

3⅓ cups Ground Beef Mix
1 (15½-ounce) can red kidney beans, undrained
1 (14½-ounce) can whole tomatoes, undrained and chopped
2 teaspoons chili powder
½ teaspoon dried whole oregano
½ teaspoon ground cumin
½ teaspoon ground coriander
½ teaspoon salt
¼ teaspoon pepper

Cook frozen Ground Beef Mix in a 3-quart saucepan over medium heat until thoroughly heated. Add beans and remaining ingredients; stir well. Bring mixture to a boil; reduce heat, and simmer, uncovered, 15 to 20 minutes, stirring occasionally. Yield: 5 cups.

Quick Spaghetti Sauce

3⅓ cups Ground Beef Mix
1 (28-ounce) can crushed tomatoes
½ cup water
¼ cup tomato paste
¼ cup chopped fresh parsley
1 bay leaf
½ teaspoon dried whole basil
½ teaspoon dried whole oregano
¼ to ½ teaspoon salt
¼ teaspoon dried whole thyme
¼ teaspoon pepper
Hot cooked spaghetti

Cook frozen Ground Beef Mix in a 3-quart saucepan over medium heat until thoroughly heated. Add crushed tomatoes and next 9 ingredients; stir well. Bring mixture to a boil; reduce heat, and simmer 20 minutes, stirring occasionally. Remove and discard bay leaf. Serve sauce over hot cooked spaghetti. Yield: 6 cups.

Top spaghetti with Quick Spaghetti Sauce for a hearty dinner to warm up a cold winter evening.

No·Rush Breakfast and Brunch

Maybe the best thing about a made-ahead breakfast is that you don't have to worry about preparing it when you wake up. Or maybe the best thing is the smell of muffins in the oven while the coffee is still brewing. Or maybe it's feeling relaxed about serving brunch to several guests.

More than any other meal, breakfast is a personal matter. Make-ahead recipes can satisfy individual preferences such as an eat-in-the-car granola bar or a quick bowl of nourishing homemade cereal and fruit. Those who like to linger over breakfast can choose French toast, grits and sausage, or a hash brown casserole.

When breakfast becomes brunch, make-ahead foods can still give you more slumber time. Welcome guests with mixed-ahead orange-cranberry coolers or mugfuls of rich coffee punch. The main course may include frozen-ahead cornbread cakes topped with rich creamed ham, delicate cream puffs retrieved from the freezer and filled with a freshly scrambled egg mixture, or a ham and broccoli casserole assembled the night before.

It suits the hour to keep things simple. The casseroles were selected because overnight refrigeration gives flavors time to mingle. The batters for muffins and pancakes can be refrigerated up to a week. Creamed ham freezes well, as do turkey sausage patties for the English muffin sandwiches. The breakfast cereal is good enough to serve as a snack, and the granola bars probably would keep for weeks in the pantry if they weren't eaten so fast!

Light and fluffy Refrigerator Buttermilk Pancakes (page 35) allow you to sleep in and still enjoy a satisfying breakfast. Stack pancakes high and top them with fresh fruit.

Coffee Punch

2 quarts strong coffee, cooled
1 cup whipping cream
1 cup milk
½ cup sugar
1½ teaspoons vanilla extract
1 quart vanilla ice cream
Garnish: grated chocolate

Combine coffee, whipping cream, milk, sugar, and vanilla; stir until sugar dissolves.

TO STORE: Refrigerate in a tightly covered container up to 2 days.

TO SERVE: Scoop ice cream into a punch bowl; gradually pour coffee mixture over ice cream. Ladle into cups, and garnish, if desired. Yield: about 1 gallon.

Blushing Orange Cooler

1 cup cranberry juice cocktail
1 (6-ounce) can frozen orange juice concentrate, thawed and undiluted
¼ cup sugar
2 cups club soda, chilled
Crushed ice
Garnishes: orange rind curls and fresh cranberries

Combine first 3 ingredients; stir until sugar dissolves.

TO STORE: Refrigerate in a tightly covered container up to 1 week.

TO SERVE: Add club soda to juice mixture. Serve over crushed ice. Garnish, if desired. Yield: about 4 cups.

Fruited Refrigerator Bran Muffins

1 cup diced mixed dried fruit
1½ cups all-purpose flour
2½ teaspoons baking powder
¼ teaspoon salt
1 cup shreds of wheat bran cereal
½ cup firmly packed brown sugar
¾ teaspoon pumpkin pie spice
1 egg, beaten
1 cup milk
¼ cup vegetable oil
1 teaspoon grated orange rind

Place fruit in a small bowl, and add boiling water to cover; let stand 5 minutes. Drain well; set aside.

Combine flour and next 5 ingredients in a medium bowl; make a well in center of mixture. Combine egg, milk, oil, and orange rind; add to dry ingredients, stirring just until moistened. Fold in fruit.

TO STORE: Refrigerate batter in a tightly covered container up to 1 week.

TO SERVE: Gently stir batter; spoon into greased muffin pans, filling three-fourths full. Bake at 400° for 15 to 20 minutes or until golden. Remove from pans immediately. Yield: 1 dozen.

Give your next brunch a special flair by welcoming guests with refreshing Blushing Orange Coolers and creamy Coffee Punch.

Refrigerator Buttermilk Pancakes

2 cups all-purpose flour
2½ teaspoons baking powder
1 teaspoon baking soda
¾ teaspoon salt
2 tablespoons sugar
2 eggs
2¼ cups buttermilk
¼ cup vegetable oil

Combine first 5 ingredients in a large bowl; stir well. Combine eggs, buttermilk, and oil; add to dry ingredients, stirring just until moistened.

TO STORE: Refrigerate batter in a tightly covered container up to 1 week.

TO SERVE: Gently stir batter. (If batter is too thick, gradually add milk or water to reach desired consistency.) For each pancake, pour about ¼ cup batter onto a hot, lightly greased griddle. Turn pancakes when tops are covered with bubbles and edges look cooked. Yield: 16 (4-inch) pancakes.

Blueberry Pancakes: Fold 1 cup fresh or frozen blueberries into batter just before cooking. Yield: 16 (4-inch) pancakes.

Overnight French Toast

8 (¾-inch-thick) slices French
  bread
4 eggs, beaten
1 cup milk
1 tablespoon sugar
½ teaspoon vanilla extract
¼ teaspoon ground cinnamon
2 tablespoons butter or
  margarine, divided
Honey-Orange Sauce

Place bread in a 13- x 9- x 2-inch baking dish. Combine eggs and next 4 ingredients; beat well. Pour egg mixture over bread; turn slices over to coat evenly.

TO STORE: Cover and refrigerate up to 8 hours.

TO SERVE: Melt 1 tablespoon butter in a large skillet over medium-high heat. Arrange 4 slices of bread in skillet; cook 3 minutes on each side or until browned. Remove to a serving plate, and keep warm. Repeat procedure with remaining 1 tablespoon butter and bread slices. Serve immediately with Honey-Orange Sauce. Yield: 4 servings.

Honey-Orange Sauce

1 cup unsweetened orange juice
2 tablespoons honey
2 teaspoons cornstarch
1 teaspoon grated orange rind
⅛ teaspoon ground ginger
1 (11-ounce) can mandarin
  oranges, drained

Combine first 5 ingredients in a saucepan. Cook over medium-high heat, stirring constantly, until mixture thickens. Remove from heat, and stir in oranges; cool.

TO STORE: Refrigerate in a tightly covered container up to 3 days.

TO SERVE: Microwave sauce at HIGH for 1½ to 2 minutes or until thoroughly heated, stirring once. Yield: 1½ cups.

You can linger over breakfast in bed when you serve Overnight French Toast with Honey-Orange Sauce.

Crunchy Granola Breakfast Bars

3½ cups regular oats, uncooked
½ cup flaked coconut
½ cup sliced almonds
½ cup wheat germ
¼ cup coarsely chopped
  cashews
¼ cup coarsely chopped pecans
¼ cup sesame seeds
¼ cup sunflower kernels
½ cup honey
¼ cup firmly packed brown
  sugar
¼ cup vegetable oil
½ cup creamy peanut butter
1 teaspoon vanilla extract

Combine first 8 ingredients in a large bowl; stir well, and set aside.

Combine honey, brown sugar, and oil in a small saucepan; cook over medium heat, stirring occasionally, until sugar dissolves and mixture is thoroughly heated. Remove from heat; add peanut butter and vanilla, stirring until peanut butter melts. Pour honey mixture over oats mixture; stir well. (Mixture will be dry at first; continue stirring until moist.)

Press mixture into a greased 15- x 10- x 1-inch jellyroll pan, using greased fingertips. Press mixture flat with the back of a wide metal spatula. Bake at 250° for 1 hour and 20 minutes or until golden brown. Cut into bars while warm; let cool completely in pan. Remove bars from pan.

TO STORE: Store in an airtight container at room temperature up to 1 week. Yield: 30 bars.

Turkey Sausage Muffin-wich

1 pound ground turkey
½ cup soft breadcrumbs
1 egg, lightly beaten
1 teaspoon ground sage
¾ teaspoon salt
¼ teaspoon crushed fennel
  seeds
¼ teaspoon dried red pepper
  flakes
⅛ teaspoon ground nutmeg
3 English muffins, split and
  toasted
6 (1-ounce) slices Cheddar
  cheese
Garnish: green pepper rings

Combine first 8 ingredients; mix well. Shape mixture into 6 patties.

TO STORE: Refrigerate patties in a tightly covered container up to 2 days. Freeze in a labeled airtight container up to 1 month.

TO SERVE: Cook patties in a large skillet over medium heat 10 to 15 minutes or until well browned. Drain on paper towels. Place 1 patty on each muffin half; top each with a slice of cheese. Broil about 6 inches from heat until cheese begins to melt. Garnish, if desired. Yield: 6 servings.

Kids of all ages will love Crunchy Granola Breakfast Bars. Packed in a lunchbox, they make a perfect mid-morning or afternoon snack.

Country Grits and Sausage Casserole

2 cups water
½ cup quick-cooking grits, uncooked
3½ cups (14 ounces) shredded extra-sharp Cheddar cheese
4 eggs, lightly beaten
1 cup milk
½ teaspoon dried whole thyme
⅛ teaspoon garlic powder
1½ pounds mild bulk pork sausage, cooked, crumbled, and drained
Garnishes: tomato wedges and fresh parsley sprigs

Bring water to a boil; stir in grits. Return to a boil; reduce heat to low, and cook 4 minutes, stirring occasionally. Add cheese, stirring until melted.

Combine eggs, milk, thyme, and garlic powder; stir well. Gradually stir about one-fourth of hot grits mixture into egg mixture; add to remaining hot mixture, stirring constantly. Stir in sausage. Pour into a lightly greased 11- x 7- x 1½-inch baking dish.

TO STORE: Cover and refrigerate up to 8 hours.

TO SERVE: Bake, uncovered, at 350° for 50 minutes or until set. Garnish, if desired. Yield: 6 to 8 servings.

Brunch Ham and Broccoli Bake

8 slices white bread, crust removed
1 cup diced cooked ham
1 cup frozen chopped broccoli, thawed and drained
3 eggs, lightly beaten
1½ cups milk
½ teaspoon dry mustard
¼ teaspoon onion salt
¼ teaspoon ground white pepper
2 cups (8 ounces) shredded Swiss cheese
Paprika

Place 4 slices of bread in a lightly greased 8-inch square baking dish. Sprinkle ham and broccoli over bread; top with remaining bread slices. Combine eggs and next 4 ingredients, stirring well; pour over bread. Sprinkle with cheese and paprika.

TO STORE: Cover and refrigerate up to 24 hours.

TO SERVE: Bake, uncovered, at 350° for 45 to 50 minutes or until puffed and golden brown. Serve immediately. Yield: 4 servings.

On cool autumn mornings, your family will enjoy waking up to the aroma of Country Grits and Sausage Casserole. Extra-sharp Cheddar cheese adds zip to this hearty dish.

Creamed Ham on Cornbread Cakes

½ cup chopped celery
½ cup chopped onion
¼ cup butter or margarine, melted
¼ cup all-purpose flour
¼ teaspoon salt
¼ teaspoon ground white pepper
2 cups milk
½ teaspoon Worcestershire sauce
2 cups diced cooked ham
½ cup diced cooked carrot
½ cup frozen English peas, thawed
1 tablespoon chopped fresh parsley
Cornbread Cakes
Garnish: fresh parsley sprigs

Sauté celery and onion in butter in a large skillet over medium heat until tender. Add flour, salt, and pepper, stirring until smooth. Cook 1 minute, stirring constantly. Gradually add milk and Worcestershire sauce; cook, stirring constantly, until mixture is thickened and bubbly. Stir in ham and next 3 ingredients. Cool slightly.

TO STORE: Refrigerate ham mixture in a tightly covered container up to 2 days. Freeze in a labeled airtight container up to 1 month.

TO SERVE: Cook over medium heat until hot, stirring often. Serve over Cornbread Cakes. Garnish, if desired. Yield: 4 to 6 servings.

Cornbread Cakes

1¾ cups self-rising cornmeal mix
1 egg, lightly beaten
1½ cups buttermilk
2 tablespoons butter or margarine, melted
¼ cup vegetable oil, divided

Combine first 4 ingredients in a large bowl, stirring just until moistened.

Heat 1 tablespoon oil in a large nonstick skillet over medium-high heat. Pour ⅓ cup batter into skillet for each corncake, cooking 3 cakes at a time. Cook 3 minutes on each side or until browned. Drain cakes on paper towels. Repeat procedure with remaining 3 tablespoons oil and batter. Cool completely.

TO STORE: Refrigerate cakes in a tightly covered container up to 2 days. Freeze in a labeled airtight container up to 1 month.

TO SERVE: Place cakes on ungreased baking sheets. Bake at 350° for 10 to 12 minutes or until thoroughly heated. Yield: 12 cakes.

Perfect for breakfast or brunch, individual servings of Creamed Ham on Cornbread Cakes are as attractive as they are delicious.

Elegant Egg and Shrimp Puffs

1 cup water
½ cup butter or margarine
1 cup all-purpose flour
⅛ teaspoon salt
4 eggs
Filling (recipe follows)

Combine water and butter in a medium saucepan; bring to a boil. Add flour and salt all at once, stirring vigorously over low heat until mixture leaves sides of pan and forms a smooth ball. Remove from heat, and cool 10 minutes.

Add eggs to flour mixture, one at a time, beating well after each addition. (Mixture may separate as each egg is added; continue beating until smooth.)

Drop batter by heaping tablespoonfuls 3 inches apart onto ungreased baking sheets. Bake at 400° for 30 to 35 minutes or until puffed and golden. Cool completely on a wire rack.

TO STORE: Freeze cream puffs in a labeled airtight container up to 1 month.

TO SERVE: Thaw at room temperature. Bake at 300° for 5 to 7 minutes. Cut tops off cream puffs; pull out and discard soft dough inside. Fill bottoms with approximately 2 tablespoons filling. Cover with tops. Yield: 10 servings.

Filling

10 eggs, lightly beaten
⅓ cup milk
½ teaspoon salt
¼ teaspoon pepper
2 tablespoons butter or margarine
2 tablespoons sliced green onions
2 tablespoons diced sweet red pepper
1 (4.5-ounce) can shrimp, rinsed and drained
¾ cup (3 ounces) shredded Cheddar cheese
2 tablespoons chopped fresh parsley

Combine first 4 ingredients, and set aside. Melt butter in a large nonstick skillet over medium-low heat. Add green onions and red pepper, and sauté until vegetables are crisp-tender. Add egg mixture; cook, without stirring, until mixture begins to set on bottom. Add shrimp, Cheddar cheese, and chopped parsley. Gently lift and fold egg mixture until cheese melts and eggs are thickened but still moist; do not stir constantly. Yield: 4 cups.

Hash Brown Potato Casserole

1 medium onion, chopped
¼ cup butter or margarine,
    melted
1 (32-ounce) package frozen
    hash brown potatoes, thawed
1 (16-ounce) carton sour cream
1 (10¾-ounce) can cream of
    celery soup, undiluted
1 cup (4 ounces) shredded
    Cheddar cheese
2 cups corn flakes cereal,
    crushed
Garnishes: tomato rose and
    fresh chives

Sauté onion in butter until tender. Combine onion mixture, hash brown potatoes, and next 3 ingredients in a large bowl; stir well. Spoon potato mixture into a lightly greased 11- x 7- x 1½-inch baking dish. Top with crushed cereal.

TO STORE: Cover and refrigerate up to 24 hours.

TO SERVE: Bake, uncovered, at 350° for 1 hour or until golden brown. Garnish, if desired. Yield: 6 to 8 servings.

Spiced Fruit Compote

1 (8-ounce) package dried figs
1 (6-ounce) package dried
    apricots
1 cup pitted prunes
¾ cup raisins
1¼ cups orange juice
¾ cup water
3 tablespoons brown sugar
2 tablespoons grated orange rind
2 (3-inch) sticks cinnamon
½ teaspoon ground allspice
½ cup slivered almonds, toasted
Vanilla yogurt (optional)

Place figs in a saucepan; add water to cover. Let stand 1 hour; drain well. Add apricots and next 8 ingredients. Bring mixture to a boil; reduce heat, and simmer 15 minutes, stirring occasionally. Let cool completely.

TO STORE: Refrigerate in a tightly covered container up to 1 week.

TO SERVE: Remove and discard cinnamon sticks. Pour fruit mixture into a saucepan; cook over low heat just until warm. Sprinkle each serving with toasted almonds. Top with yogurt, if desired. Yield: 8 servings.

Golden Fruit Medley

1 (17-ounce) can apricot halves,
    drained
1 (16-ounce) can peach halves,
    drained
1 (16-ounce) can pear halves,
    drained
1 (15¼-ounce) can pineapple
    chunks, drained
½ cup orange juice
⅓ cup firmly packed brown
    sugar
1 tablespoon lemon juice
2 (3-inch) sticks cinnamon
4 whole cloves
⅛ teaspoon ground nutmeg
Dash of salt

Cut apricot, peach, and pear halves in half; place in an 11- x 7- x 1½-inch baking dish. Add pineapple chunks.
Combine orange juice and remaining ingredients in a small saucepan; bring to a boil, reduce heat, and simmer 2 minutes. Pour orange juice mixture over fruit. Bake at 350° for 35 to 40 minutes or until hot and bubbly. Let cool completely.

TO STORE: Cover and refrigerate up to 24 hours.

TO SERVE: Remove and discard cinnamon sticks and whole cloves before serving. Bake, uncovered, at 350° for 15 minutes or until thoroughly heated. Serve fruit warm or cold. Yield: 6 to 8 servings.

Brown·Bag Snacks

A great brown-bag lunch can rescue your day. The morning may have been frantic and the afternoon may not look much better, but a midday break for a homemade beef sandwich, hot soup, pasta salad, or cookies will restore your equilibrium.

This basic remedy for a stress-filled day involves some of the easiest cooking in this book. Children can help not only with the choices but also in the preparation of some of their favorites. They may not care to help make the sandwiches, but they will gladly help themselves to pitas stuffed with chicken or French rolls filled with vegetables when they're hungry and you're not around.

Then there is the diverse and delicious selection of spreads in this chapter. These can be turned into sandwiches or packed in small containers to be eaten with vegetable dippers or crackers. The main-course salads will travel well in zip-top plastic bags or, if there is no refrigerator at work, in chilled thermal containers. Freeze the soups in microwave-safe containers for quick reheating if a microwave oven is available. If you don't have access to a microwave oven, you may want to freeze the soups in vacuum-sealed bags so that you can heat them quickly in boiling water at home, and pour them into vacuum bottles.

Another way to enjoy brown-bag lunches—and dispense with the brown bag entirely—is to savor the food at home or on a picnic! You can look forward to easy sandwiches, salads, soups, and snacks ready to be taken no further than the table, TV room, or patio for Sunday suppers, late-night refreshments, brunches, or warm-weather meals.

For a deliciously complete lunch, be sure to include Chicken Pockets (page 51), Beefy Vegetable Soup (page 46), and Jumbo Cookies (page 57).

Creamy Chicken and Broccoli Soup

½ cup sliced fresh mushrooms
½ cup chopped onion
¼ cup butter or margarine, melted
¼ cup all-purpose flour
2 cups half-and-half
1½ cups chicken broth
1 cup diced cooked chicken
1 cup frozen chopped broccoli, thawed
½ teaspoon dried whole rosemary
½ teaspoon salt
¼ teaspoon dried whole thyme
¼ teaspoon pepper

Sauté mushrooms and onion in butter in a medium saucepan over low heat until tender; add flour, stirring until smooth. Cook 1 minute, stirring constantly. Gradually add half-and-half and chicken broth; cook over medium heat, stirring constantly, until mixture is thickened and bubbly. Stir in diced chicken and remaining ingredients. Cover and simmer 10 minutes, stirring occasionally. Cool.

TO STORE: Refrigerate soup in a tightly covered container up to 2 days. Freeze in a labeled airtight container up to 1 month.

TO SERVE: Cook over low heat until thoroughly heated, stirring occasionally. Yield: 4 cups.

Beefy Vegetable Soup

2 pounds ground beef
½ cup butter or margarine
½ cup all-purpose flour
1½ quarts water
1 cup chopped onion
1 (28-ounce) can tomatoes, undrained and chopped
1 (16-ounce) package frozen mixed vegetables
1 (15-ounce) can tomato sauce with tomato bits
1½ tablespoons beef-flavored bouillon granules
1½ teaspoons salt
2 teaspoons pepper

Cook ground beef in a large Dutch oven until meat is browned, stirring to crumble. Drain well, and set aside.

Melt butter in Dutch oven over low heat; add flour, stirring until smooth. Cook 1 minute, stirring constantly. Gradually add water; cook over medium heat, stirring constantly, until mixture is thickened and bubbly.

Add ground beef, onion, and remaining ingredients to mixture in Dutch oven. Bring to a boil; reduce heat, and simmer, uncovered, 1 hour. Cool.

TO STORE: Refrigerate soup in a tightly covered container up to 3 days. Freeze in a labeled airtight container up to 2 months.

TO SERVE: Cook over low heat until thoroughly heated, stirring occasionally. Yield: 13 cups.

Take a break from a busy day to enjoy the richness of Creamy Chicken and Broccoli Soup.

Versatile Pasta Salad

4 ounces rotini pasta, uncooked
1 cup sliced fresh mushrooms
1 cup broccoli flowerets
1 cup diced Cheddar cheese
½ cup shredded carrot
½ cup chopped sweet red pepper
¼ teaspoon seasoned salt
¼ teaspoon pepper
⅓ cup vegetable oil
¼ cup white wine vinegar
1 tablespoon Dijon mustard
¼ cup finely chopped green onions
1 tablespoon minced fresh parsley
2 cloves garlic, crushed
½ teaspoon sugar
½ teaspoon dried whole basil
¼ teaspoon salt
¼ teaspoon dried whole oregano
¼ teaspoon crushed red pepper flakes

Cook rotini according to package directions; drain. Rinse with cold water; drain again. Combine cooked pasta and next 7 ingredients in a large bowl. Set aside.

Combine vegetable oil and remaining ingredients in a jar. Cover tightly, and shake vigorously. Pour dressing over pasta mixture; toss well.

TO STORE: Refrigerate in a tightly covered container at least 2 hours and up to 3 days. Yield: 4½ cups.

Summer Pasta Salad: Substitute 1 small zucchini, thinly sliced, 1 small yellow squash, thinly sliced, and 6 to 8 cherry tomatoes, halved, for mushrooms and broccoli. Yield: about 4¾ cups.

Pasta Salad Roma: Substitute 1 (14-ounce) can artichoke hearts, drained and quartered, 1 cup cubed salami, 1 cup diced mozzarella cheese, and ½ cup sliced ripe olives for broccoli, carrot, and Cheddar cheese. Yield: 4 cups.

Tuna Tabbouleh

¾ cup bulgur wheat, uncooked
1 (12½-ounce) can water-packed tuna, drained
1 medium cucumber, peeled, seeded, and finely chopped
½ cup chopped onion
½ cup chopped fresh parsley
¼ cup pine nuts, toasted
¼ cup olive oil
¼ cup fresh lemon juice
1 tablespoon chopped fresh mint
1 clove garlic, crushed
1 teaspoon grated lemon rind
½ teaspoon salt
¼ teaspoon pepper
8 to 10 cherry tomatoes, halved

Place bulgur in a colander; rinse with cold water, and drain well. Combine bulgur, tuna, cucumber, onion, parsley, and pine nuts; stir well. Set aside.

Combine oil and next 6 ingredients in a jar. Cover tightly, and shake vigorously. Pour dressing over bulgur mixture; toss well.

TO STORE: Refrigerate in a tightly covered container at least 2 hours and up to 2 days.

TO SERVE: Stir in tomato halves. Yield: 6½ cups.

Tortellini-Vegetable Salad

1 (9-ounce) package fresh
  cheese-filled tortellini
½ cup broccoli flowerets
½ cup cauliflower flowerets
6 to 8 cherry tomatoes, halved
½ small sweet red pepper, cut
  into ¼-inch strips
½ small green pepper, cut into
  ¼-inch strips
½ small purple onion, thinly
  sliced
½ cup commercial Italian salad
  dressing

Cook tortellini according to package directions; drain. Combine cooked tortellini and next 6 ingredients in a large bowl. Pour dressing over pasta mixture; toss well.

TO STORE: Refrigerate in a tightly covered container at least 2 hours and up to 3 days. Yield: 5 cups.

Chunky Peanut Butter Spread

2 cups chunky peanut butter
⅓ cup finely chopped dates
⅓ cup finely chopped dried
  apple
3 tablespoons honey
1 tablespoon orange juice
2 teaspoons grated orange rind

Combine all ingredients; stir well.

TO STORE: Refrigerate in a tightly covered container up to 1 week.

TO SERVE: Serve with crackers, or use as a spread for sandwiches, split bagels, or toast. Yield: 2⅔ cups.

Pimiento Cheese Spread

1 (8-ounce) package cream
  cheese, softened
1 cup (4 ounces) shredded
  sharp Cheddar cheese
1 cup (4 ounces) shredded
  American cheese
½ cup mayonnaise
2 (4-ounce) jars diced pimiento,
  drained
2 teaspoons Worcestershire
  sauce
1 teaspoon dry mustard
¼ teaspoon garlic powder
⅛ teaspoon hot sauce

Beat cream cheese at medium speed of an electric mixer. Stir in Cheddar cheese and remaining ingredients.

TO STORE: Refrigerate in a tightly covered container up to 2 weeks.

TO SERVE: Serve with crackers, or use as a spread for sandwiches. Yield: 3 cups.

Nutty Carrot-Cheese Spread

1 (8-ounce) package cream
  cheese, softened
1 cup shredded carrot
¾ cup (3 ounces) shredded
  Cheddar cheese
½ cup chopped pecans, toasted
¼ cup currants
¼ cup plus 2 tablespoons
  orange juice

Combine all ingredients, stirring well.

TO STORE: Refrigerate in a tightly covered container up
to 1 week.

TO SERVE: Serve with crackers, or use as a spread for
sandwiches. Yield: 2 cups.

*Chock-full of carrots, pecans, and currants, Nutty Carrot-Cheese Spread is a treat in sandwiches or on your
favorite crackers.*

Savory Ham and Cheese Spread

1 (8-ounce) package cream
   cheese, softened
1 cup ground cooked ham
¼ cup grated Parmesan cheese
¼ cup finely chopped onion
2 tablespoons mayonnaise
1 tablespoon chopped fresh
   parsley
1 teaspoon dried Italian
   seasoning

Combine all ingredients, stirring well.

TO STORE: Refrigerate in a tightly covered container up
to 1 week.

TO SERVE: Serve with crackers, or use as a spread for
sandwiches. Yield: 2 cups.

Chicken Pockets

3 cups finely chopped cooked
   chicken
⅔ cup mayonnaise or salad
   dressing
½ cup thinly sliced celery
½ cup chopped cashews
¼ cup raisins
¼ cup finely chopped dried
   apricots
2 tablespoons chopped onion
½ teaspoon salt
¼ teaspoon ground white
   pepper
4 (6-inch) whole wheat pita
   bread rounds, cut in half
Shredded lettuce

Combine first 9 ingredients; stir well. Spoon mixture
evenly into pita bread halves.

TO STORE: Refrigerate sandwiches in a tightly covered
container up to 2 days. Freeze in a labeled airtight
container up to 2 weeks.

TO SERVE: Thaw before serving. Top with shredded
lettuce. Yield: 8 servings.

Baked Ham and Swiss Sandwiches

½ cup butter or margarine,
   softened
2 tablespoons minced onion
1 tablespoon poppy seeds
1 tablespoon Dijon mustard
½ teaspoon Worcestershire
   sauce
8 hamburger buns, split
16 (1-ounce) slices cooked ham
8 (1-ounce) slices Swiss cheese

Combine first 5 ingredients, stirring well. Spread butter mixture evenly on cut sides of hamburger buns. For
each sandwich, place 2 slices of ham and 1 slice of cheese
on bottom half of each bun; cover with top half of bun.
Wrap each sandwich in aluminum foil.

TO STORE: Refrigerate up to 3 days.

TO SERVE: Place aluminum foil-wrapped sandwiches
on a baking sheet. Bake at 350° for 20 to 25 minutes or
until sandwiches are thoroughly heated and cheese is
melted. Yield: 8 servings.

Sandwich Boats Español

1 (15-ounce) can black beans,
  drained and rinsed
1 (11-ounce) can whole kernel
  corn with red and green
  peppers, drained
1 small tomato, seeded and
  chopped
½ cup (2 ounces) shredded
  sharp Cheddar cheese
½ cup (2 ounces) shredded
  Monterey Jack cheese with
  jalapeño peppers
3 tablespoons chopped purple
  onion
3 tablespoons mayonnaise or
  salad dressing
2 tablespoons catsup
¼ teaspoon salt
¼ teaspoon dried whole
  oregano
¼ teaspoon pepper
⅛ teaspoon garlic powder
8 (6-inch) French rolls
Curly leaf lettuce

Combine first 6 ingredients in a medium bowl. Combine mayonnaise, catsup, salt, oregano, pepper, and garlic powder in a small bowl, stirring well. Add mayonnaise mixture to bean mixture, stirring to coat thoroughly.

TO STORE: Refrigerate bean mixture in a tightly covered container up to 3 days.

TO SERVE: Cut a ½-inch-thick slice from top of each roll. Carefully remove soft bread from inside bottom part of each roll, leaving about ¼-inch-thick shells. (Reserve soft bread for other uses.) Line rolls with lettuce leaves, and fill evenly with bean mixture; replace tops. Yield: 8 servings.

Beef Sandwiches with Onion Marmalade

1 cup coarsely chopped onion
1 cup coarsely chopped purple
  onion
3 green onions, chopped
2 tablespoons vegetable oil
¼ cup sugar
2 tablespoons cider vinegar
1 teaspoon Worcestershire sauce
¼ teaspoon salt
⅛ teaspoon pepper
Dash of ground cloves
Curly endive leaves
4 (6-inch) French rolls, split
  lengthwise and toasted
¾ pound thinly sliced roast beef

Sauté onions in oil in a large saucepan over medium-low heat 1 hour or until very tender, stirring occasionally. Stir in sugar and next 5 ingredients. Cook over low heat, stirring occasionally, 25 to 30 minutes or until liquid evaporates. Cool completely.

TO STORE: Refrigerate in a tightly covered container up to 1 week.

TO SERVE: Bring onion mixture to room temperature. Place endive on bottom halves of toasted rolls; arrange beef over endive. Spread onion mixture evenly over beef; place top halves on rolls. Cut each sandwich in half. Yield: 4 servings.

Add a new and exciting flavor to brown-bag lunches. Beef Sandwiches with Onion Marmalade will satisfy the heartiest appetite.

Pepperoni-Vegetable Rolls _____

1 (8-ounce) package cream
  cheese, softened
1 (3½-ounce) package sliced
  pepperoni, chopped
½ cup chopped onion
½ cup chopped celery
½ cup chopped green pepper
1 clove garlic, minced
1 tablespoon tomato paste
¼ teaspoon dried Italian
  seasoning
⅛ teaspoon pepper
6 (3½-inch) French rolls

Combine first 9 ingredients in a small bowl; stir well, and set aside.

Cut a ½-inch-thick slice from top of each roll. Carefully remove soft bread from inside bottom part of each roll, leaving about ¼-inch-thick shells. (Reserve soft bread for other uses.)

Fill bottom part of each roll with ⅓ cup cream cheese mixture; replace tops.

TO STORE: Refrigerate sandwiches in a tightly covered container up to 2 days. Freeze sandwiches in a labeled airtight container up to 2 weeks.

TO SERVE: Thaw before serving. Yield: 6 servings.

Tropical Nut Bread Sandwiches _____

½ cup chopped dates
½ cup chopped pecans or
  walnuts
½ teaspoon baking soda
½ cup hot water
2 tablespoons shortening
⅓ cup sugar
1 egg
1 cup all-purpose flour
¼ teaspoon salt
½ teaspoon vanilla extract
Pineapple-Cheese Spread

Combine dates, pecans, and soda in a small bowl. Stir in hot water; set aside to cool.

Cream shortening in a medium bowl; gradually add sugar, beating well at medium speed of an electric mixer. Add egg, and beat well.

Combine flour and salt; add to creamed mixture alternately with date mixture, beginning and ending with flour mixture. Mix just until blended after each addition. Stir in vanilla.

Pour batter into 2 greased and floured 16-ounce vegetable cans. Bake at 350° for 35 to 40 minutes or until a wooden pick inserted in center comes out clean. Cool in cans 10 minutes; remove loaves from cans, and cool on wire racks. Slice loaves into ¼-inch-thick slices. Spread Pineapple-Cheese Spread evenly over half the bread slices. Top with remaining bread slices.

TO STORE: Refrigerate sandwiches in a tightly covered container up to 2 days. Freeze sandwiches in a labeled airtight container up to 2 weeks.

TO SERVE: Thaw before serving. Yield: 8 servings.

Pineapple-Cheese Spread

2 (3-ounce) packages cream
  cheese, softened
⅓ cup crushed pineapple,
  drained
¼ cup flaked coconut
2 tablespoons pineapple
  preserves

Combine all ingredients in a small bowl; stir well. Yield: 1¼ cups.

Tropical Nut Bread Sandwiches with Pineapple-Cheese Spread are a tasty snack to enjoy on the patio or by the pool.

Turkey and Cheese Rolls

1 (0.7-ounce) envelope Italian
  salad dressing mix
¼ cup Dijon mustard
2 teaspoons sugar
8 (1-ounce) slices Swiss or
  Provolone cheese
8 (2-ounce) slices cooked turkey
  breast
1 cup alfalfa sprouts

Combine first 3 ingredients; set aside.

Place 1 cheese slice on top of each turkey slice; spread evenly with mustard mixture. Top each with 2 tablespoons alfalfa sprouts, and roll up jellyroll fashion, starting at short end. Secure each roll with a wooden pick.

TO STORE: Refrigerate in a tightly covered container up to 3 days. Yield: 8 servings.

Jumbo Cookies

2 cups creamy peanut butter
½ cup butter or margarine,
  softened
1 cup sugar
1 cup plus 2 tablespoons firmly
  packed brown sugar
3 eggs
¾ teaspoon light corn syrup
¼ teaspoon vanilla extract
4½ cups regular oats, uncooked
2 teaspoons baking soda
¼ teaspoon salt
1 cup candy-coated chocolate
  pieces
1 (6-ounce) package semisweet
  chocolate morsels

Cream peanut butter and butter; gradually add sugars, beating well at medium speed of an electric mixer. Add eggs, corn syrup, and vanilla, beating well. Combine oats, soda, and salt; add to creamed mixture, mixing well. Stir in chocolate pieces and morsels. (Dough will be stiff.)

For each cookie, pack dough into a ¼-cup measure. Drop dough, 4 inches apart, onto lightly greased cookie sheets. Lightly press each cookie into a 3½-inch circle. Bake at 350° for 10 to 12 minutes or until lightly browned. Cool slightly on cookie sheets; remove cookies to wire racks to cool completely.

TO STORE: Store cookies in an airtight container at room temperature up to 1 week. Freeze in a labeled airtight container up to 1 month.

TO SERVE: Thaw cookies at room temperature. Yield: 2½ dozen.

No-Bake Chocolate Oatmeal Cookies

2 cups sugar
¼ cup cocoa
½ cup milk
¼ cup butter or margarine
2½ cups regular oats, uncooked
¾ cup creamy peanut butter
2 teaspoons vanilla extract

Combine first 4 ingredients in a heavy saucepan. Cook over medium heat, stirring occasionally, until mixture comes to a boil; boil 1 minute. Remove from heat; add oats, peanut butter, and vanilla, stirring well. Drop dough by heaping teaspoonfuls onto lightly greased wax paper. Cool completely.

TO STORE: Store in an airtight container at room temperature up to 2 weeks. Yield: 4½ dozen.

Pack Turkey and Cheese Rolls in the ice chest to take along and enjoy at your next summer outing.

Double·Duty

Make something special this weekend—maybe a big golden turkey with cornbread stuffing or a beautiful ham glazed with cranberry sauce. The recipes in this chapter show you how the leftovers of large cuts of meat and large batches of spaghetti sauce, rice, and beans are a make-ahead dividend, an already cooked ingredient for other quick meals to come.

For example, what starts out as Sunday's pot roast can become Wednesday's stroganoff. Baked ham becomes a tangy ham loaf; roast chicken turns elegant in a warm salad with walnuts and grapes.

If you can't warm up to the thought of leftovers, you may decide to freeze the surplus and retrieve it several weeks later. It will be easier to use if you divide the meat into convenient cooking quantities, measured in pounds or cups, and label the container. Sliced or diced meats will stay fresh-tasting longer if you moisten them with some of the pan juices before freezing.

In the summer, when you don't want to heat up the kitchen, it makes sense to grill extra portions of pork, beef, or poultry. Then turn the extras into cool salads and sandwiches to be eaten later.

The latter part of this chapter is devoted to beans and rice. You will find that it's well worth cooking extra amounts of these two basics to have them left over for Home-Style Baked Beans, Hearty Sausage-Bean Soup, Pork Fried Rice, and Rice Pudding.

Meaty Spaghetti Sauce (page 70) can be made ahead and frozen. Later, it can be made into Stuffed Shells Florentine (page 71).

Old-Fashioned Pot Roast

½ cup minced fresh parsley
3 tablespoons prepared
   horseradish
3 cloves garlic, minced
1 tablespoon dried whole
   marjoram
1 tablespoon dried whole thyme
1 (6- to 7-pound) chuck roast
4 medium onions, thinly sliced
   and separated into rings
1 cup Burgundy or other dry
   red wine
1½ pounds potatoes, peeled and
   quartered
1 pound carrots, scraped and
   cut into 2-inch pieces
1 pound turnips, peeled and cut
   into chunks
Salt and pepper to taste

Combine first 5 ingredients; pat evenly over roast. Cover and refrigerate 2 to 4 hours.

Combine onion rings and wine in a large Dutch oven; add roast. Insert meat thermometer into thickest part of roast. Cover and bake at 325° for 2 hours.

Add potato, carrot, and turnips; cover and bake at 325° for 1½ hours. Uncover and bake 30 minutes, or until thermometer registers 160° (medium). Let stand 15 minutes before serving.

Arrange meat and vegetables on a serving platter. Pour pan drippings into a medium saucepan; bring to a boil. Boil 3 minutes. Add salt and pepper. Serve with meat and vegetables. Yield: 10 to 15 servings.

TO STORE: Remove remaining meat from bone. Slice or chop meat as desired. Refrigerate in a tightly covered container up to 4 days. Freeze in a labeled airtight container up to 3 months.

Shortcut Stroganoff

1 medium onion, chopped
1 clove garlic, minced
1 tablespoon butter or
   margarine, melted
1 tablespoon all-purpose flour
1 teaspoon paprika
1 cup beef broth
2 tablespoons tomato paste
1 pound cooked pot roast, cut
   into thin strips
½ pound fresh mushrooms,
   sliced
1 tablespoon butter or
   margarine, melted
½ cup sour cream
½ cup chopped fresh parsley
½ teaspoon salt
¼ teaspoon pepper
Hot cooked noodles

Sauté onion and garlic in 1 tablespoon butter in a large skillet over medium heat until tender. Stir in flour and paprika; cook 1 minute, stirring constantly. Gradually add broth and tomato paste, stirring well; add beef strips. Bring mixture to a boil; reduce heat, and simmer 10 minutes.

Sauté mushrooms in 1 tablespoon butter in a large skillet over medium heat until tender; stir into meat mixture. Add sour cream, parsley, salt, and pepper, stirring well. Serve over hot noodles. Yield: 4 to 6 servings.

Beef and Bean Tostadas

1 medium onion, finely chopped
2 cloves garlic, minced
1 tablespoon vegetable oil
2 teaspoons chili powder
2 teaspoons ground cumin
1 teaspoon ground coriander
¼ teaspoon salt
¼ teaspoon ground cinnamon
½ cup tomato juice
1 (16-ounce) can pinto beans,
    drained, rinsed, and mashed
8 (6-inch) corn tortillas
½ pound shredded cooked pot
    roast
1 cup (4 ounces) shredded
    Cheddar cheese
Freshly ground pepper to taste
2 cups shredded lettuce
1 large tomato, chopped
2 green onions, thinly sliced
Sour cream
Commercial salsa

Sauté chopped onion and garlic in oil in a large skillet over medium heat until tender. Stir in chili powder and next 5 ingredients. Bring to a boil; reduce heat, and simmer 3 minutes. Stir in mashed beans.

Divide bean mixture evenly among tortillas, spreading to edges. Divide beef and cheese evenly among tortillas; sprinkle with pepper.

Place tortillas on ungreased baking sheets. Bake at 300° for 15 minutes or until thoroughly heated. Serve hot with lettuce, tomato, green onions, sour cream, and salsa. Yield: 4 servings.

Tangy Beef Salad

1 pound cooked pot roast, cut
    into thin strips
¼ cup vegetable oil
¼ cup red wine vinegar
1 teaspoon dried whole tarragon
¼ teaspoon salt
⅛ teaspoon pepper
6 cups torn mixed greens
8 cherry tomatoes, halved
Dressing (recipe follows)

Combine first 6 ingredients in a large zip-top heavy-duty plastic bag. Refrigerate 1 hour, turning occasionally. Drain meat; discard marinade.

Arrange mixed greens and tomato halves on individual plates; top with meat mixture. Spoon dressing over salad, and serve immediately. Yield: 4 servings.

Dressing

¾ cup mayonnaise
2 green onions, chopped
2 tablespoons sour cream
1 tablespoon capers, drained
    and rinsed
1 tablespoon coarse-grained
    mustard
1 clove garlic, sliced

Combine all ingredients in container of an electric blender; process until mixture is smooth. Store in refrigerator in a tightly covered container up to 2 weeks. Yield: about 1 cup.

Roast Loin of Pork

1 (5- to 6-pound) pork loin
  roast
4 cloves garlic, minced
1 tablespoon dried whole
  oregano
2 teaspoons ground cumin
½ teaspoon pepper
½ cup orange juice

Trim fat from roast. Place roast on a rack in a roasting pan. Combine garlic and next 3 ingredients; rub garlic mixture over roast. Pour orange juice over roast.

Insert meat thermometer in roast, making sure it does not touch fat or bone. Cover and bake at 325° for 2½ hours. Uncover and bake 30 minutes or until meat thermometer registers 160° (medium). Let roast stand 10 to 15 minutes before serving.

TO STORE: Remove remaining meat from bone. Slice or chop meat as desired. Refrigerate meat in a tightly covered container up to 4 days. Freeze in a labeled airtight container up to 3 months. Yield: 12 to 14 servings.

Sesame Noodles with Roast Pork

6 ounces vermicelli or thin
  spaghetti, uncooked
¼ cup plus 1 tablespoon rice
  wine vinegar
2 tablespoons dark sesame oil,
  divided
1 tablespoon vegetable oil
2 teaspoons hoisin sauce
1 teaspoon soy sauce
1 tablespoon minced fresh
  gingerroot
1 clove garlic, minced
¾ pound cooked pork roast, cut
  into thin strips
½ pound fresh spinach
3 tablespoons sesame seeds,
  toasted
Salt and pepper to taste

Cook pasta according to package directions; drain. Place pasta in a large bowl.

Combine vinegar, 1 tablespoon sesame oil, vegetable oil, hoisin sauce, soy sauce, gingerroot, and garlic in a small bowl; stir well. Pour half of dressing over pasta, tossing to combine.

Heat remaining 1 tablespoon sesame oil in a large skillet over medium-high heat. Add pork; sauté 3 to 5 minutes or until browned. Add pork to pasta mixture, tossing gently to combine.

Remove stems from spinach; wash leaves thoroughly. Cut spinach into thin strips. Cook in a large nonstick skillet over medium-high heat 3 to 4 minutes or just until spinach wilts. Add spinach to noodle mixture. Sprinkle with sesame seeds, and pour remaining dressing over pasta; toss gently to combine. Add salt and pepper to taste. Serve warm. Yield: 4 servings.

Garnished with orange twists and fresh parsley and sage sprigs, Roast Loin of Pork is an elegant entrée.

Warm Roast Pork-Potato Salad

1 (13¾-ounce) can chicken
  broth, undiluted
1½ pounds new potatoes,
  quartered
1 medium-size purple onion,
  quartered and thinly sliced
1 cup frozen English peas,
  thawed
½ cup sliced ripe olives
½ cup chopped fresh parsley
Pepper to taste
⅓ cup olive oil or vegetable oil
2½ tablespoons cider vinegar
¼ teaspoon ground cumin
⅛ teaspoon chili powder
¾ pound cubed cooked pork
  roast
2 tablespoons dry vermouth
2 hard-cooked eggs, coarsely
  chopped

Bring chicken broth to a boil in a medium saucepan. Add potato; cover, reduce heat, and simmer 10 to 15 minutes or until potato is tender. Remove potato from broth, reserving broth. Place potato in a large bowl; add onion and next 4 ingredients, tossing gently to combine.

Cook reserved broth over medium heat until reduced to ½ cup. Pour over potato mixture; toss gently to combine.

Combine oil, vinegar, cumin, and chili powder in a medium saucepan; stir well. Add pork and vermouth. Cook over medium heat until thoroughly heated. Add pork mixture to potato mixture, tossing gently. Add eggs, tossing gently to combine. Serve warm. Yield: 6 servings.

Black Beans and Pork over Rice

1 teaspoon ground cumin
½ teaspoon ground coriander
¼ teaspoon chili powder
½ pound diced cooked pork
  roast
⅓ cup orange juice
1 medium onion, chopped
1¼ cups chopped sweet red
  pepper
2 cloves garlic, minced
2 tablespoons vegetable oil
1 (16-ounce) can black beans,
  drained and rinsed
1 medium tomato, seeded and
  chopped
2 tablespoons chopped green
  chiles
¼ teaspoon salt
⅛ teaspoon pepper
3 cups hot cooked rice
Garnish: fresh cilantro sprigs

Combine cumin, coriander, and chili powder; toss pork in spice mixture to coat. Heat a large skillet over medium-high heat until hot; add pork. Cook, stirring constantly, 2 minutes or until thoroughly heated. Remove pork from skillet, and place in a medium bowl; add orange juice, stirring well. Set aside.

Sauté onion, sweet pepper, and garlic in oil in skillet until vegetables are tender. Stir in reserved pork mixture, beans, and next 4 ingredients. Cook, stirring occasionally, until thoroughly heated. Serve over rice. Garnish, if desired. Yield: 4 servings.

Green chiles, cumin, and garlic give Black Beans and Pork over Rice an authentic south-of-the-border flavor.

Roast Pork Sandwiches

½ cup mayonnaise
1 tablespoon orange juice
1 teaspoon grated orange rind
Dash of hot sauce
1 (16-ounce) loaf Italian bread,
    sliced in half lengthwise
1 pound thinly sliced cooked
    pork roast
1 medium tomato, thinly sliced
1 small purple onion, thinly
    sliced and separated into rings
Salt and pepper to taste

Combine first 4 ingredients; stir well. Spread cut sides of bread with mayonnaise mixture. Layer pork, tomato, and onion on bottom slice of bread; sprinkle with salt and pepper. Cover with top slice of bread. Cut sandwich into fourths. Yield: 4 servings.

Cranberry-Glazed Ham

1 (12- to 14-pound) smoked,
    fully cooked ham
2 tablespoons Dijon mustard
Whole cloves
1 (16-ounce) can jellied
    cranberry sauce
2 tablespoons red wine vinegar
1 tablespoon soy sauce
1 tablespoon minced fresh
    gingerroot
1 teaspoon dry mustard
¼ teaspoon ground cardamom
¼ teaspoon ground cinnamon
⅛ teaspoon ground nutmeg
Garnishes: flowering cabbage
    and fresh cranberries
1½ cups ruby port wine
¾ cup sugar
1 (12-ounce) package fresh
    cranberries

Trim skin from ham, leaving ¼-inch thickness of fat. Brush ham with Dijon mustard. Score fat on ham in a diamond design, and stud with cloves. Place ham, fat side up, on a rack in a shallow roasting pan. Insert meat thermometer, making sure it does not touch fat or bone. Bake, uncovered, at 250° for 2 hours.

Place cranberry sauce in a medium saucepan; add vinegar and soy sauce. Cook over low heat, stirring frequently, until cranberry sauce melts. Stir in gingerroot and next 4 ingredients. Spread one-third of cranberry sauce mixture over ham. Cover and bake at 350° for 1 hour or until thermometer registers 140° (18 to 24 minutes per pound), basting with cranberry sauce mixture after 30 minutes. Let stand 20 minutes before slicing. Garnish, if desired.

Add wine and sugar to remaining cranberry sauce mixture; bring to a boil. Stir in cranberries, and cook over medium heat 15 minutes or until cranberries pop. Remove from heat; let stand 20 minutes. Serve with ham.

TO STORE: Remove remaining meat from bone. Slice or chop meat as desired. Refrigerate in a tightly covered container up to 1 week. Freeze in a labeled airtight container up to 3 months. (Ham bone may be frozen in a labeled airtight container up to 6 months for later use.) Yield: 20 to 25 servings.

Ham and Bean Soup

1 pound dried Great Northern
    beans
6 cups water, divided
1 medium onion, chopped
2 cloves garlic, crushed
1 medium-size hot red pepper
1 bay leaf
2 teaspoons salt
½ teaspoon dried whole thyme
¼ teaspoon pepper
4 medium potatoes, peeled and
    cubed
3 medium carrots, scraped and
    cut into ½-inch slices
2 cups coarsely chopped cooked
    ham

Sort and wash beans; place in a Dutch oven. Cover with water 2 inches above beans; let soak 8 hours.

Drain beans and return to Dutch oven. Add 4 cups water and next 7 ingredients. Bring to a boil; cover, reduce heat, and simmer 1½ hours, stirring occasionally. Add remaining 2 cups water, potato, carrot, and ham. Cover and simmer 30 minutes, or until vegetables are tender. Remove hot red pepper and bay leaf before serving. Yield: 10 cups.

Cranberry-Glazed Ham is a welcome addition to any holiday meal. String fresh cranberries for a garnish with extra flair.

Scalloped Ham and Potatoes

¼ cup butter or margarine
¼ cup all-purpose flour
2 cups half-and-half
¾ teaspoon salt
¼ teaspoon ground white
  pepper
4 medium potatoes, peeled and
  thinly sliced
2 cups chopped cooked ham
2 small onions, thinly sliced and
  separated into rings
¼ cup chopped green pepper
2 cloves garlic, minced

Melt butter in a heavy saucepan over low heat; add flour, stirring until smooth. Cook 1 minute, stirring constantly. Gradually add half-and-half; cook over medium heat, stirring constantly, until mixture is thickened and bubbly. Stir in salt and white pepper.

Spoon ¼ cup sauce mixture into a greased 10-inch ovenproof skillet. Combine potato and remaining ingredients in a large bowl; stir well. Layer half of potato mixture over sauce. Top with half of remaining sauce. Repeat layers. Cover and bake at 350° for 1 hour or until potato is tender. Yield: 8 servings.

Crustless Ham Quiche

1 cup diced cooked ham
½ pound fresh mushrooms,
  sliced
1 tablespoon butter or
  margarine, melted
4 eggs
1 cup sour cream
1 cup small-curd cottage cheese
½ cup grated Parmesan cheese
¼ cup all-purpose flour
½ teaspoon dried whole
  dillweed
½ teaspoon dry mustard
⅛ teaspoon ground nutmeg
⅛ teaspoon pepper
1 cup (4 ounces) shredded
  Swiss cheese
½ cup chopped fresh parsley

Cook ham in a skillet over medium heat until lightly browned; set aside. Sauté mushrooms in butter in a skillet over medium heat until tender (about 10 minutes). Sprinkle mushrooms and reserved ham evenly in a greased 10-inch quiche dish.

Combine eggs and next 8 ingredients in container of an electric blender; process until smooth. Stir cheese and parsley into egg mixture; pour over ham and mushrooms. Bake at 350° for 40 to 45 minutes or until set. Let stand 10 minutes before serving. Yield: one 10-inch quiche.

Put leftover ham to use in Crustless Ham Quiche. This hearty meat and egg pie is a tasty, no-fuss dish.

Sweet-Sour Ham Loaf

1 pound ground cooked ham
1 pound ground pork
2 eggs, lightly beaten
¾ cup soft breadcrumbs
½ cup milk
¼ cup plus 1 tablespoon
  Chinese sweet-and-sour sauce,
  divided
2 tablespoons brown sugar
2 tablespoons soy sauce, divided
1 tablespoon plus 1 teaspoon
  Dijon mustard, divided

Combine first 5 ingredients, mixing well. Add 3 tablespoons sweet-and-sour sauce, brown sugar, 2 teaspoons soy sauce, and 2 teaspoons mustard; mix well. Press mixture into a greased 9- x 5- x 3-inch loafpan.

Combine remaining 2 tablespoons sweet-and-sour sauce, 1 tablespoon plus 1 teaspoon soy sauce, and 2 teaspoons mustard in a small bowl; stir well. Pour sauce over ham loaf. Bake at 350° for 1 hour and 15 minutes. Yield: 6 to 8 servings.

Meaty Spaghetti Sauce

2 pounds lean ground beef
2 pounds ground pork or veal
1 pound Italian sausage, casings removed
2 large onions, chopped
2 medium-size green peppers, chopped
5 cloves garlic, minced
2 (28-ounce) cans whole tomatoes, undrained and chopped
2 (6-ounce) cans tomato paste
2 cups Burgundy or other dry red wine
2 cups water
1 cup chopped fresh parsley
3 bay leaves
1½ teaspoons salt
2 teaspoons dried whole oregano
2 teaspoons dried whole basil, crushed
2 teaspoons brown sugar
Hot cooked spaghetti
Grated Parmesan cheese

Combine first 6 ingredients in a stockpot; cook over medium-high heat until meat is browned, stirring to crumble meat; drain well. Stir in tomatoes and next 9 ingredients. Bring to a boil; cover, reduce heat, and simmer 2 hours, stirring occasionally. Uncover and simmer 1 hour, or to desired consistency, stirring occasionally. Remove bay leaves. Serve over hot spaghetti; sprinkle with Parmesan cheese. Yield: about 16 cups.

TO STORE: Refrigerate remaining spaghetti sauce in a tightly covered container up to 1 week. Freeze remaining sauce in desired amounts in labeled airtight containers up to 3 months.

Skillet Pizza Supreme

1 package dry yeast
¼ cup warm water (105° to 115°)
2½ cups all-purpose flour, divided
1 teaspoon sugar
1 teaspoon salt
1 tablespoon vegetable oil
½ to ¾ cup milk
2 cups Meaty Spaghetti Sauce
1 small green pepper, thinly sliced into rings
½ cup sliced fresh mushrooms
½ cup sliced ripe olives
2 cups (8 ounces) shredded mozzarella cheese
¼ teaspoon dried whole oregano
¼ teaspoon pepper
¼ cup grated Parmesan cheese

Dissolve yeast in warm water in a small bowl; let stand 5 minutes. Combine 2 cups flour, sugar, and salt in a large bowl; stir in yeast mixture and oil. Add enough milk to make a soft dough. Cover and let stand 15 minutes.

Turn dough out onto a floured surface. Knead 5 to 8 times, working in remaining ½ cup flour to make a smooth dough. Pat dough evenly in bottom and halfway up sides of a lightly greased 10-inch cast-iron skillet. Bake at 425° for 8 minutes.

Cook Meaty Spaghetti Sauce in a small saucepan over medium heat until thoroughly heated, stirring occasionally. Spoon sauce over crust. Top with pepper rings and remaining ingredients. Bake 10 to 12 minutes or until cheese melts. Yield: 6 servings.

Eggplant Parmesan

1 large eggplant (about 1½ pounds)
Salt
2 eggs, beaten
1¼ cups cracker crumbs
Vegetable oil
4 cups Meaty Spaghetti Sauce
2 cups (8 ounces) shredded mozzarella cheese
½ cup grated Parmesan cheese

Peel eggplant, and cut into ¼-inch slices. Sprinkle both sides of slices with salt; let stand 30 minutes. Rinse eggplant, and pat dry. Dip eggplant in egg; coat with cracker crumbs. Fry a few slices at a time in hot oil until golden brown. Drain on paper towels.

Cook Meaty Spaghetti Sauce in a saucepan over medium heat until thoroughly heated; stir occasionally.

Place half of eggplant slices in a lightly greased 13- x 9- x 2-inch baking dish; spread half of Meaty Spaghetti Sauce over eggplant. Top with half each of mozzarella and Parmesan cheeses. Repeat layers. Bake at 350° for 40 to 45 minutes or until eggplant is tender. Let stand 10 minutes before serving. Yield: 8 servings.

Stuffed Shells Florentine

24 jumbo macaroni shells
1 (10-ounce) package frozen chopped spinach, thawed and drained
2 cups (8 ounces) shredded mozzarella cheese
2 cups ricotta cheese
½ cup grated Parmesan cheese
3 green onions, minced
2 tablespoons minced fresh parsley
1 teaspoon dried whole basil
¼ teaspoon salt
¼ teaspoon ground nutmeg
¼ teaspoon pepper
4 cups Meaty Spaghetti Sauce
¼ cup grated Parmesan cheese

Cook macaroni shells according to package directions; drain well, and set aside.

Combine spinach and next 9 ingredients in a large bowl; stir well.

Cook Meaty Spaghetti Sauce in a saucepan over medium heat until thoroughly heated, stirring occasionally. Fill each shell with ¼ cup spinach mixture, and place in a lightly greased 13- x 9- x 2-inch baking dish. Pour sauce evenly over shells; sprinkle with Parmesan cheese. Bake at 350° for 35 to 40 minutes or until hot and bubbly. Let stand 10 minutes before serving. Yield: 8 servings.

Lasagna

1 (8-ounce) package lasagna noodles
1 (15-ounce) carton ricotta cheese
⅓ cup grated Parmesan cheese
2 eggs, lightly beaten
¼ cup minced fresh parsley
½ teaspoon salt
⅛ teaspoon pepper
6 cups Meaty Spaghetti Sauce
2 cups (8 ounces) shredded mozzarella cheese

Cook lasagna noodles according to package directions; drain and set aside.

Combine ricotta cheese and next 5 ingredients in a medium bowl, stirring well; set aside. Cook Meaty Spaghetti Sauce in a large saucepan over medium heat until thoroughly heated, stirring occasionally.

Arrange 3 lasagna noodles in a lightly greased 13- x 9- x 2-inch baking dish. Layer one-third each of cheese mixture, sauce, and mozzarella cheese over noodles. Repeat layers twice. Bake at 350° for 30 to 35 minutes or until hot and bubbly. Let stand 10 minutes before serving. Yield: 8 servings.

Savory Roast Chickens

2 (3½- to 4-pound)
  broiler-fryers
½ teaspoon salt
½ teaspoon garlic powder
2 carrots, scraped and sliced
2 stalks celery with leaves,
  sliced
1 large onion, cut into wedges
10 fresh parsley sprigs
2 teaspoons dried whole
  rosemary
2 teaspoons dried whole
  tarragon
¼ cup butter or margarine,
  melted
1 cup chicken broth

Remove giblets and necks from chickens; reserve for other uses. Rinse chickens thoroughly inside and out with cold water; pat dry. Sprinkle body cavities of chickens with salt and garlic powder; set aside.

Combine carrot and next 5 ingredients in a medium bowl. Lightly pack the vegetable mixture into body cavities of chickens. Close cavities with skewers and truss. Tie ends of legs together with string. Lift wingtips up and over back, and tuck under chickens.

Place chickens, breast side up, on a rack in a roasting pan. Brush chickens with butter. Pour chicken broth over chickens.

Insert meat thermometer in breast or meaty part of thigh, making sure it does not touch bone. Cover and bake at 325° for 1½ hours, basting frequently with chicken broth. Uncover and bake an additional 1½ hours or until meat thermometer registers 185°, basting frequently with chicken broth. If chicken starts to brown too much, cover with aluminum foil. Let stand 10 minutes before serving. Yield: 8 to 10 servings.

TO STORE: Remove remaining meat from bone. Slice or chop meat as desired. Refrigerate in a tightly covered container up to 3 days. Freeze in a labeled airtight container up to 3 months.

Warm Chinese Chicken Salad

¼ cup cider vinegar
2 tablespoons walnut oil
2 tablespoons vegetable oil
2 tablespoons chicken broth
1 teaspoon dried whole tarragon
½ teaspoon Dijon mustard
½ teaspoon Worcestershire
  sauce
¼ teaspoon salt
⅛ teaspoon ground nutmeg
2 cups torn Chinese cabbage
2 cups torn romaine lettuce
⅔ cup chopped walnuts, toasted
3 cups coarsely chopped cooked
  chicken
1½ cups halved seedless red
  grapes

Combine first 9 ingredients in a small bowl, stirring well. Toss cabbage and lettuce with half of dressing mixture in a large shallow bowl. Sprinkle walnuts over cabbage mixture.

Combine chicken and 3 tablespoons remaining dressing mixture in a skillet over medium heat. Cook, stirring occasionally, until chicken is thoroughly heated. Toss hot chicken mixture and grape halves with cabbage mixture. Serve salad warm with remaining dressing. Yield: 4 servings.

A tangy dressing gives cooked chicken an Oriental flavor in elegant Warm Chinese Chicken Salad.

Chicken Flautas with Avocado Sauce

1 ripe avocado, peeled and
   mashed
½ cup finely chopped fresh
   cilantro
¼ cup sour cream
2 tablespoons fresh lime juice
1 green onion, thinly sliced
¼ teaspoon salt
¼ teaspoon pepper
1 small onion, minced
2 cloves garlic, minced
½ cup chicken broth
2 cups shredded cooked chicken
¼ cup drained chopped green
   chiles
¼ teaspoon salt
¼ teaspoon chili powder
10 (6-inch) corn tortillas
Vegetable oil
Garnish: chopped fresh tomato

Combine first 7 ingredients, stirring well; set avocado sauce aside.

Place onion, garlic, and broth in a medium skillet; cover and cook over medium-low heat 15 minutes. Stir in chicken, chiles, ¼ teaspoon salt, and chili powder; cook over medium heat until thoroughly heated.

Place 3 tablespoons chicken mixture in center of each tortilla; roll up tortillas, and secure with wooden picks.

Fry tortilla rolls in hot oil (375°) in a large skillet until golden brown on all sides. Drain on paper towels. Serve with reserved avocado sauce. Garnish, if desired. Yield: 4 servings.

Chicken Fettuccine

½ pound fresh mushrooms,
   sliced
1 small sweet red pepper, cut
   into thin strips
1 small onion, chopped
1 clove garlic, crushed
2 tablespoons butter or
   margarine, melted
3 cups chopped cooked chicken
1 (8-ounce) package fettuccine
½ cup whipping cream
½ cup butter or margarine
½ cup grated Parmesan cheese
2 tablespoons chopped fresh
   parsley
¼ teaspoon ground white
   pepper

Sauté first 4 ingredients in 2 tablespoons butter in a large skillet over medium heat until vegetables are tender. Add chicken, and cook until thoroughly heated. Set aside, and keep warm.

Cook fettuccine according to package directions; drain and place in a large bowl.

Combine whipping cream and ½ cup butter in a small saucepan; cook over low heat until butter melts. Stir in Parmesan cheese, chopped parsley, and white pepper. Pour whipping cream mixture over hot fettuccine; add chicken mixture. Toss until fettuccine is thoroughly coated. Yield: 6 to 8 servings.

Chicken Fettuccine is impressive, yet easy to make. Add bread and a favorite beverage for a complete meal.

Toasted Chicken and Swiss Sandwiches —————

3 tablespoons mayonnaise
1½ tablespoons coarse-grained mustard
8 slices rye or pumpernickel bread
½ pound thinly sliced cooked chicken
4 slices bacon, cooked
4 (1-ounce) slices Swiss cheese
2 eggs, lightly beaten
3 tablespoons milk
1 to 4 tablespoons butter or margarine

Combine mayonnaise and mustard, stirring well. Spread mayonnaise mixture on one side of each slice of bread. Arrange chicken on 4 slices of bread; top with bacon, cheese, and remaining bread slices.

Combine eggs and milk, stirring well. Melt 1 tablespoon butter in a large skillet over medium heat. Carefully dip one sandwich into egg mixture, coating both sides. Cook in melted butter until golden brown and cheese is slightly melted, turning once. Repeat procedure with remaining sandwiches, adding 1 tablespoon butter to skillet each time, if necessary. Yield: 4 servings.

Roast Turkey with Cornbread Stuffing

2 medium onions, chopped
1¼ cups chopped celery
2 large cloves garlic, minced
3 tablespoons butter or
   margarine, melted
4 slices white bread
4 cups crumbled cornbread
1 cup finely chopped fresh
   parsley
1 teaspoon rubbed sage
1 teaspoon dried whole
   rosemary
½ teaspoon salt
½ teaspoon dried whole thyme
⅛ teaspoon ground nutmeg
⅛ teaspoon pepper
2 cups chicken broth, divided
3 eggs, lightly beaten
1 (14- to 16-pound) turkey
Melted butter or margarine or
   vegetable oil
Garnishes: fresh parsley sprigs,
   fresh thyme sprigs, fresh sage
   sprigs, and crab apples

Sauté onion, celery, and garlic in 3 tablespoons butter in a large skillet over medium heat until tender. Set aside. Trim crust from bread slices; reserve crust for other uses. Cut bread into cubes. Combine bread, cornbread, and next 7 ingredients in a large bowl. Add onion mixture, 1 cup chicken broth, and eggs; stir until bread mixture is moistened.

Remove giblets and neck from turkey; reserve for other uses, if desired. Rinse turkey thoroughly with cold water; pat dry. Lightly pack stuffing into body cavities of turkey. Tuck legs under flap of skin around tail, or close cavity with skewers and truss. Tie ends of legs to tail with cord. Lift wingtips up and over back; tuck under turkey.

Place turkey on a rack in a roasting pan, breast side up; brush entire turkey with butter. Insert meat thermometer in meaty part of thigh, making sure it does not touch bone. Pour remaining 1 cup broth in bottom of pan. Cover turkey with heavy-duty aluminum foil, and bake at 325° for 3 hours. Uncover and bake an additional 2 to 2½ hours or until thermometer reaches 185°, basting every 30 minutes with butter.

When turkey is two-thirds done, cut the cord or band of skin holding the drumstick ends to the tail; this will ensure that the thighs are cooked internally. Turkey is done when drumsticks are easy to move up and down. Let stand 15 minutes before carving. Garnish, if desired.

TO STORE: Remove remaining meat from bones. Slice or chop meat as desired. Refrigerate in a tightly covered container up to 3 days. Freeze in a labeled airtight container up to 3 months. (Turkey carcass may be frozen in a labeled airtight container up to 6 months for later use.) Yield: 24 to 26 servings.

Day-After-Thanksgiving Sandwiches

4 ounces cream cheese, softened
½ cup jellied cranberry sauce
8 slices white bread or whole
   wheat bread
Curly leaf lettuce
¾ pound sliced cooked turkey
Salt and pepper to taste

Beat cream cheese at medium speed of an electric mixer until smooth. Spread cream cheese and cranberry sauce evenly over one side of 4 slices of bread. Top each slice with lettuce; divide turkey evenly over lettuce. Sprinkle with salt and pepper; top with remaining bread slices. Yield: 4 servings.

Make tender Roast Turkey with Cornbread Stuffing the centerpiece of your holiday table.

Lattice-Topped Turkey Pie

2 cups chopped cooked turkey
1 (10-ounce) package frozen
   English peas and carrots,
   thawed
1 cup diced celery
1 cup (4 ounces) shredded
   Cheddar cheese
1 cup mayonnaise
½ cup soft breadcrumbs
¼ cup chopped onion
¼ teaspoon salt
⅛ teaspoon pepper
3 dashes of hot sauce
1 (8-ounce) can crescent
   dinner rolls

Combine first 10 ingredients in a large bowl; stir well. Spoon into a lightly greased 10- x 6- x 2-inch baking dish; set aside.

Unroll crescent roll dough into two rectangles; press long sides together to make one large rectangle. Cut dough into ¾-inch strips. Arrange strips in a lattice design over turkey mixture. Bake at 350° for 20 to 25 minutes or until lightly browned. Yield: 6 to 8 servings.

Lattice-Topped Turkey Pie is a time-saving entrée that is pretty enough to serve company.

Turkey-Rice Pilaf

1 (6-ounce) package long-grain and wild rice mix
2 teaspoons sesame oil or vegetable oil
2 cups shredded Chinese cabbage
2 cups chopped cooked turkey
1 (10-ounce) package frozen English peas, thawed
½ cup chopped pecans, toasted
¼ cup chicken broth
2 tablespoons dry sherry
2 tablespoons white wine vinegar
¼ teaspoon salt
¼ teaspoon pepper

Prepare rice mix according to package directions; set rice aside.

Heat oil in a large heavy skillet over medium heat; add cabbage, and cook 3 minutes or until wilted. Add prepared rice, turkey, and remaining ingredients. Cook 3 to 5 minutes or until thoroughly heated, stirring frequently. Yield: 6 to 8 servings.

Turkey Tortilla Casserole

8 (6-inch) corn tortillas
Vegetable oil
1 large onion, chopped
2 small cloves garlic, minced
1 tablespoon vegetable oil
1 (10-ounce) can tomatoes and green chiles, undrained and chopped
1 (7½-ounce) can whole tomatoes, undrained and chopped
1½ teaspoons dried whole cilantro
¼ teaspoon salt
3 cups chopped cooked turkey
2 cups (8 ounces) shredded Monterey Jack cheese
Sour cream

Fry tortillas, one at a time, in ¼ inch hot oil (375°) about 5 seconds on each side or just until softened. Drain on paper towels. Line an 11- x 7- x 1½-inch baking dish with tortillas, letting tortillas extend ½ inch above sides of dish. Set aside.

Sauté onion and garlic in 1 tablespoon oil in a large skillet until tender. Stir in tomatoes, cilantro, and salt. Simmer, uncovered, 8 to 10 minutes, stirring occasionally; stir in turkey. Pour mixture over tortillas. Bake at 350° for 20 minutes. Sprinkle with cheese, and bake an additional 5 minutes or until cheese melts. Serve with sour cream. Yield: 6 to 8 servings.

Curried Turkey Salad

3 cups chopped cooked turkey
2 stalks celery, sliced
½ cup frozen English peas,
　thawed
½ cup finely chopped fresh
　parsley
⅓ cup mayonnaise
2 tablespoons sour cream
2 teaspoons fresh lime juice or
　lemon juice
1½ teaspoons curry powder
½ teaspoon ground cumin
¼ teaspoon salt
¼ teaspoon pepper
⅛ teaspoon ground cinnamon
⅛ teaspoon ground nutmeg
½ cup sliced almonds, toasted
Lettuce leaves

Combine turkey, celery, peas, and parsley in a medium bowl; stir well. Combine mayonnaise and next 8 ingredients in a small bowl; pour over turkey mixture, tossing well. Chill thoroughly.

Before serving, add almonds to salad, and toss well. Serve on lettuce leaves. Yield: 4 servings.

Turkey Vegetable Soup

1 turkey carcass
3 quarts water
1 bay leaf
6 small potatoes, peeled and
　diced
4 large carrots, scraped and
　diced
2 stalks celery, diced
1 large onion, chopped
1 (28-ounce) can tomatoes,
　undrained and chopped
1 (16-ounce) can tomato sauce
½ cup barley, uncooked
1 tablespoon chopped fresh
　parsley
1½ teaspoons salt
1 teaspoon dried whole basil
¼ teaspoon dried whole thyme
¼ teaspoon pepper

Place turkey carcass, water, and bay leaf in a large Dutch oven; bring to a boil. Cover, reduce heat, and simmer 2 hours. Remove carcass from broth, and pick meat from bones. Remove and discard bay leaf. Skim fat from broth, if necessary.

Return meat to broth; add potato and remaining ingredients. Cover and simmer 1 hour or until vegetables are tender. Yield: 3½ quarts.

Curried Turkey Salad, served on a bed of lettuce, is a dish that appeals to the eye as well as the palate.

Ham-Simmered Beans

2 pounds dried white, kidney,
  or pinto beans
3 quarts water
1 large smoked ham hock
2 large onions, chopped
3 large cloves garlic, minced
1 teaspoon salt
1 teaspoon dried whole thyme
1 teaspoon dried whole
  marjoram
3 bay leaves

Sort and wash beans; place in a large Dutch oven. Cover with water 2 inches above beans; let soak overnight. Drain beans, and return to Dutch oven. Add 3 quarts water and remaining ingredients to beans. Bring to a boil; cover, reduce heat, and simmer 1½ to 2 hours or until beans are tender. Remove ham hock and bay leaves. If desired, cut ham from hock and chop; return to beans. Yield: 16 cups.

TO STORE: Refrigerate remaining beans in a tightly covered container up to 5 days. Freeze in desired amounts in labeled airtight containers up to 6 months.

Hearty Sausage-Bean Soup

2 pounds bulk turkey sausage
1 large onion, chopped
4 cups Ham-Simmered Beans
3 cups water
2 (14½-ounce) cans tomatoes,
  undrained and chopped
2 medium potatoes, peeled and
  cubed
½ cup chopped green pepper
1 large bay leaf
½ teaspoon salt
½ teaspoon dried whole thyme
¼ teaspoon garlic powder
¼ teaspoon pepper

Cook sausage and onion in a large Dutch oven over medium heat until sausage is browned, stirring to crumble meat; drain. Stir in beans and remaining ingredients; bring to a boil. Cover, reduce heat, and simmer 1 hour. Remove bay leaf before serving. Yield: 14 cups.

Refried Beans

2 tablespoons vegetable oil
2 cups Ham-Simmered Beans
½ teaspoon garlic salt
½ cup (2 ounces) shredded
  Monterey Jack cheese with
  jalapeño peppers

Heat oil in a medium skillet; add beans and garlic salt. Mash beans. Add cheese, and cook over medium heat, stirring often, until cheese melts. Yield: 4 servings.

Warm up a winter evening with Hearty Sausage-Bean Soup. This soup teams nicely with a crisp green salad.

Tuna and Bean Salad

2 tablespoons olive oil
2 tablespoons red wine vinegar
2 teaspoons Dijon mustard
¼ teaspoon salt
⅛ teaspoon pepper
2 (6½-ounce) cans tuna in
   water, drained and flaked
2 cups Ham-Simmered Beans
1 medium-size sweet red
   pepper, cut into thin strips
½ small purple onion, thinly
   sliced and separated into rings
1 tablespoon minced fresh
   parsley
2 teaspoons minced fresh basil
Curly leaf lettuce

Combine oil, vinegar, mustard, salt, and pepper in a jar. Cover tightly, and shake vigorously. Chill thoroughly.

Combine tuna and next 5 ingredients. Pour chilled dressing over tuna mixture; toss gently. Serve on lettuce leaves. Yield: 5 cups.

Home-Style Baked Beans

8 slices bacon
2 medium onions, finely
   chopped
4 cups Ham-Simmered Beans
1 cup catsup
¼ cup firmly packed brown
   sugar
1 tablespoon plus 1 teaspoon
   spicy brown mustard
¼ teaspoon ground cloves
¼ teaspoon pepper

Cook bacon in a medium skillet until crisp; drain well, reserving 3 tablespoons drippings in skillet. Crumble bacon, and set aside.

Add onion to drippings; sauté over medium heat until tender. Stir in reserved bacon, beans, and remaining ingredients. Spoon bean mixture into a 2-quart casserole. Cover and bake at 400° for 30 minutes. Yield: 6 to 8 servings.

Your family will request Home-Style Baked Beans often because it's delicious; you will like it because it's so easy to prepare.

Basic Rice

4 cups water
1 teaspoon salt
2 cups long-grain rice, uncooked

Bring water and salt to a boil in a medium saucepan; add rice. Cover, reduce heat, and simmer 20 minutes or until rice is tender and water is absorbed. Yield: 6 cups.

TO STORE: Refrigerate remaining rice in a tightly covered container up to 1 week. Freeze in desired amounts in labeled airtight containers up to 1 month.

Pork Fried Rice

½ pound diced cooked pork
2 tablespoons vegetable oil, divided
⅛ teaspoon pepper
1 medium carrot, diced
1 stalk celery, sliced
½ cup chicken broth
¼ cup soy sauce, divided
3 cups cooked Basic Rice
2 eggs, lightly beaten
¼ teaspoon garlic powder
¼ teaspoon ground ginger
1 cup frozen English peas, thawed
½ cup sliced green onions

Sauté pork in 1 tablespoon oil in a large skillet over medium-high heat until pork is browned; remove from skillet with a slotted spoon. Sprinkle pork with pepper; set aside.

Sauté carrot and celery in remaining 1 tablespoon oil until crisp-tender (about 6 minutes). Add broth and 2 tablespoons soy sauce; cook until broth is reduced by half. Add rice, and cook until thoroughly heated.

Combine eggs, 1 tablespoon soy sauce, garlic powder, and ginger. Push rice mixture to sides of skillet, forming a well in center. Pour egg mixture into well, and cook until set, stirring occasionally. Stir rice mixture into eggs; add reserved pork, peas, green onions, and remaining 1 tablespoon soy sauce, stirring well. Cook 2 minutes or until thoroughly heated. Yield: 4 servings.

Rice Pudding

2 eggs, lightly beaten
1½ cups milk
¼ cup sugar
1 tablespoon butter or margarine, melted
½ teaspoon grated lemon rind
1 teaspoon lemon juice
1 teaspoon vanilla extract
⅛ teaspoon salt
2 cups cooked Basic Rice
⅓ cup raisins
2 tablespoons brown sugar
½ teaspoon ground cinnamon

Combine first 8 ingredients in a medium bowl; stir well. Stir in rice and raisins. Spoon mixture into a lightly greased 1-quart baking dish. Combine brown sugar and cinnamon; sprinkle over pudding. Bake at 325° for 1 hour or until set. Yield: 4 servings.

Pork Fried Rice gives leftover pork a delicious Oriental flavor.

Appetizers and Beverages

Some cooks find entertaining easy. If they are relaxed, it's because they know how to prepare for the event.

This chapter will help you to be a relaxed hostess and enjoy your own party because it allows you to anticipate social gatherings well in advance. Delectable morsels like Smoked Salmon Tarts and Chicken Cocktail Puffs will keep picture-perfect in the refrigerator or freezer. Quick back-ups for a casual bid to "stop by for drinks" include Delta Shrimp that can be cooked earlier and left to marinate until the cocktail hour. Hot Artichoke Spread and Tuna Spread take 10 to 15 minutes to put together the night before. Frozen Daiquiris and fruity White Sangría can be ready when the doorbell rings.

For the holidays or when you are expecting a houseful of guests, be prepared by keeping several pecan-studded Smoky Cheese Balls in the refrigerator and a batch of Crunchy Cheese Snacks in the freezer.

But don't reserve appetizers for company only. Serve them as festive meal-starters for the family, and turn the meal into a party. The appetizer soups fit well into everyday meals too. The soups are cool and summery; in contrast, the beverages Mocha-Cinnamon Cocoa and Hot Spiced Tea are winter-warmers—giving you choices for all seasons.

Entertain a hungry crowd during football season with these winning appetizers: Delta Shrimp (page 93), Crunchy Cheese Snacks (page 91), and White Sangría (page 98).

Hot Artichoke Spread

1 (14-ounce) can artichoke
  hearts, drained and chopped
1 (8-ounce) can water
  chestnuts, drained and
  chopped
½ cup grated Romano cheese
¼ cup sliced green onions
½ cup mayonnaise
½ cup sour cream
Dash of hot sauce
Paprika

Combine first 7 ingredients in a medium bowl; spoon into a lightly greased 1-quart baking dish. Sprinkle with paprika.

TO STORE: Cover and refrigerate up to 24 hours.

TO SERVE: Bake at 350° for 30 to 35 minutes or until hot and bubbly. Serve spread with assorted crackers. Yield: 3¾ cups.

Tuna Spread

2 (6½-ounce) cans tuna in
  water, drained and flaked
1 (8-ounce) package cream
  cheese, softened
2 tablespoons grated onion
2 tablespoons commercial
  cocktail sauce
1 tablespoon minced fresh
  parsley
1 tablespoon prepared
  horseradish
1 teaspoon lemon juice

Combine all ingredients in a medium bowl; stir well to combine.

TO STORE: Refrigerate spread in a tightly covered container up to 2 days.

TO SERVE: Serve with crackers, or use as a spread for sandwiches. Yield: 3 cups.

Smoky Cheese Ball

1 (8-ounce) package cream
  cheese, softened
1 cup (4 ounces) shredded
  sharp Cheddar cheese
1 cup (4 ounces) shredded
  smoked Cheddar cheese
2 tablespoons milk
2 teaspoons prepared mustard
½ cup chopped pecans, toasted
¼ cup minced fresh parsley

Combine first 5 ingredients in a medium bowl; beat at medium speed of an electric mixer until smooth. Cover and chill at least 3 hours. Shape mixture into a ball. Combine pecans and parsley; roll cheese ball in pecan mixture.

TO STORE: Refrigerate in a tightly covered container up to 1 week.

TO SERVE: Let stand at room temperature 30 minutes before serving. Serve with crackers or party pumpernickel bread. Yield: one 3½-inch ball.

Crunchy Cheese Snacks

1 cup (4 ounces) shredded
   Cheddar cheese
¾ cup all-purpose flour
¾ cup coarsely crushed crisp
   rice cereal
6 slices bacon, cooked and
   crumbled
¼ teaspoon salt
¼ teaspoon dry mustard
⅛ teaspoon garlic powder
⅛ teaspoon crushed red pepper
⅓ cup butter or margarine,
   softened
2 tablespoons cold water
24 pecan halves

Combine first 8 ingredients in a large bowl, stirring well. Add butter; stir with a fork until blended. Sprinkle water evenly over surface; stir with a fork until dough forms a ball.

Drop dough by level tablespoonfuls onto greased baking sheets. Press a pecan half into center of each cheese snack. Bake at 350° for 15 to 18 minutes or until lightly browned. Cool on wire racks.

TO STORE: Freeze cheese snacks in a labeled airtight container up to 3 months.

TO SERVE: Thaw at room temperature. Yield: 2 dozen.

Chicken Cocktail Puffs

1 cup water
½ cup butter or margarine
1 cup all-purpose flour
⅛ teaspoon salt
4 eggs
Chicken Salad
1¼ cups (5 ounces) shredded
   Cheddar cheese

Combine water and butter in a medium saucepan; bring to a boil. Add flour and salt all at once, stirring vigorously over low heat, until mixture leaves sides of pan and forms a smooth ball. Remove from heat, and cool 10 minutes. Add eggs, one at a time, beating well after each addition. (Mixture may separate as each egg is added; continue beating until smooth.)

Drop batter by heaping teaspoonfuls onto an ungreased baking sheet. Bake at 400° for 30 to 35 minutes, or until puffed and golden. Cool on a wire rack.

TO STORE: Freeze cream puffs in a labeled airtight container up to 1 month.

TO SERVE: Thaw at room temperature. Cut tops off cream puffs; pull out and discard soft dough inside. Fill bottoms with 1 tablespoon Chicken Salad; top with 1 teaspoon cheese. Cover with tops. Bake at 400° for 12 to 15 minutes or until cheese begins to melt. Yield: 5 dozen.

Chicken Salad

3 cups finely chopped cooked
   chicken
⅔ cup mayonnaise or salad
   dressing
½ cup chopped celery
2 hard-cooked eggs, chopped
2 tablespoons chopped fresh
   chives
2 tablespoons sliced ripe olives
1 tablespoon lemon juice
2 teaspoons prepared mustard

Combine all ingredients in a large bowl; stir well. Yield: 4 cups.

TO STORE: Refrigerate in a tightly covered container up to 2 days.

Smoked Salmon Tarts

4 (9-inch) refrigerated piecrusts
1½ cups half-and-half
4 eggs, beaten
¼ pound smoked salmon,
   chopped
½ cup (2 ounces) shredded
   Monterey Jack cheese
¼ cup minced green onions
½ teaspoon dried whole
   dillweed
¼ teaspoon salt
⅛ teaspoon pepper

Cut each piecrust into 14 circles, using a 2½-inch round cutter. Place rounds in greased miniature (1¾-inch) muffin cups; trim excess pastry.

Combine half-and-half and eggs in a medium bowl; stir with a wire whisk until well blended. Stir in salmon and remaining ingredients.

Spoon 1 tablespoon salmon mixture into each pastry shell. Bake at 375° for 25 to 30 minutes or until set. Remove from pans, and cool on wire racks.

TO STORE: Freeze tarts in a labeled airtight container up to 2 weeks.

TO SERVE: Thaw at room temperature. Place on baking sheets; cover and bake at 375° for 5 to 10 minutes or until hot. Yield: about 4 dozen.

Smoked Salmon Tarts look elegant when offered from a silver tray. Serve them anytime you want a dressy appetizer.

Party Pizzas

1 (10-ounce) package frozen chopped spinach, thawed and well drained
2 cups (8 ounces) shredded Monterey Jack cheese
½ cup mayonnaise
2 tablespoons sliced green onions
2 tablespoons chopped fresh chives
¼ teaspoon dried whole oregano
¼ teaspoon dried whole basil
⅛ teaspoon pepper
10 slices bacon, cooked and crumbled
30 slices party rye bread

Combine first 8 ingredients; stir well.

TO STORE: Refrigerate spinach mixture in a tightly covered container up to 3 days. Freeze cooked and crumbled bacon in a labeled airtight container up to 3 days.

TO SERVE: Place bread slices on a large baking sheet. Bake at 350° for 3 to 4 minutes on each side. Spread 1 tablespoon spinach mixture on one side of each bread slice; sprinkle evenly with bacon. Broil 6 inches from heat 3 to 4 minutes or until bubbly. Serve immediately. Yield: 2½ dozen.

Delta Shrimp

2 quarts water
½ large lemon, sliced
2½ pounds unpeeled large fresh shrimp
1 cup vegetable oil
2 tablespoons hot sauce
1½ teaspoons olive oil
1½ teaspoons minced garlic
1 teaspoon minced fresh parsley
¾ teaspoon salt
¾ teaspoon Old Bay seasoning
¾ teaspoon dried whole basil
¾ teaspoon dried whole oregano
¾ teaspoon dried whole thyme
Leaf lettuce
Commercial cocktail sauce

Bring water and lemon to a boil; add shrimp, and cook 3 to 5 minutes. Drain well; rinse with cold water. Peel and devein shrimp, leaving tails intact; place shrimp in a large bowl.
Combine vegetable oil and next 9 ingredients; stir with a wire whisk. Pour over shrimp; toss to coat shrimp.

TO STORE: Refrigerate in a tightly covered container up to 8 hours.

TO SERVE: Drain shrimp, and arrange in a large lettuce-lined bowl. Serve with cocktail sauce. Yield: 12 appetizer servings.

Vichyssoise

1 large leek
½ cup chopped onion
2 tablespoons butter or
  margarine, melted
3 medium potatoes, peeled and
  sliced
2 cups chicken broth
1½ cups milk
¼ teaspoon salt
¼ teaspoon ground white
  pepper
1 cup whipping cream
Garnish: chopped fresh chives

Remove and discard root, tough outer leaves, and green top from leek. Thinly slice remaining white portion of leek. Sauté leek and onion in butter in a large saucepan over low heat until tender. Stir in potato and chicken broth; bring to a boil. Cover, reduce heat, and simmer 35 minutes or until potato is tender.

Spoon half of potato mixture into container of a food processor or electric blender; process until smooth. Repeat procedure with remaining half of potato mixture.

Return pureed mixture to saucepan; stir in milk, salt, and pepper. Cook over medium heat until thoroughly heated, stirring frequently. Cool; stir in whipping cream.

TO STORE: Refrigerate in a tightly covered container up to 24 hours.

TO SERVE: Ladle chilled soup into individual bowls. Garnish, if desired. Yield: about 6 cups.

Cool Carrot-Pineapple Soup

1 pound carrots, scraped and
  sliced
¾ cup water
2 (8-ounce) cans unsweetened
  crushed pineapple, undrained
1 cup unsweetened orange juice
½ teaspoon ground coriander
¼ teaspoon ground cardamom
¼ teaspoon ground ginger
Garnishes: vanilla yogurt and
  chopped fresh mint

Combine carrot and water in a medium saucepan. Bring to a boil; cover, reduce heat, and simmer 15 minutes or until carrot is tender. Drain.

Place carrot, pineapple, and next 4 ingredients in container of a food processor or electric blender; process until smooth.

TO STORE: Refrigerate in a tightly covered container up to 3 days.

TO SERVE: Ladle chilled soup into individual bowls. Garnish, if desired. Yield: about 4 cups.

*Serve chilled Summer Garden Soup for warm-weather parties.
Prepare the soup ahead to allow the flavors to mingle.*

Summer Garden Soup

2¼ cups tomato juice
1 medium carrot, scraped and
  sliced
1 stalk celery, sliced
½ cup seeded, chopped
  cucumber
2 green onions, chopped
1 (¼-inch-thick) slice lemon
½ teaspoon celery salt
½ teaspoon Worcestershire
  sauce
⅛ teaspoon hot pepper sauce
Garnish: green onion fans

Place first 9 ingredients in container of a food processor or electric blender; process until smooth.

TO STORE: Refrigerate in a tightly covered container up to 3 days.

TO SERVE: Ladle chilled soup into individual bowls. Garnish, if desired. Yield 3 cups.

Frozen Daiquiris

2 (6-ounce) cans frozen limeade
  concentrate, thawed and
  undiluted
2 cups light rum
⅓ cup sifted powdered sugar
Ice cubes
Garnish: lime slices

Combine half of each of the first 3 ingredients in container of an electric blender. Process 30 seconds. Gradually add enough ice cubes to bring mixture to 4-cup level; blend until smooth. Pour mixture into a large freezer container. Repeat procedure with remaining half of ingredients.

TO STORE: Cover tightly, and freeze up to 1 month.

TO SERVE: Thaw 20 minutes or until mixture becomes slushy. Stir and serve immediately. Garnish, if desired. Yield: 9 cups.

Frozen Strawberry Daiquiris

1 (6-ounce) can frozen limeade
  concentrate, thawed and
  undiluted
1 cup light rum
¼ cup sifted powdered sugar
1 cup sliced fresh strawberries
Ice cubes
Garnish: fresh strawberries

Combine first 4 ingredients in container of an electric blender. Process 30 seconds. Gradually add enough ice cubes to bring mixture to 4-cup level; blend until smooth.

TO STORE: Freeze beverage in a labeled airtight container up to 1 month.

TO SERVE: Thaw 20 minutes or until mixture becomes slushy. Stir and serve immediately. Garnish, if desired. Yield: about 4 cups.

Frozen Peach Daiquiris: Substitute 2 medium peaches, peeled and chopped, for strawberries. Garnish with fresh peach wedges, if desired.

Frozen Pineapple Daiquiris: Substitute 1 cup fresh pineapple chunks for strawberries. Garnish with fresh pineapple chunks, if desired.

Special Iced Coffee

3 cups boiling water
2 tablespoons instant coffee
  granules
4 (3-inch) sticks cinnamon
6 whole cloves
6 whole allspice
2 (3- x ¼-inch) strips orange
  rind
2 (3- x ¼-inch) strips lemon
  rind
⅓ cup Kahlúa or other
  coffee-flavored liqueur
⅓ cup amaretto or other
  almond-flavored liqueur
8 cups cold coffee
Garnishes: sweetened whipped
  cream and orange rind curls

Combine first 7 ingredients; cover and let stand at room temperature 2 hours. Strain and discard spices and rind. Pour liquid evenly into 2 ice cube trays.

TO STORE: Freeze coffee mixture until firm; transfer frozen cubes to a labeled zip-top heavy-duty plastic bag. Freeze up to 1 month.

TO SERVE: For each serving, place 3 coffee cubes in a tall glass. Add 2 teaspoons each of Kahlúa and amaretto. Add 1 cup cold coffee to each glass, stirring well. Garnish, if desired. Yield: 8 servings.

Take the heat out of a summer afternoon by sipping frosty Frozen Daiquiris or Frozen Strawberry Daiquiris in the shade.

Frozen Margaritas

2 (6-ounce) cans frozen limeade
  concentrate, thawed and
  undiluted
1½ cups tequila
½ cup Triple Sec or other
  orange-flavored liqueur
2 tablespoons sifted powdered
  sugar
Ice cubes
Lime wedges
Coarse salt
Garnish: lime slices

Combine half of each of the first 4 ingredients in container of an electric blender. Process 30 seconds. Gradually add enough ice cubes to bring mixture to 3½-cup level; blend until smooth. Pour mixture into a large freezer container. Repeat procedure with remaining half of ingredients.

TO STORE: Cover tightly, and freeze up to 1 month.

TO SERVE: Thaw 20 minutes or until mixture becomes slushy. Rub rims of cocktail glasses with lime wedge. Place salt in saucer; spin rim of each glass in salt. Pour beverage into prepared glasses. Garnish, if desired. Serve immediately. Yield: about 7 cups.

White Sangría

2 cups unsweetened apple juice
1 (12-ounce) can frozen
  lemonade concentrate, thawed
  and undiluted
1 medium apple, cored and cut
  into thin wedges
1 medium orange, thinly sliced
1 lemon, thinly sliced
1 (750-milliliter) bottle Chablis
  or other dry white wine,
  chilled
1 (10-ounce) bottle club soda,
  chilled

Combine apple juice and lemonade; stir well. Add apple, orange, and lemon.

TO STORE: Freeze fruit mixture in a labeled airtight container up to 1 month.

TO SERVE: Thaw 2 hours at room temperature. Pour fruit mixture into a large bowl. Add chilled wine and club soda, stirring gently to mix. Serve immediately. Yield: 2½ quarts.

Minted Wine Coolers for a Crowd

1¼ cups water
1 cup sugar
¼ cup pineapple juice
¼ cup fresh lime juice
2 tablespoons grated orange rind
¼ cup fresh orange juice
1 tablespoon grated lemon rind
¼ cup fresh lemon juice
¾ cup coarsely chopped fresh
  mint
5 cups Chablis or other dry
  white wine, chilled
2½ cups club soda, chilled
Garnishes: fresh mint leaves and
  citrus slices

Combine water and sugar in a medium saucepan; bring to a boil, stirring until sugar dissolves. Pour mixture into a medium bowl; add pineapple juice and next 6 ingredients, stirring well. Cover and let stand at room temperature 4 hours; strain and discard grated citrus rind and chopped mint.

TO STORE: Pour strained mixture into a labeled airtight container. Freeze up to 3 months.

TO SERVE: Thaw 30 minutes or until mixture is slushy. Pour mixture into a large bowl or pitcher; stir in chilled wine and club soda. Serve immediately. Garnish individual servings, if desired. Yield: about 2 quarts.

Enjoy the flavor of cinnamon in these mixes when you drink Hot Spiced Tea and Mocha-Cinnamon Cocoa.

Mocha-Cinnamon Cocoa Mix

2¼ cups sifted powdered sugar
2 cups instant nonfat dry milk
  powder
2 cups powdered non-dairy
  coffee creamer
2 cups chocolate milk mix
¾ cup instant coffee granules
3 tablespoons ground cinnamon
Garnishes: whipped cream and
  ground cinnamon

Combine first 6 ingredients; stir well.

TO STORE: Store in an airtight container at room temperature up to 3 months.

TO SERVE: For each serving, place ¼ cup mix in a cup. Add ¾ cup boiling water; stir well. Garnish, if desired. Yield: 32 servings or 8 cups mix.

Hot Spiced Tea Mix

2 cups instant orange-flavored
  breakfast drink
2 cups sugar
½ cup instant tea
1 (.31 ounce) package
  unsweetened lemon-flavored
  drink mix
1 teaspoon ground cinnamon
1 teaspoon ground cloves
Garnish: cinnamon sticks

Combine first 6 ingredients; mix well.

TO STORE: Store in an airtight container at room temperature up to 3 months.

TO SERVE: For each serving, place 1½ to 2 tablespoons mix in a cup. Add ¾ cup boiling water; stir well. Garnish, if desired. Yield: 32 servings or 4 cups mix.

Main Dishes

What distinguishes main courses from other foods is that you almost always have to serve one. And these dishes take some thought if you want to provide a variety of meals.

Many of the entrées in this chapter can be assembled quickly the night before cooking; some are left to marinate, while others can be frozen. With many of the recipes for meats and poultry, advance preparation actually improves results because the additional time can help to tenderize and allow seasonings to permeate and blend.

Chicken marinates well, but not for more than a day; after cooking, it will retain better flavor in the freezer if submerged in a sauce. Beef and pork are sturdier; they can be marinated up to two days. Large cuts of lamb improve in flavor if marinated several days before cooking. Seafood is the most fragile fare; only very firm types, such as shrimp or salmon, should be marinated more than a couple of hours. Use heavy-duty zip-top plastic bags for easiest marinating; just by turning the bag you can turn the food over for even penetration of the marinade.

Although most fully cooked main courses can be cooled in the refrigerator and then frozen, some guidelines apply. It is best to omit vegetables such as potatoes, mushrooms, and peas from combination dishes, because they do not freeze well. These vegetables will retain better color, texture, and nutrient content if added during reheating instead of prior to freezing.

For the same reason, it is also best to refrigerate or freeze seafood soups and stews without the seafood, which can be added during reheating. For safety's sake, do not freeze stuffed poultry, and do not defrost poultry at room temperature—whether cooked or uncooked.

Stuffed with fresh asparagus and green onions, Oriental Flank Steak Rolls (page 102) is an impressive make-ahead main dish.

Bohemian Beef Brisket

1 (3-pound) beef brisket
2 medium onions, thinly sliced
   and separated into rings
1 (12-ounce) can beer
1 (10½-ounce) can beef broth,
   undiluted
1 tablespoon sugar
1 bay leaf
½ teaspoon salt
¼ teaspoon garlic powder
¼ teaspoon pepper

Trim fat from brisket. Place brisket and onion in a Dutch oven. Combine beer and remaining ingredients; pour over meat. Bring to a boil; cover, reduce heat, and simmer 2 to 2½ hours or until brisket is tender. Remove and discard bay leaf. Cool.

TO STORE: Refrigerate brisket in a tightly covered container up to 2 days. Freeze in a labeled airtight container up to 1 month.

TO SERVE: Thaw in refrigerator. Cook in a Dutch oven over low heat until thoroughly heated. Slice across the grain into thin slices before serving. Yield: 6 servings.

Oriental Flank Steak Rolls

¾ cup light sesame oil
¾ cup soy sauce
¼ cup balsamic vinegar
¼ cup Worcestershire sauce
¼ cup catsup
3 tablespoons brown sugar
2 tablespoons Dijon mustard
1 teaspoon coarsely ground
   pepper
¼ teaspoon garlic powder
¼ pound fresh asparagus spears
4 green onions
¼ cup butter or margarine,
   melted and divided
1 (1½-pound) flank steak

Combine first 9 ingredients in a medium saucepan. Cook over low heat, stirring frequently, 8 to 10 minutes or until sugar dissolves. Set aside.

Snap off tough ends of asparagus. Remove scales from stalks with a knife or vegetable peeler, if desired. Split stalks in half lengthwise; set aside. Remove roots, tough outer leaves, and tops from green onions, leaving 3 inches of dark leaves. Split onions in half lengthwise. Sauté asparagus and onions in 2 tablespoons melted butter 3 minutes or until crisp-tender. Set aside.

Place steak between 2 sheets of heavy-duty plastic wrap, and flatten to ¼-inch thickness, using a meat mallet or rolling pin. Score steak on one side in 1½-inch squares.

Place asparagus and onions across narrow end of scored side of steak. Roll up steak, jellyroll fashion, starting with narrow end. Secure at 1-inch intervals with string. Place in a shallow dish; pour reserved marinade over steak roll.

TO STORE: Cover and refrigerate up to 24 hours, turning occasionally.

TO SERVE: Place remaining 2 tablespoons melted butter in a skillet over medium heat. Add steak roll, and cook on all sides until browned. Place roll in a 13- x 9- x 2-inch baking pan; bake at 450° for 20 to 22 minutes or to desired degree of doneness. Remove string, and cut steak into 1-inch slices before serving. Yield: 4 servings.

Caribbean Swiss Steak

1 (2-pound) round steak
3 tablespoons all-purpose flour
¼ teaspoon salt
¼ teaspoon pepper
2 tablespoons vegetable oil
1 (8-ounce) can crushed
  pineapple, undrained
1 (8-ounce) can tomato sauce
1 (1.25-ounce) envelope onion
  soup mix
1 tablespoon dark brown sugar
1 tablespoon lime juice
½ teaspoon ground allspice
¼ teaspoon ground ginger
¼ teaspoon dry mustard

Place steak between 2 sheets of heavy-duty plastic wrap, and flatten to ¼-inch thickness, using a meat mallet or rolling pin. Cut into serving-size pieces.

Combine flour, salt, and pepper. Dredge steak pieces in flour mixture. Brown steak pieces on both sides in hot oil in a large skillet; drain.

Return steak pieces to skillet. Combine pineapple and remaining ingredients; pour over steak pieces. Bring to a boil; cover, reduce heat, and simmer 1½ hours or until tender. Cool.

TO STORE: Refrigerate steak in a tightly covered container up to 2 days. Freeze in a labeled airtight container up to 1 month.

TO SERVE: Thaw in refrigerator. Cook in a large skillet over medium-low heat 10 to 15 minutes or until thoroughly heated. Yield: 6 to 8 servings.

Creamy Beef Stroganoff

1 (1½-pound) sirloin steak
2 tablespoons vegetable oil
1½ cups sliced fresh
  mushrooms
½ cup chopped onion
1 clove garlic, minced
½ cup dry sherry
½ cup beef broth
1 tablespoon grated lemon rind
1 teaspoon dried whole chervil
1 teaspoon dried whole parsley
½ teaspoon salt
Freshly ground pepper
1 (3-ounce) package cream
  cheese
1 cup sour cream
Hot cooked noodles or rice

Partially freeze steak; slice diagonally across grain into ¼-inch strips. Brown meat in hot oil in a large skillet; remove meat from skillet, reserving pan drippings. Sauté mushrooms, onion, and garlic in reserved pan drippings until tender.

Return steak to skillet; add sherry and next 6 ingredients. Cook over medium-low heat 10 to 12 minutes or until most of liquid evaporates. Remove from heat; add cream cheese, stirring until cheese melts. Cool.

TO STORE: Refrigerate beef mixture in a tightly covered container up to 2 days. Freeze mixture in a labeled airtight container up to 2 weeks.

TO SERVE: Thaw in refrigerator. Cook in a large saucepan over medium heat until simmering, stirring frequently. Stir in sour cream; cook just until hot. (Do not boil.) Serve stroganoff over noodles or rice. Yield: 4 to 6 servings.

Marinated Steak Teriyaki

1 (1½-pound) boneless sirloin
  steak
4 green onions, finely chopped
¾ cup vegetable oil
½ cup soy sauce
3 tablespoons honey
2 tablespoons vinegar
2 cloves garlic, minced
2 teaspoons ground ginger

Place steak in a large shallow dish. Combine onions and remaining ingredients, stirring well. Pour over steak, turning to coat.

TO STORE: Cover and refrigerate 8 hours, turning steak occasionally.

TO SERVE: Remove steak from marinade, reserving marinade. Pour marinade into a small saucepan. Bring to a boil; reduce heat, and simmer 5 minutes. Grill steak over medium-hot coals 10 minutes on each side or to desired degree of doneness, basting frequently with marinade. To serve, slice steak diagonally across grain into thin slices. Yield: 4 to 6 servings.

Beef Stew with Leeks

1 cup Burgundy or other dry
  red wine
1 clove garlic, minced
1 bay leaf
2 whole cloves
1 teaspoon salt
½ teaspoon freshly ground
  pepper
¼ teaspoon dried whole thyme
2 pounds boneless beef, cut into
  1-inch cubes
¼ cup olive oil
2 (10½-ounce) cans beef broth,
  undiluted
2 leeks
12 small fresh mushroom caps
3 carrots, scraped and cut into
  2-inch pieces
3 medium potatoes, peeled and
  quartered

Combine first 7 ingredients; mix well. Place meat in a zip-top heavy-duty plastic bag. Pour marinade over meat.

TO STORE: Refrigerate meat in marinade up to 8 hours, turning occasionally.

TO SERVE: Remove meat from marinade, reserving marinade. Remove and discard bay leaf and cloves. Heat oil in a Dutch oven over medium heat; brown beef in oil. Add broth and reserved marinade. Bring to a boil; cover, reduce heat, and simmer 1½ hours.

Remove and discard root, tough outer leaves, and tops from leeks. Thoroughly wash leeks, and cut into 2-inch pieces. Add leeks, mushroom caps, carrot, and potato to beef mixture. Cover and cook 30 minutes or until vegetables are tender. Yield: 9 cups.

Thick and Hearty Beef-Vegetable Soup

2 pounds boneless beef
3 tablespoons olive oil
6 large carrots, scraped and cut
   diagonally into 1-inch slices
3 stalks celery, cut diagonally
   into 1-inch slices
2 medium onions, quartered
1 medium-size green pepper, cut
   into 1-inch pieces
1 tablespoon grated lemon rind
1 teaspoon dried whole chervil
½ teaspoon pepper
4 cups vegetable juice cocktail
½ cup water
½ cup uncooked rice

Cut beef into ½-inch cubes. Cook beef in hot oil in a Dutch oven over medium-high heat until browned on all sides; drain. Add carrot and next 8 ingredients. Bring to a boil; cover, reduce heat, and simmer 1½ to 2 hours or until meat and vegetables are tender. Cool.

TO STORE: Refrigerate soup in a tightly covered container up to 3 days. Freeze in a labeled airtight container up to 1 month.

TO SERVE: Thaw in refrigerator. Place soup in Dutch oven over medium-high heat. Bring to a boil, stirring frequently. Add rice; cover and cook over medium heat, stirring frequently, 20 to 25 minutes or until rice is tender. Yield: 9½ cups.

Piquant Little Meat Loaves

1½ pounds ground chuck
⅔ cup soft breadcrumbs
⅓ cup chopped onion
2 eggs, lightly beaten
2 tablespoons milk
1 teaspoon salt
⅛ teaspoon pepper
¾ cup firmly packed brown
   sugar
¾ cup catsup
1½ teaspoons dry mustard
1 teaspoon Worcestershire sauce

Combine first 7 ingredients in a large bowl; stir until blended. Shape mixture into six 4- x 2½-inch loaves; place on lightly greased rack of a broiler pan.

TO STORE: Cover and refrigerate up to 24 hours.

TO SERVE: Bake, uncovered, at 400° for 40 to 45 minutes. Combine brown sugar and remaining ingredients; stir well. Remove meat loaves from oven; pour brown sugar mixture over loaves. Return meat loaves to oven; bake an additional 5 to 7 minutes. Yield: 6 servings.

Mexican Rice and Beef

1 pound ground beef
½ cup chopped onion
1 clove garlic, minced
3 cups cooked rice
1 (28-ounce) can tomatoes,
   undrained and chopped
1 (4-ounce) can chopped green
   chiles, drained
½ cup sliced ripe olives
1 (1.14-ounce) package taco
   seasoning mix
1 tablespoon chopped fresh
   cilantro
1 cup (4 ounces) shredded
   Monterey Jack cheese

Cook ground beef, onion, and garlic in a large skillet over medium-high heat until meat is browned, stirring to crumble meat; drain. Stir in rice and next 5 ingredients. Bring mixture to a boil; reduce heat, and simmer 10 minutes. Spoon mixture into a lightly greased 2-quart casserole.

TO STORE: Cover and refrigerate up to 24 hours.

TO SERVE: Bake, uncovered, at 350° for 35 to 40 minutes or until thoroughly heated. Sprinkle with cheese, and bake an additional 5 minutes or until cheese melts. Yield: 4 to 6 servings.

Southwestern Burgers

2 pounds ground beef
1⅓ cups fine, dry breadcrumbs
⅔ cup Burgundy or other dry
  red wine
2 tablespoons finely chopped
  onion
2 tablespoons finely chopped
  green pepper
2 teaspoons prepared
  horseradish
2 teaspoons Dijon mustard
2 teaspoons Worcestershire
  sauce
1 teaspoon salt
½ teaspoon pepper
¼ teaspoon garlic powder
⅛ teaspoon hot sauce
8 hamburger buns
1 (8-ounce) package sliced
  Monterey Jack cheese with
  jalapeño peppers
Commercial mild salsa

Combine first 12 ingredients; shape into 8 patties.

TO STORE: Refrigerate in a tightly covered container up to 24 hours. Separate patties with wax paper, and freeze in a labeled airtight container up to 1 month.

TO SERVE: Thaw in refrigerator. Grill patties over medium-hot coals 8 minutes on each side or to desired degree of doneness. Place burgers on bottom halves of buns; top with cheese slices, salsa, and top halves of buns. Yield: 8 servings.

Lemony Veal Rolls

⅓ cup diced onion
1 clove garlic, minced
2 tablespoons butter or
   margarine, melted
½ cup fine, dry breadcrumbs
4 slices bacon, cooked and
   crumbled
2 tablespoons chopped fresh
   parsley
½ teaspoon grated lemon rind
6 veal cutlets (about 1½
   pounds)
1 tablespoon butter or
   margarine
1 tablespoon all-purpose flour
1 cup milk
¼ teaspoon salt
¼ teaspoon lemon-pepper
   seasoning
¼ teaspoon dried whole
   dillweed
3 tablespoons butter or
   margarine, melted

Sauté onion and garlic in 2 tablespoons butter in a large skillet over medium heat until tender. Stir in breadcrumbs, bacon, parsley, and lemon rind.

Place each veal cutlet between 2 pieces of heavy-duty plastic wrap, and flatten to ¼-inch thickness, using a meat mallet or rolling pin. Place 2 tablespoons onion mixture in center of each cutlet. Roll up jellyroll fashion, starting with short end; secure with wooden picks. Place rolls in a lightly greased 2-quart baking dish.

Melt 1 tablespoon butter in a saucepan over low heat; add flour, stirring until smooth. Cook 1 minute, stirring constantly. Gradually add milk; cook over medium heat, stirring constantly, until mixture is thickened. Stir in salt, lemon-pepper seasoning, and dillweed.

TO STORE: Cover veal rolls. Place sauce in a tightly covered container. Refrigerate veal rolls and sauce up to 24 hours.

TO SERVE: Drizzle veal rolls with 3 tablespoons melted butter. Cover and bake at 350° for 25 minutes. Uncover and bake 10 minutes or until browned. Cook sauce in a small saucepan over low heat 5 minutes or until thoroughly heated, stirring frequently. Spoon sauce over veal rolls. Yield: 6 servings.

Baked Lemon Pork Chops

½ cup fine, dry breadcrumbs
¼ cup grated Parmesan cheese
½ teaspoon salt
½ teaspoon dried whole
   rosemary, crushed
½ teaspoon lemon-pepper
   seasoning
1 egg, lightly beaten
¼ cup Chablis or other dry
   white wine
1 tablespoon lemon juice
1 teaspoon vegetable oil
6 (1-inch-thick) pork chops
Garnish: lemon slices

Combine first 5 ingredients in a small bowl; stir well, and set aside.

Combine egg, wine, lemon juice, and oil; stir well. Dip chops in egg mixture; dredge in breadcrumb mixture.

TO STORE: Refrigerate in a tightly covered container up to 24 hours.

TO SERVE: Place chops on lightly greased rack in a roasting pan. Bake at 350° for 40 to 45 minutes or until tender. Garnish, if desired. Yield: 6 servings.

For a festive summer cookout with plenty of flavor, serve grilled Southwestern Burgers.

Sweet-and-Sour Pork

1 (20-ounce) can pineapple
  chunks, undrained
1½ pounds boneless pork,
  trimmed
1 tablespoon vegetable oil
½ cup water
⅓ cup vinegar
¼ cup firmly packed brown
  sugar
1 tablespoon soy sauce
½ teaspoon salt
2 tablespoons cornstarch
½ cup water
1 medium onion, cut into thin
  wedges
1 small green pepper, cut into
  strips
1 small sweet red pepper, cut
  into strips
Hot cooked rice

Drain pineapple, reserving juice. Refrigerate pineapple chunks in a tightly covered container. Set juice aside.

Partially freeze pork; slice diagonally across grain into 2- x 1- x ¼-inch strips. Sauté pork strips in hot oil in a large skillet until browned; drain. Stir in reserved pineapple juice, ½ cup water, and next 4 ingredients. Cover, reduce heat to low, and simmer 30 minutes, stirring occasionally.

Combine cornstarch and ½ cup water, stirring until smooth. Add to pork mixture, stirring constantly; cook over medium-low heat 2 minutes or until sauce is clear and thickened. Cool.

TO STORE: Refrigerate in a tightly covered container up to 2 days.

TO SERVE: Cook pork mixture in a large skillet over medium heat until simmering, stirring occasionally. Stir in onion, peppers, and reserved pineapple chunks; cover and cook, stirring occasionally, 2 minutes or until vegetables are crisp-tender and thoroughly heated. Serve with hot cooked rice. Yield: 4 to 6 servings.

Italian Stuffed Peppers

4 medium-size green peppers
½ pound hot Italian sausage
½ pound ground chuck
1 cup chopped onion
1 clove garlic, minced
1 cup cooked rice
1 (8-ounce) can tomato sauce
1 (2¼-ounce) can sliced ripe
  olives, drained
½ teaspoon salt
½ teaspoon dried whole basil
½ teaspoon pepper
½ cup (2 ounces) shredded
  Cheddar cheese

Cut off tops of green peppers, and remove seeds. Cook peppers 5 minutes in boiling water to cover; drain peppers, and set aside.

Cook sausage, ground chuck, onion, and garlic in a large skillet until meat is browned, stirring to crumble meat; drain. Stir in rice and next 5 ingredients. Stuff peppers with meat mixture, and place in a lightly greased 8-inch square baking dish.

TO STORE: Cover and refrigerate up to 24 hours.

TO SERVE: Bake, uncovered, at 350° for 30 minutes. Sprinkle tops of peppers with cheese; bake an additional 5 minutes or until cheese melts. Yield: 4 servings.

Sweet-and-Sour Pork is colorful and attractive. Served over hot cooked rice, this is a filling one-dish meal.

Spaghetti Squash Italiano

1½ pounds bulk pork sausage
1 cup sliced fresh mushrooms
½ cup sliced green onions
1 clove garlic, minced
2 (15-ounce) cans tomato sauce
2 medium tomatoes, peeled and chopped
2 tablespoons dried whole basil
1 tablespoon dried whole oregano
½ teaspoon pepper
1 (3-pound) spaghetti squash
2 cups (8 ounces) shredded Cheddar cheese

Cook sausage in a large skillet until browned, stirring to crumble. Drain sausage, reserving 2 tablespoons drippings; set sausage aside. Sauté mushrooms, onions, and garlic in reserved pan drippings until tender. Stir in sausage, tomato sauce, and next 4 ingredients. Bring to a boil; reduce heat, and simmer, uncovered, 15 to 20 minutes, stirring occasionally. Cool.

TO STORE: Refrigerate sauce in a tightly covered container up to 3 days. Freeze in a labeled airtight container up to 2 weeks.

TO SERVE: Thaw sauce in refrigerator. Wash squash; pierce with a fork several times. Place squash in a shallow baking dish. Bake at 350° for 1 hour or until squash yields to pressure. Let cool to touch.

Cut squash in half lengthwise; remove and discard seeds. Using a fork, remove spaghetti-like strands from squash. Place half of squash in a 13- x 9- x 2-inch baking dish; pour half of sauce over squash. Repeat layers. Spread cheese evenly over top. Bake at 350° for 30 to 35 minutes or until bubbly. Yield: 6 to 8 servings.

Herbed Leg of Lamb

1 cup olive oil
½ cup balsamic vinegar
½ cup chopped onion
2 tablespoons Dijon mustard
6 fresh parsley sprigs
3 cloves garlic, crushed
2 bay leaves
½ teaspoon salt
½ teaspoon dried whole oregano
½ teaspoon dried whole basil
½ teaspoon dried whole rosemary
½ teaspoon dried whole dillweed
½ teaspoon dried whole marjoram
½ teaspoon pepper
1 (5- to 7-pound) boneless leg of lamb, rolled and tied
Commercial mint jelly (optional)

Combine first 14 ingredients; stir well. Place lamb in a large shallow dish; pour marinade over lamb.

TO STORE: Cover and refrigerate up to 2 days, turning occasionally.

TO SERVE: Remove lamb from marinade; discard marinade. Place lamb on rack in a large roasting pan. Insert meat thermometer into thickest part of lamb, making sure it does not touch fat or bone. Bake at 325° for 2½ to 3 hours or until thermometer registers 140° (rare) or 160° (medium). Let stand 10 minutes before carving. Serve with mint jelly, if desired. Yield: 8 to 10 servings.

Take a break from ordinary pasta by serving Spaghetti Squash Italiano. The spaghetti-like strands of this vegetable give this family favorite a new twist.

Hearty Lamb Ragout

2 pounds boneless lamb, cut into 1½-inch cubes
¼ cup plus 1 tablespoon all-purpose flour
2 tablespoons vegetable oil
3 cups water
1 (10½-ounce) can beef broth, undiluted
¼ cup tomato puree
1 teaspoon salt
1 teaspoon dried whole thyme
1 teaspoon dried parsley flakes
1 clove garlic, crushed
1 small bay leaf
4 medium potatoes, peeled and cubed
12 baby carrots, scraped
1 cup frozen English peas, thawed

Dredge meat in flour, and cook in hot oil in a large Dutch oven until meat is browned on all sides. Stir in water and next 7 ingredients; cover, reduce heat, and simmer 1 hour. Cool.

TO STORE: Refrigerate in a tightly covered container up to 2 days.

TO SERVE: Remove and discard fat layer from top of beef mixture; pour into a large Dutch oven. Cook beef mixture over medium heat until simmering, stirring frequently. Add potato, carrots, and peas; cover and cook over medium-low heat, stirring occasionally, 45 minutes or until vegetables are tender. Remove and discard bay leaf. Yield: 13 cups.

Roasted Teriyaki Chicken

1 (3- to 3½-pound) broiler-fryer
⅓ cup dry sherry
¼ cup soy sauce
¼ cup honey
2 tablespoons orange juice
½ teaspoon five-spice powder
¼ teaspoon garlic powder

Remove giblets and neck from chicken; reserve for other uses, if desired. Rinse chicken with cold water; pat dry. Place chicken in a zip-top heavy-duty plastic bag.

Combine sherry and remaining ingredients in a small bowl; stir well. Pour marinade over chicken.

TO STORE: Refrigerate chicken up to 24 hours, turning occasionally.

TO SERVE: Remove chicken from marinade, reserving marinade. Place marinade in a small saucepan. Bring to a boil; reduce heat, and simmer 5 minutes. Place chicken, skin side up, on rack in a roasting pan. Bake chicken, uncovered, at 375° for 1½ hours or until done, basting occasionally with marinade. Yield: 6 servings.

Orange-Herb Chicken

1 (2½- to 3-pound)
    broiler-fryer, cut up
1 cup orange juice
¼ cup vegetable oil
¼ cup orange marmalade
2 tablespoons Grand Marnier or
    other orange-flavored liqueur
2 teaspoons grated orange rind
1 teaspoon dried whole basil
1 teaspoon dried whole oregano
½ teaspoon salt
½ teaspoon dried whole thyme
¼ teaspoon pepper

Place chicken in a 13- x 9- x 2-inch baking dish. Combine orange juice and remaining ingredients in a small saucepan; cook over medium heat 5 minutes or until marmalade melts, stirring occasionally. Pour orange juice mixture over chicken.

TO STORE: Cover and refrigerate up to 24 hours.

TO SERVE: Remove chicken from marinade, reserving marinade. Place marinade in a small saucepan. Bring to a boil; reduce heat, and simmer 5 minutes. Cover and bake chicken at 350° for 30 minutes; uncover and bake 30 to 35 minutes or until tender, basting occasionally with marinade. Yield: 4 servings.

No one can resist a bowlful of Hearty Lamb Ragout, a savory blend of lamb, vegetables, and seasonings.

Fiesta Chicken Rolls

8 chicken breast halves, skinned and boned
¼ cup (1 ounce) shredded Cheddar cheese
1 (3-ounce) package cream cheese, softened
2 tablespoons butter or margarine, softened
2 tablespoons chopped green chiles
2 tablespoons grated onion
¼ teaspoon salt
⅛ teaspoon black pepper
1¾ cups bite-size Cheddar cheese crackers, crushed
1 teaspoon chili powder
¼ teaspoon ground cumin
¼ teaspoon ground red pepper
⅛ teaspoon garlic powder
¼ cup butter or margarine, melted

Place chicken between 2 sheets of heavy-duty plastic wrap; flatten to ¼-inch thickness, using a meat mallet or rolling pin. Set aside. Combine Cheddar cheese and next 6 ingredients in a small bowl; stir well.

Spoon cheese mixture evenly over center of each chicken breast half. Roll up jellyroll fashion, starting with short end; secure with wooden picks.

Combine cracker crumbs, chili powder, cumin, red pepper, and garlic powder in a small bowl; stir well. Dip chicken in melted butter; dredge in crumb mixture. Place seam side down in a 13- x 9- x 2-inch baking dish.

TO STORE: Cover and refrigerate up to 24 hours.

TO SERVE: Bake, uncovered, at 400° for 20 to 25 minutes or until done. Remove wooden picks before serving. Yield: 8 servings.

Company Chicken-Artichoke Bake

¼ cup butter or margarine
6 chicken breast halves, skinned and boned
1 cup chopped onion
1 clove garlic, minced
3 tablespoons all-purpose flour
¼ teaspoon salt
1¼ cups Chablis or other dry white wine
1 cup chicken broth
1 (3-ounce) package cream cheese
1 (14-ounce) can artichoke hearts, drained and halved
½ cup sliced natural almonds, toasted

Melt butter in a large skillet over medium heat. Add chicken, and cook 5 minutes on each side or until browned. Remove chicken from skillet, reserving pan drippings; place chicken in a 2-quart casserole. Set aside.

Sauté onion and garlic in reserved pan drippings until tender. Add flour and salt, stirring until smooth. Cook 1 minute, stirring constantly. Gradually add wine and broth; cook over medium heat, stirring constantly, until mixture is thickened and bubbly. Add cream cheese, stirring until cheese melts. Remove from heat; set aside.

Arrange halved artichoke hearts over chicken. Spoon cream cheese mixture over chicken and artichokes. Cool.

TO STORE: Cover and refrigerate up to 24 hours.

TO SERVE: Bake, covered, at 350° for 45 to 50 minutes or until bubbly. Sprinkle with toasted almonds. Yield: 4 to 6 servings.

Entertaining is easy with Company Chicken-Artichoke Bake. White wine enhances the flavor of this special dish.

Chicken Romano

8 chicken breast halves, skinned
  and boned
2 tablespoons butter or
  margarine, melted
2 tablespoons olive oil
½ pound sweet Italian sausage
½ cup finely chopped onion
½ cup sliced fresh mushrooms
1 clove garlic, minced
1 (6-ounce) can tomato paste
1 cup Chablis
¼ cup water
1 teaspoon dried whole basil
½ teaspoon dried whole
  oregano
¼ teaspoon dried whole
  marjoram
¼ teaspoon salt
¼ teaspoon pepper
½ cup (2 ounces) shredded
  mozzarella cheese

Sauté chicken in butter and olive oil in a large skillet over medium heat until browned on both sides. Transfer chicken to a lightly greased 13- x 9- x 2-inch baking dish, reserving drippings in skillet.

Cook sausage, onion, mushrooms, and garlic in reserved drippings until meat is browned, stirring to crumble meat. Drain. Return sausage mixture to skillet; stir in tomato paste and next 7 ingredients. Bring to a boil; reduce heat, and simmer, uncovered, 15 minutes, stirring occasionally. Pour sauce over chicken.

TO STORE: Cover and refrigerate up to 24 hours.

TO SERVE: Bake, covered, at 350° for 25 minutes. Uncover and bake 20 minutes or until thoroughly heated. Sprinkle with cheese, and bake an additional 5 minutes or until cheese melts. Yield: 8 servings.

Country Chicken Pot Pies

1 cup chopped onion
1 cup chopped celery
1 cup chopped carrot
⅓ cup butter or margarine,
  melted
½ cup all-purpose flour
2 cups chicken broth
1 cup half-and-half
4 cups chopped cooked chicken
1 cup frozen English peas,
  thawed
1 teaspoon salt
¼ teaspoon pepper
Basic Pastry

Sauté first 3 ingredients in butter in a skillet over medium heat until tender. Add flour; stir until smooth. Cook 1 minute, stirring constantly. Add chicken broth and half-and-half; cook, stirring constantly, until thickened and bubbly. Stir in chicken, peas, salt, and pepper.

Divide Basic Pastry into 8 equal portions. Roll 4 portions of pastry to 10-inch circles on a floured surface. Place in four 6-inch disposable pie pans. Divide chicken mixture over pastry in pans. Roll remaining 4 portions of pastry to 7-inch circles on a floured surface. Place pastry circles over filling; fold edges under and flute. Cut slits in tops to allow steam to escape.

TO STORE: Cover tightly, and freeze up to 1 month.

TO SERVE: Bake, uncovered, at 400° for 1 hour or until crust is golden brown. Yield: 4 servings.

Basic Pastry

4 cups all-purpose flour
2 teaspoons salt
1½ cups plus 1 tablespoon
  shortening
⅓ to ½ cup cold water

Combine flour and salt; cut in shortening with a pastry blender until mixture resembles coarse meal. Sprinkle cold water (1 tablespoon at a time) over surface; stir with a fork until dry ingredients are moistened. Shape into a ball; chill. Yield: pastry for four 6-inch pies.

Country Chicken Pot Pies are filled with chicken and vegetables and topped with a flaky homemade crust.

Chicken Tetrazzini

1 (8-ounce) package spaghetti
1 medium-size green pepper, chopped
¼ cup butter or margarine, melted
2½ tablespoons all-purpose flour
1 cup milk
1 (10¾-ounce) can cream of mushroom soup, undiluted
½ cup grated Parmesan cheese
¼ cup Chablis or other dry white wine
1 (4-ounce) can sliced mushrooms, drained
1 (2-ounce) jar diced pimiento, drained
⅛ teaspoon garlic powder
3 cups (12 ounces) shredded American cheese, divided
3 cups coarsely chopped cooked chicken
½ cup sliced almonds, toasted

Cook spaghetti according to package directions; drain and set aside.

Sauté green pepper in butter in a Dutch oven over medium heat until tender. Add flour, stirring until smooth. Cook 1 minute, stirring constantly. Gradually add milk and next 6 ingredients; cook over medium heat, stirring constantly, 10 minutes or until thickened. Remove from heat; add 2 cups cheese and chicken, stirring until cheese melts.

Spread half of cooked spaghetti in a greased 13- x 9- x 2-inch baking dish; top with half of chicken mixture. Repeat layers.

TO STORE: Cover and refrigerate up to 24 hours.

TO SERVE: Bake, uncovered, at 350° for 30 to 35 minutes. Sprinkle with remaining 1 cup cheese and almonds. Bake an additional 5 minutes or until cheese melts. Yield: 6 to 8 servings.

Cornish Hens Mandarin

4 (1- to 1½-pound) Cornish hens
½ cup soy sauce
½ cup orange marmalade
2 tablespoons butter or margarine, melted
1 clove garlic, crushed
½ teaspoon ground ginger
½ teaspoon dry mustard
¼ teaspoon ground white pepper

Remove giblets from hens; reserve for other uses, if desired. Rinse hens with cold water; pat dry. Place hens in a large shallow dish.

Combine soy sauce and remaining ingredients in a small bowl; stir well. Pour marinade over hens.

TO STORE: Cover and refrigerate up to 24 hours, turning hens occasionally.

TO SERVE: Remove hens from marinade, reserving marinade. Place marinade in a small saucepan. Bring to a boil; reduce heat, and simmer 5 minutes. Place hens, breast side up, on rack in a shallow roasting pan. Bake at 350° for 1 to 1½ hours or until juices run clear when thigh is pierced with a fork, basting frequently with marinade. Yield: 4 servings.

Turkey and Wild Rice Casserole

1 (6-ounce) package long-grain
  and wild rice mix
½ pound bulk pork sausage
1 cup sliced fresh mushrooms
½ cup sliced celery
1 tablespoon cornstarch
1 cup milk
1 tablespoon Worcestershire
  sauce
3 cups chopped cooked turkey
1 cup dried cranberries

Prepare rice mix according to package directions, and set aside.

Cook sausage, mushrooms, and celery in a large skillet until sausage is browned, stirring to crumble meat. Drain sausage mixture, reserving 1 tablespoon drippings in skillet. Set sausage mixture aside.

Add cornstarch to drippings in skillet, stirring until smooth. Cook 1 minute, stirring constantly. Gradually add milk and Worcestershire sauce; cook over medium heat, stirring constantly, until mixture is thickened.

Combine rice, sausage mixture, sauce, turkey, and cranberries. Spoon mixture into a lightly greased 11- x 7- x 1½-inch baking dish.

TO STORE: Cover and refrigerate up to 2 days. Cover tightly, and freeze up to 2 weeks.

TO SERVE: Thaw in refrigerator. Bake, uncovered, at 375° for 40 to 45 minutes. Yield: 6 to 8 servings.

Turkey Lasagna Rolls

11 lasagna noodles, uncooked
1 pound ground turkey
1 cup chopped onion
1 clove garlic, minced
1 (26-ounce) jar commercial
  spaghetti sauce with
  mushrooms and ripe olives
¼ cup Chablis or other dry
  white wine
3 tablespoons chopped fresh
  parsley
½ teaspoon salt
3 cups ricotta cheese
1 cup (4 ounces) shredded
  mozzarella cheese
2 eggs, lightly beaten
2 tablespoons grated Parmesan
  cheese
⅓ cup fine, dry breadcrumbs
1 teaspoon dried Italian
  seasoning
½ cup grated Parmesan cheese

Cook lasagna noodles according to package directions; drain. Cut in half crosswise, and set aside.

Cook turkey, onion, and garlic in a large skillet until turkey is browned, stirring to crumble meat. Drain. Add spaghetti sauce, wine, parsley, and salt, stirring well. Cover and simmer 10 minutes, stirring occasionally. Remove from heat, and set aside.

Combine ricotta cheese and next 5 ingredients, stirring well. Spread ricotta mixture evenly over lasagna noodles. Roll up jellyroll fashion, starting at narrow end. Place lasagna rolls, seam side down, in a lightly greased 13- x 9- x 2-inch baking dish. Pour meat sauce over rolls, and sprinkle with ½ cup Parmesan cheese.

TO STORE: Cover and refrigerate up to 24 hours. Cover tightly, and freeze up to 2 weeks.

TO SERVE: Thaw in refrigerator. Bake, covered, at 375° for 30 minutes. Uncover and bake 15 minutes or until thoroughly heated. Yield: 8 to 10 servings.

Grilled Salmon Steaks

½ cup lemon juice
2 tablespoons minced fresh dillweed
2 tablespoons olive oil
½ teaspoon salt
¼ teaspoon ground white pepper
4 (8-ounce) salmon steaks (about 1-inch thick)
Tarragon-Dill Mayonnaise
Garnishes: lemon slices and fresh dillweed sprigs

Combine first 5 ingredients in a jar. Cover tightly, and shake vigorously. Set aside.

Arrange salmon steaks in a shallow baking dish. Pour marinade over steaks, turning to coat both sides.

TO STORE: Cover and refrigerate up to 8 hours, turning steaks occasionally.

TO SERVE: Remove steaks from marinade, reserving marinade. Pour marinade into a small saucepan. Bring to a boil over medium heat; reduce heat, and simmer 5 minutes. Grill steaks over hot coals 7 to 8 minutes on each side or until salmon flakes easily when tested with a fork, basting frequently with reserved marinade. Serve with Tarragon-Dill Mayonnaise. Garnish, if desired. Yield: 4 servings.

Tarragon-Dill Mayonnaise

½ cup mayonnaise
½ cup sour cream
1 tablespoon Dijon mustard
1 teaspoon white wine Worcestershire sauce
1 clove garlic, crushed
1 teaspoon dried whole tarragon
½ teaspoon dried whole dillweed
¼ teaspoon seasoned salt
Dash of ground white pepper

Combine all ingredients in a small bowl, stirring well.

TO STORE: Refrigerate in a tightly covered container up to 3 days. Yield: 1 cup.

Shrimp and Vegetable Kabobs

1½ pounds unpeeled medium-size fresh shrimp
1 (8-ounce) bottle Italian salad dressing
¼ cup grated Parmesan cheese
¼ cup water
½ teaspoon crushed red pepper
8 boiling onions
16 small fresh mushrooms
2 small zucchini, cut into 1-inch slices
1 large sweet red pepper, cut into 1-inch pieces

Peel shrimp, leaving tails intact. Place shrimp in a zip-top heavy-duty plastic bag. Combine salad dressing and next 3 ingredients; stir well, and pour over shrimp.

TO STORE: Refrigerate shrimp up to 24 hours, turning occasionally.

TO SERVE: Parboil onions 5 minutes; drain well, and set aside. Remove shrimp from marinade, reserving marinade. Pour marinade into a small saucepan. Bring to a boil over medium heat; reduce heat, and simmer 5 minutes, stirring frequently.

Alternate shrimp and vegetables on eight 12-inch skewers. Grill kabobs over medium-hot coals 4 minutes on each side or to desired degree of doneness, turning and basting frequently with marinade. Yield: 4 servings.

Shrimp and Vegetable Kabobs are a marvelous entrée from the grill.

Shrimp Creole

¾ cup chopped onion
¾ cup sliced celery
¾ cup chopped sweet red
   pepper
3 cloves garlic, minced
2 tablespoons vegetable oil
1 (15-ounce) can tomato sauce
⅓ cup Chablis or other dry
   white wine
3 tablespoons chopped fresh
   parsley
2 bay leaves
¾ teaspoon dried whole thyme
½ teaspoon salt
½ teaspoon ground red pepper
1 pound medium-size fresh
   shrimp, peeled and deveined
Hot cooked rice
4 slices bacon, cooked and
   crumbled

Sauté onion, celery, sweet red pepper, and garlic in hot oil in a large skillet over medium heat until crisp-tender. Stir in tomato sauce and next 6 ingredients. Bring to a boil; cover, reduce heat, and simmer 15 minutes. Remove from heat; cool. Remove and discard bay leaves.

TO STORE: Refrigerate vegetable mixture in a tightly covered container up to 24 hours. Freeze vegetable mixture in a labeled airtight container up to 2 weeks.

TO SERVE: Thaw in refrigerator. Cook over medium heat until simmering, stirring occasionally. Add shrimp, and cook 3 to 5 minutes or until shrimp are done. Serve over hot cooked rice. Sprinkle with crumbled bacon. Yield: 4 servings.

Shrimp Gumbo

¼ cup all-purpose flour
¼ cup vegetable oil
½ cup chopped onion
½ cup chopped green pepper
2 cloves garlic, minced
2 cups tomato juice
1 cup chicken broth
2 tablespoons chopped fresh
   parsley
2 bay leaves
1 teaspoon salt
¼ teaspoon ground nutmeg
¼ teaspoon ground red pepper
2 medium tomatoes, peeled,
   seeded, and chopped
1 (10-ounce) package frozen cut
   okra, thawed
1 (12-ounce) package frozen
   peeled shrimp, thawed
Hot cooked rice
Gumbo filé (optional)

Combine flour and oil in a large Dutch oven; cook over medium heat, stirring constantly, until roux is the color of chocolate (20 to 25 minutes). Stir in onion, green pepper, and garlic; cook until vegetables are tender.

Gradually add tomato juice and broth, stirring until smooth. Add parsley and next 5 ingredients, stirring well. Bring to a boil; cover, reduce heat, and simmer 25 minutes. Remove and discard bay leaves. Cool.

TO STORE: Refrigerate mixture in a tightly covered container up to 3 days. Freeze mixture in a labeled airtight container up to 1 month.

TO SERVE: Thaw in refrigerator. Cook mixture in a large saucepan over medium heat until simmering, stirring occasionally. Add okra and shrimp; cook an additional 5 minutes or until shrimp are done, stirring occasionally. Serve over hot cooked rice. Sprinkle with gumbo filé, if desired. Yield: 4 to 6 servings.

Favorite Tuna-Noodle Casserole

1 (8-ounce) package medium egg
  noodles
1 cup chopped celery
½ cup chopped onion
2 tablespoons butter or
  margarine, melted
1 (12½-ounce) can tuna in
  water, drained and flaked
1 (10¾-ounce) can cream of
  mushroom soup, undiluted
1 (10-ounce) package frozen
  chopped broccoli, thawed and
  drained
1 cup milk
1 (4½-ounce) jar sliced
  mushrooms, drained
1 (2-ounce) jar sliced pimiento,
  drained
¼ teaspoon salt (optional)
¼ cup grated Parmesan cheese
Garnishes: red pepper rings and
  fresh parsley sprigs

Cook noodles according to package directions; drain well, and set aside.

Sauté chopped celery and onion in melted butter in a Dutch oven until tender. Stir in cooked noodles, tuna, and next 5 ingredients. Add salt, if desired. Spoon mixture into a lightly greased 2½-quart casserole; sprinkle with Parmesan cheese.

TO STORE: Cover and refrigerate up to 24 hours.

TO SERVE: Bake, uncovered, at 375° for 50 to 60 minutes or until hot and bubbly. Garnish, if desired. Yield: 6 servings.

Vegetable Lasagna

½ pound fresh mushrooms,
  coarsely chopped
2 cups shredded carrot
1 cup chopped onion
3 tablespoons butter or
  margarine, melted
2 cups small-curd cottage cheese
2 eggs, lightly beaten
½ cup grated Parmesan cheese
3 tablespoons chopped fresh
  parsley
1 teaspoon dried whole oregano
½ teaspoon dried whole basil
1 (15½-ounce) jar commercial
  spaghetti sauce
1 (6-ounce) can tomato paste
6 lasagna noodles, uncooked
1 (10-ounce) package frozen
  chopped spinach, thawed and
  well drained
2 medium tomatoes, peeled and
  coarsely chopped
2 cups (8 ounces) shredded
  mozzarella cheese

Sauté mushrooms, carrot, and onion in butter in a large skillet over medium heat until tender; drain and set aside. Combine cottage cheese and next 5 ingredients; stir well, and set aside.

Combine spaghetti sauce and tomato paste; stir well. Spread half of spaghetti sauce mixture in a 13- x 9- x 2-inch baking dish. Arrange 3 lasagna noodles over sauce. Spread reserved vegetable mixture over noodles. Spoon half of reserved cottage cheese mixture over vegetable mixture. Arrange remaining 3 lasagna noodles over cottage cheese mixture, and top with remaining sauce mixture, spinach, remaining cottage cheese mixture, and chopped tomato.

TO STORE: Cover and refrigerate up to 24 hours.

TO SERVE: Bake, covered, at 350° for 40 minutes. Uncover and sprinkle with mozzarella cheese; bake 15 minutes or until lasagna is thoroughly heated and cheese melts. Let stand 10 minutes before serving. Yield: 6 to 8 servings.

Accompaniments

Do-ahead accompaniments fall into three basic categories. First, there are breads and pasta or rice dishes. Some of the breads keep as refrigerated or frozen dough, such as Angel Biscuits and Refrigerator Potato Rolls, and some are baked, frozen, and ready to reheat, such as Country Corn Cakes and Wild Rice-Pecan Muffins. The rice and the pasta dishes, such as Broccoli-Rice Combo and Noodles Romanoff, may be prepared a couple of days ahead and can be used in place of a bread in the meal. Second, there are recipes that must be refrigerated to congeal or to allow flavors to blend, such as Congealed Beet Salad Piquant, Refrigerator Pickled Vegetable Medley, and Gingered Summer Fruit Compote. Third, there are the side dishes that are prepared in two stages. These include casseroles like Italian Green Bean and Artichoke Casserole, which can be assembled one day and baked the next, and Zesty Stuffed Onions, filled with a flavorful mixture one day and baked the next day.

There are also foods that take more time to prepare but keep well, like Smoky Red Beans and Rice. The bean mixture simmers for 2 hours initially. When ready to serve, reheat the bean mixture while the rice cooks.

For big parties, consider the salads and marinated vegetables that will hold up as well on a buffet table as they do in the refrigerator. The recipes for these dishes can be doubled or tripled easily. The vegetable salads are great for picnics and covered-dish suppers too.

Holiday meals will be less hectic when you serve festive made-ahead side dishes such as Pecan-Kissed Squash (page 143) and Baked Cranberry-Orange Sauce (page 133).

Herbed Bread Italiano

1 (16-ounce) loaf unsliced
   Italian bread
¼ cup butter or margarine,
   softened
¼ cup finely chopped pepperoni
3 tablespoons grated Parmesan
   cheese
1 clove garlic, crushed
1 tablespoon minced fresh
   parsley
½ teaspoon dried whole basil
½ teaspoon dried whole
   oregano

Cut bread diagonally into 1-inch slices, cutting to but not through bottom of loaf. Combine butter and remaining ingredients; spread on cut sides of bread.

TO STORE: Wrap in heavy-duty aluminum foil. Refrigerate up to 2 days. Label and freeze up to 2 weeks.

TO SERVE: Thaw loaf in refrigerator. Loosen foil. Bake at 400° for 20 minutes or until bread is thoroughly heated. Yield: 1 loaf.

Poppy Seed-Dill Biscuits

2 cups all-purpose flour
1 tablespoon baking powder
1 teaspoon salt
1 teaspoon dried whole dillweed
⅓ cup shortening
¾ cup milk
Poppy seeds

Combine first 4 ingredients in a large bowl; cut in shortening with a pastry blender until mixture resembles coarse meal. Add milk to mixture, stirring until dry ingredients are moistened. Turn dough out onto a lightly floured surface, and knead 4 or 5 times.

Roll dough to ½-inch thickness; cut with a 2½-inch biscuit cutter. Place biscuits ½ inch apart on a lightly greased baking sheet. Brush tops of biscuits lightly with water; sprinkle with poppy seeds, gently pressing seeds into biscuits.

TO STORE: Cover tightly, and freeze 2 hours or until firm. Place frozen biscuits in a zip-top heavy-duty plastic bag. Freeze up to 1 week.

TO SERVE: Place frozen biscuits on an ungreased baking sheet. Bake at 425° for 20 to 25 minutes or until golden brown. Yield: 9 biscuits.

Country Corn Cakes are a delightful, old-fashioned way to round out a menu that features fresh summer vegetables.

Country Corn Cakes

1 (10-ounce) package frozen
   whole kernel corn, thawed
2 tablespoons finely chopped
   onion
2 tablespoons finely chopped
   celery
1 (2-ounce) jar diced pimiento,
   drained
1½ cups buttermilk
1 egg, lightly beaten
2 tablespoons butter or
   margarine, melted
¼ teaspoon salt
1¾ cups self-rising cornmeal
¼ cup vegetable oil, divided

Finely chop ½ cup corn. Combine chopped and unchopped corn, onion, and next 6 ingredients in a medium bowl; stir well. Gradually add cornmeal, stirring just until moistened.

Heat 2 tablespoons oil in a large skillet over medium-high heat. Pour ¼ cup batter into skillet for each corn cake, cooking 3 or 4 cakes at a time. Cook 4 to 5 minutes on each side or until browned. Drain cakes on paper towels. Repeat procedure using remaining batter and adding oil to skillet, if necessary. Cool.

TO STORE: Refrigerate corn cakes in a tightly covered container up to 2 days. Freeze corn cakes in a labeled airtight container up to 1 month.

TO SERVE: Place cakes on ungreased baking sheets. Bake at 350° for 10 to 12 minutes or until thoroughly heated. Yield: 14 corn cakes.

Wild Rice-Pecan Muffins

1 cup whole wheat flour
½ cup all-purpose flour
1 teaspoon baking powder
1 teaspoon baking soda
½ teaspoon salt
3 tablespoons brown sugar
1 egg, lightly beaten
1 (8-ounce) carton plain yogurt
¼ cup vegetable oil
½ teaspoon vanilla extract
½ cup cooked wild rice
¼ cup chopped pecans, toasted

Combine first 6 ingredients in a large bowl; make a well in center of mixture. Combine egg, yogurt, oil, and vanilla; add to dry ingredients, stirring just until moistened. Fold in rice and pecans.

Spoon batter into greased muffin pans, filling two-thirds full. Bake at 400° for 18 to 20 minutes or until golden brown. Remove from pans immediately. Cool on wire racks.

TO STORE: Freeze muffins in a labeled airtight container up to 2 weeks.

TO SERVE: Thaw at room temperature. Serve muffins warm or at room temperature. Yield: 1 dozen.

Angel Biscuits

1 package dry yeast
¼ cup warm water (105° to 115°)
2 cups buttermilk
5 cups all-purpose flour
1 tablespoon baking powder
1 teaspoon baking soda
1 teaspoon salt
¼ cup sugar
1 cup shortening

Combine yeast and warm water; let stand 5 minutes. Add buttermilk to yeast mixture, and set aside.

Combine flour and next 4 ingredients in a large bowl; cut in shortening with a pastry blender until mixture resembles coarse meal. Add buttermilk mixture, stirring just until dry ingredients are moistened. Turn dough out onto a lightly floured surface, and knead 4 or 5 times. Shape dough into a ball.

TO STORE: Refrigerate in a tightly covered container up to 1 week.

TO SERVE: Roll dough to ½-inch thickness; cut with a 2-inch biscuit cutter. Place on lightly greased baking sheets. Bake at 400° for 13 to 15 minutes or until golden brown. Yield: 4½ dozen.

Refrigerator Potato Rolls

1 medium potato, peeled and quartered
1 package dry yeast
1 teaspoon sugar
¼ cup butter or margarine, melted
2 tablespoons shortening, melted
¼ cup honey
1 egg, lightly beaten
1½ teaspoons salt
3 to 3½ cups all-purpose flour, divided

Cook potato in boiling water to cover 15 minutes or until tender. Drain, reserving ½ cup liquid; set potato aside. Cool reserved liquid to 105° to 115°; stir in yeast and sugar. Let stand 5 minutes.

Mash enough potato to measure ½ cup; place in a large mixing bowl. Add butter, shortening, honey, egg, salt, yeast mixture, and 1¼ cups flour. Beat at medium speed of an electric mixer 2 minutes. Gradually stir in enough remaining flour to make a soft dough.

Turn dough out onto a well-floured surface, and knead until smooth and elastic (6 to 8 minutes). Divide dough in half. Shape each half into 12 balls, and place in 2 greased 8-inch round pans.

TO STORE: Cover and refrigerate up to 4 days.

TO SERVE: Cover and let rise in a warm place (85°), free from drafts, 1 hour and 30 minutes to 1 hour and 45 minutes or until doubled in bulk. Bake at 375° for 15 to 20 minutes or until golden. Yield: 2 dozen.

Your family and friends will rave when you serve freshly baked Refrigerator Potato Rolls.

Broccoli-Rice Combo

1 (6-ounce) package long-grain
  and wild rice mix
1 (10¾-ounce) can cream of
  chicken soup, undiluted
1 (10-ounce) package frozen
  chopped broccoli, thawed
1 (8-ounce) can sliced water
  chestnuts, drained
1 cup (4 ounces) shredded
  Cheddar cheese
½ cup sliced celery
½ cup chopped onion
½ cup milk
1 (2-ounce) jar sliced pimiento,
  drained
½ cup coarsely crushed chow
  mein noodles

Cook rice according to package directions, using 2 cups water. Combine rice and next 8 ingredients, stirring well. Spoon mixture into a lightly greased 2-quart casserole.

TO STORE: Cover and refrigerate up to 2 days.

TO SERVE: Bake, uncovered, at 350° for 35 to 40 minutes. Sprinkle with crushed chow mein noodles, and bake an additional 5 minutes. Yield: 4 to 6 servings.

Noodles Romanoff

1 (8-ounce) package
  medium-size curly egg noodles
1 cup small-curd cottage cheese
1 (8-ounce) carton sour cream
½ cup sliced ripe olives
½ cup sliced green onions
1 teaspoon Worcestershire sauce
½ teaspoon salt
⅛ teaspoon ground red pepper
½ cup (2 ounces) shredded
  Cheddar cheese

Cook noodles according to package directions, omitting salt. Drain well. Combine noodles, cottage cheese, and next 6 ingredients, stirring well. Spoon mixture into a lightly greased 11- x 7- x 1½-inch baking dish.

TO STORE: Cover and refrigerate up to 2 days.

TO SERVE: Bake, uncovered, at 350° for 30 to 35 minutes. Sprinkle with shredded Cheddar cheese, and bake an additional 5 minutes or until cheese melts. Yield: 6 to 8 servings.

The rich, creamy texture and cheesy flavor of Noodles Romanoff will make it a popular addition to many meals.

Smoky Red Beans and Rice

½ pound dried red beans
6 cups water, divided
¾ cup chopped onion
½ cup chopped celery
½ cup chopped green pepper
2 cloves garlic, minced
2 tablespoons chopped fresh
  parsley
1 bay leaf
½ teaspoon salt
½ teaspoon crushed red pepper
½ pound smoked Polish
  sausage, cut into ¼-inch
  pieces
Hot cooked rice

Combine dried red beans and 3 cups water in a large saucepan. Bring to a boil; reduce heat, and simmer 2 minutes. Remove from heat; cover and let stand 1 hour. Drain well.

Return beans to saucepan. Add remaining 3 cups water, onion, and next 7 ingredients. Bring to a boil; cover, reduce heat, and simmer 2 hours or until beans are tender, stirring occasionally. Add sausage, and simmer, uncovered, an additional 30 minutes. Remove and discard bay leaf. Cool.

TO STORE: Refrigerate bean mixture in a tightly covered container up to 3 days. Freeze in a labeled airtight container up to 2 weeks.

TO SERVE: Thaw in refrigerator. Place bean mixture in a large saucepan. Cook over medium-low heat until thoroughly heated, stirring occasionally. Serve over rice. Yield: 8 servings.

Smoky Red Beans and Rice, a traditional Southern favorite, can be presented as a flavorful side dish.

Baked Cranberry-Orange Sauce _____

4 cups fresh cranberries
2 cups sugar
½ teaspoon ground cinnamon
1 (13-ounce) jar orange marmalade
1 cup coarsely chopped walnuts, toasted
2 tablespoons lemon juice

Wash cranberries and drain. Combine sugar and cinnamon in a large bowl; add cranberries, stirring well. Place cranberry mixture in a 9-inch square pan. Cover and bake at 350° for 45 minutes. Add marmalade, walnuts, and lemon juice; stir well. Cool.

TO STORE: Refrigerate in a tightly covered container up to 4 days.

TO SERVE: Serve hot or cold. Yield: 5 cups.

Scalloped Pineapple _____

1 (20-ounce) can crushed pineapple, undrained
3 cups 1-inch cubes white bread
1½ cups sugar
3 eggs, beaten
⅓ cup butter or margarine

Combine first 4 ingredients, stirring well. Pour into a lightly greased 10- x 6- x 2-inch baking dish. Dot evenly with butter.

TO STORE: Cover and refrigerate up to 24 hours.

TO SERVE: Bake, uncovered, at 350° for 50 minutes or until bubbly and top is lightly browned. Yield: 6 servings.

Congealed Beet Salad Piquant _____

1 (15.2-ounce) can sliced beets
1 tablespoon sugar
1 tablespoon prepared horseradish
2 teaspoons grated lemon rind
½ teaspoon ground cinnamon
¼ teaspoon ground allspice
¼ teaspoon ground cloves
1 (3-ounce) package orange-flavored gelatin
⅓ cup water
⅓ cup cider vinegar
⅓ cup Burgundy or other dry red wine
Curly leaf lettuce

Drain beets; reserve liquid. Add enough water to beet liquid to measure 1 cup; set aside. Dice beets; set aside.
Combine beet liquid, sugar, and next 5 ingredients in a medium saucepan. Bring to a boil over medium heat; reduce heat, and simmer 1 minute. Dissolve gelatin in boiling liquid. Stir in water, vinegar, and wine; chill until the consistency of unbeaten egg white. Fold in beets. Spoon mixture into a lightly oiled 4-cup mold.

TO STORE: Cover salad, and refrigerate until firm and up to 2 days.

TO SERVE: Unmold salad onto lettuce leaves. Yield: 6 servings.

Festive Raspberry Ribbon Salad

1 (3-ounce) package
   raspberry-flavored gelatin
¾ cup boiling water
1 (10-ounce) package frozen
   raspberries in syrup, thawed
   and undrained
1 (8-ounce) can crushed
   pineapple, undrained
¼ cup chopped pecans
1 (8-ounce) carton sour cream
Curly leaf lettuce

Dissolve gelatin in boiling water in a large bowl; add raspberries, pineapple, and pecans, stirring until blended.

Spoon half of raspberry mixture into a lightly oiled 8-inch square dish; chill until firm. Store remaining raspberry mixture at room temperature.

Spread sour cream evenly over congealed gelatin layer. Spoon reserved gelatin mixture over sour cream.

TO STORE: Cover salad, and refrigerate until firm and up to 2 days.

TO SERVE: Cut salad into squares, and serve on lettuce leaves. Yield: 9 servings.

Gingered Summer Fruit Compote

1 tablespoon sugar
2 teaspoons cornstarch
½ teaspoon ground ginger
1 cup pineapple juice
1½ cups fresh pineapple chunks
1½ cups fresh strawberries,
   hulled
1 cup sliced fresh peaches
1 cup fresh blueberries
Garnish: fresh mint sprigs

Combine first 3 ingredients in a small saucepan; gradually add pineapple juice, stirring until smooth. Bring mixture to a boil over medium heat; boil 1 minute, stirring constantly. Remove from heat; cool.

Combine pineapple, strawberries, peaches, and blueberries in a large bowl. Pour sauce over fruit; toss gently.

TO STORE: Refrigerate in a tightly covered container up to 8 hours.

TO SERVE: Spoon fruit mixture into individual serving bowls. Garnish, if desired. Yield: 5 cups.

Gingered Summer Fruit Compote stars as a colorful addition to any menu. For a finishing touch, garnish individual servings with fresh mint sprigs.

Frozen Individual Waldorf Salads

1 (8¼-ounce) can crushed
  pineapple, undrained
2 eggs, lightly beaten
½ cup sugar
2½ cups chopped apple
¼ cup lemon juice
⅔ cup chopped celery
⅔ cup chopped walnuts
⅔ cup miniature marshmallows
¼ cup mayonnaise
1 cup whipping cream, whipped

Drain pineapple, reserving juice. Set pineapple aside. Combine reserved pineapple juice, eggs, and sugar in a large saucepan. Cook over medium heat, stirring constantly, until thickened and smooth. Remove from heat; cool slightly.

Combine chopped apple and lemon juice in a small bowl; add to thickened mixture. Add reserved pineapple, celery, and next 3 ingredients, stirring well. Fold in whipped cream. Spoon salad into paper-lined muffin pans, filling each three-fourths full.

TO STORE: Cover and freeze until firm. Remove salads from muffin pans, and place in large zip-top heavy-duty plastic bags. Freeze up to 1 month.

TO SERVE: Let stand at room temperature 5 minutes before serving. Serve immediately. Yield: 18 servings.

Eight-Layer Salad

1 small head iceberg lettuce,
  torn into bite-size pieces
1 small head romaine lettuce,
  torn into bite-size pieces
½ pound bacon, cooked and
  crumbled
1 small purple onion, chopped
1 (10-ounce) package frozen
  English peas, thawed
1 medium-size sweet red
  pepper, chopped
1 (8-ounce) can sliced water
  chestnuts, drained
1 cup (4 ounces) shredded
  sharp Cheddar cheese
¾ cup mayonnaise
¾ cup sour cream
Garnish: sweet red pepper rings

Layer first 8 ingredients in order listed in a large salad bowl. Combine mayonnaise and sour cream, stirring well; spread over top of salad, sealing to edge of bowl.

TO STORE: Cover and refrigerate up to 24 hours.

TO SERVE: Garnish, if desired. Yield: 12 servings.

Eight-Layer Salad, with a variety of crisp, flavorful ingredients, offers cool refreshment for summer dining.

Fire and Ice Bean Salad

1 (16-ounce) can cut green
  beans, drained
1 (16-ounce) can garbanzo
  beans, drained
1 (15-ounce) can pinto beans,
  drained
1 large sweet red pepper, cut
  into strips
1 small purple onion, thinly
  sliced and separated into rings
½ cup cider vinegar
⅓ cup vegetable oil
1 tablespoon sugar
1 clove garlic, crushed
½ teaspoon crushed red pepper
½ teaspoon chili powder
¼ teaspoon ground cumin
¼ teaspoon ground coriander
Lettuce leaves

Combine beans, red pepper strips, and onion in a large bowl; stir well. Combine vinegar and next 7 ingredients in a jar. Cover tightly, and shake vigorously. Pour dressing over bean mixture; toss gently.

TO STORE: Refrigerate in a tightly covered container up to 24 hours.

TO SERVE: Drain well, and serve in a lettuce-lined bowl. Yield: 6 to 8 servings.

Refrigerator Pickled Vegetable Medley

½ pound small fresh brussels
  sprouts
½ pound baby carrots, scraped
½ pound small fresh
  mushrooms
1 small purple onion, thinly
  sliced and separated into rings
1 small sweet red pepper, cut
  into thin strips
2 cups white vinegar
2 cups water
½ cup sugar
4 (3-inch) sticks cinnamon,
  broken into pieces
1 teaspoon whole cloves
1 teaspoon salt

Wash brussels sprouts thoroughly, and remove discolored leaves. Cut off stem ends, and slash bottom of each sprout with a shallow X. Place brussels sprouts and carrots in a vegetable steamer over boiling water; cover and steam 6 to 8 minutes or until crisp-tender. Drain.

Combine brussels sprouts, carrots, mushrooms, onion, and pepper in a large bowl; toss well, and set aside.

Combine vinegar and remaining ingredients in a medium saucepan. Bring to a boil; cover, reduce heat, and simmer 10 minutes. Remove from heat; strain mixture, and discard spices. Pour hot vinegar mixture over vegetables. Cool.

TO STORE: Refrigerate in a tightly covered container up to 4 days.

TO SERVE: Serve with a slotted spoon. Yield: 8 cups.

Winter Vegetable Salad

2 cups cauliflower flowerets
2 cups broccoli flowerets
3 medium carrots, scraped and cut into ¼-inch slices
1 (15-ounce) can artichoke hearts, drained and halved
¼ cup mayonnaise
¼ cup sour cream
¼ cup Dijon mustard
¼ cup chopped fresh parsley
½ teaspoon dried whole tarragon
½ teaspoon celery salt
½ teaspoon cracked pepper

Cook cauliflower, broccoli, and carrot in a small amount of boiling water 3 minutes or until crisp-tender. Drain and rinse with cold water. Combine cooked vegetables and artichokes in a large bowl; set aside.

Combine mayonnaise and remaining ingredients in a small bowl, stirring well. Pour mayonnaise mixture over vegetables, tossing gently to coat.

TO STORE: Refrigerate in a tightly covered container up to 24 hours.

TO SERVE: Toss gently before serving. Yield: 4 to 6 servings.

Italian Green Bean and Artichoke Casserole

2 (16-ounce) cans cut green beans, drained
1 (14-ounce) can artichoke hearts, drained and quartered
1 (2-ounce) jar diced pimiento, drained
1 (8-ounce) bottle Italian salad dressing
¼ cup fine, dry breadcrumbs
¼ cup Parmesan cheese

Combine beans, artichoke hearts, and pimiento in a shallow dish. Add salad dressing, tossing gently to coat.

TO STORE: Cover and refrigerate up to 24 hours, stirring occasionally.

TO SERVE: Drain vegetables; spoon into a greased 2-quart casserole. Combine breadcrumbs and cheese; sprinkle over vegetables. Bake, uncovered, at 350° for 30 minutes or until thoroughly heated. Yield: 6 servings.

Sweet-and-Sour Red Cabbage

5 cups shredded red cabbage
2 cups water
4 slices bacon
2 tablespoons brown sugar
1 tablespoon all-purpose flour
½ cup red wine vinegar
⅓ cup water
1 small onion, thinly sliced and separated into rings
1 small apple, chopped
½ teaspoon salt
⅛ teaspoon pepper

Place cabbage and 2 cups water in a saucepan. Bring to a boil over medium-high heat; cover, reduce heat, and simmer 5 to 8 minutes or until crisp-tender. Drain; set aside. Cook bacon in a skillet until crisp. Drain bacon on paper towels, reserving 1 tablespoon drippings in skillet. Crumble bacon; set aside.

Add brown sugar and flour to drippings in skillet; stir until smooth. Gradually add vinegar and ⅓ cup water, stirring until smooth. Add onion and remaining ingredients; cook 5 minutes or until slightly thickened, stirring frequently. Stir in cabbage and bacon. Cool.

TO STORE: Refrigerate in a tightly covered container up to 3 days.

TO SERVE: Place cabbage mixture in a large saucepan. Cook over medium heat until thoroughly heated, stirring frequently. Serve immediately. Yield: 6 servings.

Zesty Stuffed Onions

6 medium onions
¼ cup fine, dry breadcrumbs
2 tablespoons grated Parmesan cheese
1½ tablespoons butter or margarine, melted
1 tablespoon minced fresh parsley
1 teaspoon commercial steak sauce
¼ teaspoon salt
⅛ teaspoon pepper
Pinch of ground cloves

Peel onions, and cut a thin slice from tops; discard slices. Cook onions in boiling water to cover 8 to 10 minutes or just until tender; drain. Remove centers of onions, leaving ½-inch shells intact; chop centers.

Combine chopped onion, breadcrumbs, and remaining ingredients in a small bowl, stirring well. Stuff onion shells with breadcrumb mixture. Place stuffed onions in a lightly greased 8-inch square baking dish.

TO STORE: Cover and refrigerate up to 24 hours.

TO SERVE: Bake, covered, at 350° for 25 to 30 minutes or until tender. Yield: 6 servings.

When friends come to dinner, offer Zesty Stuffed Onions, a pretty and practical way to round out a menu.

Mushroom-Stuffed Potatoes

4 medium-size baking potatoes
½ cup chopped fresh mushrooms
¼ cup thinly sliced green onions
2 tablespoons butter or margarine, melted
½ (3-ounce) package cream cheese, softened
1 egg yolk
1 tablespoon chopped fresh parsley
½ teaspoon salt
¼ teaspoon ground white pepper
1 to 2 tablespoons butter or margarine, melted
¼ cup grated Parmesan cheese
1 teaspoon paprika

Scrub potatoes, and pat dry. Prick each potato several times with a fork. Arrange potatoes on a baking sheet. Bake at 400° for 1 hour or until tender. Allow potatoes to cool to touch. Cut each potato in half lengthwise; carefully scoop out pulp, leaving shells intact. Sauté mushrooms and green onions in 2 tablespoons butter in a skillet over medium heat until tender. Set aside.

Combine potato pulp, cream cheese, and next 4 ingredients in a medium mixing bowl. Beat at medium speed of an electric mixer until light and fluffy. Combine potato mixture and mushroom mixture, stirring well; spoon evenly into potato shells.

TO STORE: Refrigerate stuffed potatoes in a tightly covered container up to 24 hours. Freeze potatoes in a labeled airtight container up to 2 weeks.

TO SERVE: Thaw in refrigerator. Brush potatoes with 1 to 2 tablespoons melted butter; sprinkle with Parmesan cheese and paprika. Bake at 375° for 20 minutes or until puffed and lightly browned. Yield: 8 servings.

Stuffed Baked Sweet Potatoes

4 medium-size sweet potatoes
½ cup apricot nectar
¼ cup milk
2 tablespoons butter or margarine, melted
1 teaspoon grated orange rind
¼ teaspoon salt
¼ teaspoon ground nutmeg
¼ cup finely chopped pecans, toasted
1 to 2 tablespoons butter or margarine, melted

Scrub sweet potatoes, and pat dry. Prick each potato several times with a fork. Arrange potatoes on a baking sheet. Bake at 400° for 1 hour or until tender. Allow potatoes to cool to touch. Cut a 1-inch lengthwise strip from top of each potato; carefully scoop out pulp, leaving shells intact.

Combine potato pulp, apricot nectar, and next 5 ingredients in a medium bowl. Beat at medium speed of an electric mixer until light and fluffy. Stir in pecans. Spoon mixture evenly into potato shells.

TO STORE: Refrigerate stuffed potatoes in a tightly covered container up to 24 hours. Freeze potatoes in a labeled airtight container up to 2 weeks.

TO SERVE: Thaw in refrigerator. Brush potatoes with 1 to 2 tablespoons melted butter. Bake at 425° for 20 to 25 minutes or until thoroughly heated. Yield: 4 servings.

Company Potato Rosettes

2 medium potatoes, peeled and quartered
½ cup (2 ounces) shredded sharp Cheddar cheese
1 egg, lightly beaten
2 tablespoons minced green onions
2 tablespoons sour cream
½ teaspoon salt
¼ teaspoon ground white pepper
1 (2-ounce) jar diced pimiento, drained and minced

Cook potatoes in boiling water to cover 15 minutes or until tender; drain. Mash potatoes in a medium bowl. Add cheese and next 5 ingredients, stirring to blend. Stir in pimiento. Cool slightly.

Spoon potato mixture into a decorating bag fitted with a large star tip. Pipe mixture into 12 rosettes on a wax paper-lined baking sheet.

TO STORE: Cover and freeze 3 hours or until firm. Place rosettes in a zip-top heavy-duty freezer bag. Freeze up to 1 month.

TO SERVE: Place frozen rosettes on a lightly greased baking sheet. Bake at 350° for 25 to 30 minutes or until lightly browned. Yield: 6 servings.

Pecan-Kissed Squash

2 large acorn squash (about 1¼ pounds each)
20 round buttery crackers, crushed
½ cup coarsely chopped pecans
¼ cup butter or margarine, melted
¼ cup firmly packed brown sugar
¼ teaspoon pumpkin pie spice

Cut squash in half crosswise; remove and discard seeds. Place squash halves, cut side up, in a shallow baking dish. Combine cracker crumbs and remaining ingredients, stirring well. Spoon mixture evenly into squash cavities.

TO STORE: Cover and refrigerate up to 24 hours.

TO SERVE: Pour hot water to a depth of ½ inch into dish with squash. Bake at 350° for 1 hour or until squash is tender. Yield: 4 servings.

Curried Vegetable Combo

2 cups cauliflower flowerets
2 cups scraped, sliced carrot
2 cups sliced celery
½ cup chopped onion
1 (10¾-ounce) can cream of chicken soup, undiluted
⅓ cup mayonnaise
½ teaspoon salt
½ teaspoon curry powder
¼ teaspoon ground coriander
⅛ teaspoon ground ginger
½ cup (2 ounces) shredded Cheddar cheese
½ cup soft breadcrumbs
2 tablespoons butter or margarine, melted

Cook cauliflower, carrot, celery, and onion in a small amount of boiling water 3 minutes or until crisp-tender. Drain and set aside.
Combine soup and next 5 ingredients in a large bowl, stirring well. Stir in vegetables. Spoon mixture into a 1½-quart casserole.

TO STORE: Cover and refrigerate up to 24 hours.

TO SERVE: Combine cheese, breadcrumbs, and butter; sprinkle mixture over casserole. Bake, uncovered, at 350° for 30 to 35 minutes or until bubbly. Yield: 4 to 6 servings.

Plain potatoes become exciting when piped into pretty swirls for Company Potato Rosettes.

Desserts

With a little planning, you can always have dessert on hand for a birthday, an anniversary, a holiday celebration, or a late-night craving. The selections are as delicious as Raspberry-Almond Chocolate Cake, Sour Cream-Streusel Pound Cake, Favorite Apple Pie, or Old-Fashioned Vanilla Ice Cream.

Keep these points in mind when preparing make-ahead desserts. It is better to freeze cakes without the frosting. Wrap a cooled sheet cake in heavy-duty aluminum foil, or place cake layers in zip-top heavy-duty plastic bags and freeze. Defrost the cake in the wrapping at room temperature, allowing about 1 hour for cake layers and up to 3 hours for a sheet cake to thaw. Frost the cake when you are ready to serve it.

Cookies generally freeze well. Bar cookies may be cut and frozen individually. Or bake and freeze bar cookies in disposable aluminum pans; cut into bars or squares after thawing.

Pie pastry will be crisper if pies are frozen unbaked. Wrap the pie with heavy-duty aluminum foil, and place in a box or a large freezer bag for best protection.

Homemade ice creams and sherbets made with a cooked custard base will keep 2 to 4 weeks in the freezer if the temperature is 0°. After opening, place plastic wrap directly on the surface of the ice cream or sherbet to prevent ice crystals from forming.

Add a flavorful dimension to vanilla ice cream by topping a scoop with refreshing Lemon Curd or Praline-Pecan Sauce. These sauces will keep in the refrigerator for a couple of weeks and can be put in jars and tied with ribbons for attractive gifts.

Serve Favorite Apple Pie (page 155) with Old-Fashioned Vanilla Ice Cream (page 160). These two all-American desserts are guaranteed to please the entire family.

Basic Chocolate Cake

¾ cup butter or margarine, softened
2 cups sugar
2 eggs
4 (1-ounce) squares unsweetened chocolate, melted
2 cups all-purpose flour
1 teaspoon baking soda
1 cup buttermilk
½ cup water
1 teaspoon vanilla extract
Kahlúa Frosting
Garnish: pecan halves

Cream butter; gradually add sugar, beating well at medium speed of an electric mixer. Add eggs, one at a time, beating well after each addition. Add melted chocolate, beating until blended. Combine flour and baking soda; set aside. Combine buttermilk and water. Add flour mixture to creamed mixture alternately with buttermilk mixture, beginning and ending with flour mixture. Mix after each addition. Stir in vanilla.

Pour batter into 2 greased and floured 9-inch round cakepans. Bake at 350° for 40 minutes or until a wooden pick inserted in center comes out clean. Cool in pans 10 minutes; remove from pans, and cool completely on wire racks.

TO STORE: Wrap individual layers in heavy-duty plastic wrap. Freeze wrapped layers in a labeled airtight container up to 1 month.

TO SERVE: Thaw layers at room temperature. Spread Kahlúa Frosting between layers and on top and sides of cake. Garnish, if desired. Yield: one 2-layer cake.

Kahlúa Frosting

¼ cup butter or margarine, softened
1 (8-ounce) package cream cheese, softened
1 (16-ounce) package powdered sugar, sifted
3 tablespoons Kahlúa

Cream butter and cream cheese. Gradually add powdered sugar, beating until mixture is smooth. Add Kahlúa, beating until mixture reaches spreading consistency. Yield: 2¾ cups.

Raspberry-Almond Chocolate Cake

1 cup butter or margarine, softened
3 cups sifted powdered sugar
2 tablespoons milk
1 teaspoon almond extract
⅔ cup red raspberry preserves
2 layers Basic Chocolate Cake
Garnish: toasted sliced almonds

Cream butter; gradually add powdered sugar, beating until smooth. Add milk, beating until mixture reaches spreading consistency. Stir in almond extract.

Spread preserves between layers of Basic Chocolate Cake; spread frosting on top and sides of cake. Garnish, if desired. Yield: one 2-layer cake.

White Chocolate Party Cake, topped with festive candles and white chocolate curls, makes a striking presentation.

White Chocolate Party Cake

1 cup butter or margarine,
  softened
2 cups sugar
4 eggs
4 (1-ounce) squares white
  chocolate, melted
2¼ cups all-purpose flour
1 teaspoon baking powder
1 cup buttermilk
1 cup flaked coconut
1 cup finely chopped almonds
1¼ teaspoons vanilla extract
Almond Butter Frosting
Garnish: white chocolate curls

Cream butter; gradually add sugar, beating well at medium speed of an electric mixer. Add eggs, one at a time, beating well after each addition. Add melted chocolate, beating until blended. Combine flour and baking powder. Add to creamed mixture alternately with buttermilk, beginning and ending with flour mixture. Mix after each addition. Stir in coconut, almonds, and vanilla.

Pour batter into 3 greased and floured 8-inch round cakepans. Bake at 350° for 30 to 35 minutes or until a wooden pick inserted in center comes out clean. Cool in pans 10 minutes; remove from pans, and cool completely on wire racks.

TO STORE: Wrap individual layers in heavy-duty plastic wrap. Freeze wrapped layers in a labeled airtight container up to 1 month.

TO SERVE: Thaw layers at room temperature. Spread Almond Butter Frosting between layers and on top and sides of cake. Garnish, if desired. Yield: one 3-layer cake.

Almond Butter Frosting

⅔ cup butter, softened
6 cups sifted powdered sugar
¼ cup amaretto or other
  almond-flavored liqueur
1 to 2 tablespoons milk
1 teaspoon vanilla extract

Cream butter; gradually add powdered sugar, beating until smooth. Add amaretto and milk, beating until mixture reaches spreading consistency. Stir in vanilla. Yield: 3 cups.

Carrot-Pineapple Cake

2 cups all-purpose flour
2½ teaspoons baking powder
¾ teaspoon salt
2 teaspoons ground cinnamon
2 cups sugar
2 cups shredded carrot
1¼ cups vegetable oil
4 eggs, beaten
1 (8¼-ounce) can crushed
  pineapple, undrained
¾ cup chopped pecans
Cream Cheese Frosting

Cream Cheese Frosting

½ cup butter or margarine,
  softened
1 (8-ounce) package cream
  cheese, softened
1 (16-ounce) package powdered
  sugar, sifted
1 teaspoon vanilla extract

Combine first 5 ingredients in a large bowl; stir in carrot, oil, eggs, pineapple, and pecans, mixing well.

Pour batter into a greased and floured 13- x 9- x 2-inch baking pan. Bake 325° for 45 to 55 minutes or until a wooden pick inserted in center comes out clean. Cool completely on a wire rack.

TO STORE: Cover tightly, and freeze up to 2 weeks.

TO SERVE: Thaw at room temperature. Spread Cream Cheese Frosting over cake. Yield: 15 servings.

Cream butter and cream cheese. Gradually add powdered sugar; beat until mixture is light and fluffy. Stir in vanilla. Yield: 3 cups.

Refreshing Lemon Cheesecake

1½ cups graham cracker crumbs
2 tablespoons sugar
¼ cup plus 2 tablespoons butter
  or margarine, melted
3 (8-ounce) packages cream
  cheese, softened
¾ cup sugar
3 eggs
1 tablespoon grated lemon rind
¼ cup fresh lemon juice
1 teaspoon vanilla extract
2 cups sour cream
3 tablespoons sugar
Garnishes: lemon roses, lemon
  rind curls, and fresh mint
  sprig

Combine first 3 ingredients, stirring well. Firmly press mixture evenly on bottom and 1 inch up sides of a 9-inch springform pan. Bake at 350° for 5 minutes. Cool.

Beat cream cheese at high speed of an electric mixer until light and fluffy; gradually add ¾ cup sugar, beating well. Add eggs, one at a time, beating well after each addition. Stir in grated lemon rind, lemon juice, and vanilla. Pour mixture into prepared crust. Bake at 375° for 40 to 45 minutes or until set.

Combine sour cream and 3 tablespoons sugar; stir well. Spread mixture evenly over cheesecake. Bake at 500° for 5 minutes. Cool completely on a wire rack.

TO STORE: Cover and refrigerate at least 8 hours and up to 2 days. Cover tightly, and freeze up to 2 weeks.

TO SERVE: Thaw in refrigerator. Carefully remove sides of springform pan. Garnish, if desired. Yield: one 9-inch cheesecake.

Serve Refreshing Lemon Cheesecake for a delicious ending to an outdoor summer dinner. Lemon roses and lemon rind curls are the perfect garnish.

Peaches and Cream Cheesecake

¾ cup all-purpose flour
1 teaspoon baking powder
1 (3⅛-ounce) package vanilla
   pudding mix
3 tablespoons butter or
   margarine, softened
1 egg
½ cup milk
1 (16-ounce) can sliced peaches,
   undrained
1 (8-ounce) package cream
   cheese, softened
½ cup sugar
1½ teaspoons sugar
¼ teaspoon ground nutmeg

Combine first 6 ingredients in a mixing bowl; beat at medium speed of an electric mixer until smooth. Pour batter into a greased 8-inch round cakepan. Drain peaches, reserving 3 tablespoons liquid. Set peach liquid aside; arrange peach slices over batter.

Combine cream cheese, ½ cup sugar, and reserved peach liquid in a small mixing bowl; beat 2 minutes at medium speed of an electric mixer. Spoon mixture over peaches in center of batter, leaving a 1-inch border around edge of cakepan.

Combine 1½ teaspoons sugar and nutmeg; sprinkle over cream cheese mixture. Bake at 350° for 35 minutes; remove from oven. Cool completely on a wire rack.

TO STORE: Cover and refrigerate up to 24 hours. Cover tightly, and freeze up to 2 weeks.

TO SERVE: Thaw at room temperature 2 hours before serving. Yield: one 8-inch cheesecake.

Sour Cream-Streusel Pound Cake

½ cup firmly packed brown
   sugar
¼ cup chopped pecans
2 tablespoons butter or
   margarine, softened
2 tablespoons all-purpose flour
1 teaspoon ground cinnamon
1 cup butter or margarine,
   softened
3 cups sugar
6 eggs
3 cups all-purpose flour
¼ teaspoon baking powder
¼ teaspoon baking soda
¼ teaspoon salt
1 (8-ounce) carton sour cream
2 teaspoons vanilla extract

Combine first 5 ingredients, stirring well. Set aside.

Cream 1 cup butter; gradually add 3 cups sugar, beating well at medium speed of an electric mixer. Add eggs, one at a time, beating after each addition.

Combine 3 cups flour, baking powder, soda, and salt; add to creamed mixture alternately with sour cream, beginning and ending with flour mixture. Mix just until blended after each addition. Stir in vanilla.

Pour half of batter into a greased and floured 12-cup Bundt pan. Sprinkle pecan mixture over batter; pour remaining batter over pecan mixture. Bake at 325° for 1 hour and 15 minutes or until a wooden pick inserted in center comes out clean. Cool in pan 10 minutes; remove from pan, and cool completely on a wire rack.

TO STORE: Cover and store at room temperature up to 3 days. Cover tightly, and freeze up to 1 month.

TO SERVE: Thaw at room temperature. Yield: one 10-inch cake.

Chocolate Pecan Bars

1¾ cups all-purpose flour
⅓ cup firmly packed brown
  sugar
¾ cup butter or margarine,
  softened
1 cup firmly packed brown
  sugar
4 eggs, lightly beaten
1 cup light corn syrup
3 tablespoons butter or
  margarine, melted
1 teaspoon vanilla extract
2 cups chopped pecans
1 (6-ounce) package semisweet
  chocolate morsels

Combine flour and ⅓ cup brown sugar in a small bowl. Cut in ¾ cup butter with a pastry blender until mixture resembles coarse meal. Press mixture in the bottom of a greased 13- x 9- x 2-inch pan. Bake at 350° for 15 to 17 minutes.

Combine 1 cup brown sugar and next 4 ingredients, stirring well. Stir in pecans. Pour mixture over prepared crust. Bake at 350° for 40 to 45 minutes or until firm. Remove from oven, and sprinkle with chocolate morsels; let stand 5 minutes or until morsels are softened; spread evenly. Cool completely, and cut into bars.

TO STORE: Freeze bars in a labeled airtight container up to 1 month.

TO SERVE: Thaw at room temperature before serving. Yield: 4 dozen.

Lemon Cheese Squares

⅓ cup butter or margarine,
  softened
⅓ cup firmly packed brown
  sugar
1 cup all-purpose flour
½ cup finely chopped pecans
1 (8-ounce) package cream
  cheese, softened
½ cup sugar
1 egg
1 teaspoon grated lemon rind
3 tablespoons lemon juice
2 tablespoons milk
½ teaspoon vanilla extract

Cream butter; gradually add brown sugar, beating at medium speed of an electric mixer. Gradually add flour, mixing well. Stir in pecans. Reserve ¾ cup crumb mixture. Press remaining crumb mixture in the bottom of an ungreased 8-inch square baking pan. Bake at 350° for 12 to 15 minutes.

Combine cream cheese and remaining ingredients in a bowl; mix well. Pour cream cheese mixture over prepared crust; sprinkle with reserved crumb mixture. Bake at 350° for 25 to 30 minutes or until golden. Cool.

TO STORE: Cover and refrigerate up to 5 days. Cover tightly, and freeze up to 1 month.

TO SERVE: Thaw at room temperature, and cut into squares. Yield: 16 squares.

No-Bake Raspberry Confections

5½ cups chocolate wafer
  crumbs
1 cup finely chopped pecans
1 cup raspberry preserves
½ (12-ounce) package
  semisweet chocolate
  mini-morsels
2 tablespoons dark rum
1 cup sifted powdered sugar

Combine first 5 ingredients in a large bowl, stirring well. Shape mixture into 1¼-inch balls; roll balls in powdered sugar.

TO STORE: Refrigerate in a tightly covered container up to 1 week. Yield: 5 dozen.

Vanilla Chip Cookies

½ cup butter or margarine,
   softened
¼ cup plus 2 tablespoons sugar
¼ cup plus 2 tablespoons firmly
   packed brown sugar
1 egg
¾ teaspoon vanilla extract
1¼ cups all-purpose flour
½ teaspoon baking soda
½ teaspoon salt
1 cup vanilla milk chips
½ cup chopped pecans

Cream butter in a large mixing bowl; gradually add sugars, beating at medium speed of an electric mixer. Add egg and vanilla, mixing well.

Combine flour, soda, and salt; gradually add to creamed mixture, mixing well. Stir in chips and pecans. Shape dough into a 15-inch roll.

TO STORE: Wrap roll in wax paper, and refrigerate at least 2 hours and up to 24 hours. To freeze, wrap roll in wax paper, and then in heavy-duty aluminum foil. Freeze up to 1 month.

TO SERVE: Unwrap roll, and cut into ½-inch slices; place cut side down on ungreased baking sheets. Bake at 350° for 8 to 10 minutes or until cookies are light golden brown. Cool slightly; remove to wire racks to cool completely. Yield: about 2½ dozen.

Date-Nut Dessert Cheese

⅔ cup walnuts, lightly toasted
⅔ cup chopped dates
8 ounces sharp Cheddar cheese,
   cut into 1-inch pieces
1 (8-ounce) package cream
   cheese, softened and cut into
   1-inch pieces
3 to 4 tablespoons dark rum

Position knife blade in food processor bowl. Add walnuts; top with cover, and pulse 6 times or until coarsely chopped. Remove walnuts, and set aside.

Position knife blade in processor bowl; add dates, and top with cover. Process 1 minute or until finely chopped. Add Cheddar cheese, cream cheese, and rum. Process 2 minutes, scraping sides of processor bowl occasionally.

Line a 2-cup mold with plastic wrap, extending plastic wrap over edges of mold. Spoon cheese mixture into mold, pressing firmly with the back of a spoon. Bring ends of plastic wrap over cheese mixture.

TO STORE: Cover and refrigerate at least 4 hours and up to 4 days.

TO SERVE: Unmold cheese, and remove plastic wrap. Press reserved walnuts on top and sides of cheese. Serve with gingersnaps and apple and pear slices. Yield: 2 cups.

Offer Date-Nut Dessert Cheese with gingersnaps and sliced apples and pears. Serve this whenever you want a not-too-sweet dessert.

Chocolate-Orange Crème in Meringue Shells

3 egg whites
¼ teaspoon cream of tartar
½ teaspoon vanilla extract
Dash of salt
½ cup sugar
Chocolate-Orange Crème
Garnishes: kumquat slices or
   small orange wedges

Beat egg whites (at room temperature) and cream of tartar at high speed of an electric mixer just until foamy; add vanilla and salt, beating until soft peaks form. Gradually add sugar, 1 tablespoon at a time, beating until stiff peaks form and sugar dissolves (2 to 4 minutes).

Line a baking sheet with heavy brown paper. Draw eight 3-inch circles on paper. Pipe meringue onto circles on brown paper, building up sides to form a shell. Bake at 200° for 1 hour and 15 minutes to 1 hour and 30 minutes. Turn oven off. Cool completely in oven at least 2 hours or overnight with oven door closed.

TO STORE: Place meringue shells in an airtight container, and store in a cool, dry place up to 2 weeks.

TO SERVE: Fill shells with Chocolate-Orange Crème. Garnish, if desired. Yield: 8 servings.

Chocolate-Orange Crème

¼ cup plus 2 tablespoons sugar
⅓ cup water
1 (6-ounce) package semisweet
   chocolate morsels
3 eggs, separated
2 teaspoons grated orange rind
½ teaspoon vanilla extract
½ teaspoon orange extract
¼ teaspoon cream of tartar
3 tablespoons sugar
¾ cup whipping cream,
   whipped

Combine ¼ cup plus 2 tablespoons sugar and water in a medium saucepan. Cook over medium-low heat until sugar dissolves, stirring constantly. Reduce heat to low; add chocolate, and cook until chocolate melts, stirring occasionally. Remove from heat.

Beat egg yolks in a medium bowl until thick and lemon colored. Gradually stir about one-fourth of chocolate mixture into yolks; add to remaining chocolate mixture, stirring constantly. Place mixture over medium heat, and bring to a boil. Cook 2 minutes, stirring constantly. Remove from heat, and stir in orange rind and flavorings. Let cool, stirring occasionally.

Beat egg whites (at room temperature) and cream of tartar at high speed of an electric mixer just until foamy. Gradually add 3 tablespoons sugar, 1 tablespoon at a time, beating until stiff peaks form and sugar dissolves. Fold beaten egg whites and whipped cream into chocolate mixture.

TO STORE: Cover and refrigerate up to 24 hours. Yield: 4 cups.

Chocolate-Orange Crème in Meringue Shells is a showy dessert that is surprisingly easy to prepare.

Favorite Apple Pie

Pastry for double-crust 9-inch
  pie
6½ cups peeled, sliced cooking
  apple
1 tablespoon lemon juice
¼ cup golden raisins
½ cup sugar
½ cup firmly packed brown
  sugar
¼ cup all-purpose flour
1 teaspoon grated lemon rind
1 teaspoon ground cinnamon
¼ teaspoon ground nutmeg
¼ teaspoon ground cloves
3 tablespoons butter or
  margarine

Roll half of pastry to ⅛-inch thickness on a lightly floured surface. Place in a 9-inch pieplate; trim off excess pastry along edges. Set aside.

Combine apple, lemon juice, and raisins in a large bowl, tossing to coat; set aside. Combine ½ cup sugar and next 6 ingredients in a small bowl. Spread half of sugar mixture over bottom of pastry shell. Spoon apple mixture over sugar mixture; sprinkle with remaining sugar mixture. Dot with butter.

Roll remaining pastry to ⅛-inch thickness, and place over filling. Trim off excess pastry along edges. Fold edges under and flute. Make decorative cutouts for top crust using excess pastry, if desired. Cut several slits in top crust to allow steam to escape.

TO STORE: Carefully wrap pie in heavy-duty aluminum foil. Label and freeze up to 1 month.

TO SERVE: Place frozen pie on a baking sheet. Bake, uncovered, at 475° for 15 minutes. Shield edge of pie with aluminum foil to prevent overbrowning. Reduce heat to 375°, and bake 1 hour or until golden brown. Cool before serving. Yield: one 9-inch pie.

Lemon-Orange Tarts

1½ cups all-purpose flour
2 tablespoons sugar
½ teaspoon baking powder
½ teaspoon salt
¼ cup butter or margarine,
    softened
¼ cup shortening
3 tablespoons milk
Lemon-Orange Filling
Garnishes: whipped cream,
    orange zest strips, and fresh
    mint sprigs

Combine first 4 ingredients in a large bowl; cut in butter and shortening with a pastry blender until mixture resembles coarse meal. Sprinkle milk (1 tablespoon at a time) over surface of mixture; stir with a fork until dry ingredients are moistened. Shape dough into a ball; chill 2 hours.

Divide dough into 8 equal portions. Roll each portion to ⅛-inch thickness on a lightly floured surface. Fit pastry into eight 4-inch tart pans. Prick bottom and sides of crust generously with a fork.

Bake at 450° for 8 to 10 minutes or until edges of pastry are lightly browned. Cool.

TO STORE: Refrigerate tart shells in a tightly covered container up to 24 hours. Freeze shells in a labeled airtight container up to 1 month.

TO SERVE: Thaw at room temperature. Spoon Lemon-Orange Filling into tart shells. Garnish, if desired. Yield: eight 4-inch tarts.

Lemon-Orange Filling

2 cups sugar
1 cup butter or margarine
1 tablespoon grated lemon rind
1 tablespoon grated orange rind
⅓ cup fresh lemon juice
⅓ cup fresh orange juice
6 egg yolks, beaten

Combine first 6 ingredients in top of a double boiler. Bring water to a boil. Reduce heat to low; cook over simmering water, stirring constantly, until butter melts. Gradually stir about one-fourth of hot mixture into egg yolks; add to remaining hot mixture, stirring constantly. Cook over simmering water, stirring constantly, until mixture thickens and coats a metal spoon (15 to 20 minutes). Remove from heat; cool.

TO STORE: Refrigerate filling in a tightly covered container up to 3 days. Yield: 3 cups.

For your next party, serve individual Lemon-Orange Tarts. They look pretty garnished with whipped cream, orange zest, and fresh mint sprigs.

Elegant Raspberry Tart

1 cup all-purpose flour
¾ cup quick-cooking oats,
    uncooked
½ cup finely chopped pecans
2 tablespoons brown sugar
½ teaspoon ground cinnamon
½ cup butter or margarine,
    softened
Filling (recipe follows)
3 cups fresh raspberries
Garnish: fresh mint sprigs

Combine first 5 ingredients in a medium bowl; cut in butter with a pastry blender until mixture resembles coarse meal. Press dough into a greased and floured 9-inch tart pan with removable bottom. Prick bottom and sides of pastry generously with a fork. Bake at 350° for 15 minutes or until lightly browned. Cool. Pour filling into baked tart shell. Cool 30 minutes.

TO STORE: Cover and refrigerate up to 24 hours.

TO SERVE: Top with raspberries. Garnish, if desired. Yield: one 9-inch tart.

Filling

½ cup sugar
3 tablespoons cornstarch
⅛ teaspoon salt
2 egg yolks, lightly beaten
2 cups milk
1 tablespoon butter or
    margarine
¾ teaspoon vanilla extract

Combine first 3 ingredients in a medium saucepan, stirring until blended. Combine egg yolks and milk; stir into sugar mixture. Cook over medium heat, stirring constantly, just until mixture comes to a boil. Reduce heat, and simmer 1 minute. Remove from heat; stir in butter and vanilla. Yield: 2¼ cups.

Summer Fruit Cobbler

1 cup sugar
3 tablespoons cornstarch
½ teaspoon ground cinnamon
¼ teaspoon salt
1 cup water
4 cups sliced fresh peaches
3 cups fresh blueberries
2 teaspoons lemon juice
1 teaspoon vanilla extract
Pastry for 9-inch pie
Vanilla ice cream (optional)

Combine first 4 ingredients in a large saucepan; gradually stir in water. Cook over medium heat, stirring constantly, until mixture comes to a boil. Cook 1 minute, stirring constantly. Remove from heat; stir in peaches, blueberries, lemon juice, and vanilla. Spoon fruit mixture into a 9-inch square pan.
Roll pastry to a 12-inch square on a lightly floured surface. Place pastry over fruit mixture; seal pastry to sides of pan. Flute edges of pastry, if desired. Cut several slits in top crust to allow steam to escape.

TO STORE: Wrap tightly in heavy-duty aluminum foil. Label and freeze up to 1 month.

TO SERVE: Remove foil. Bake frozen cobbler at 350° for 1½ hours or until bubbly and golden brown. Serve with vanilla ice cream, if desired. Yield: 6 to 8 servings.

Blueberry-Apple Crisp

1 large cooking apple, peeled
  and chopped
2 tablespoons lemon juice
2 cups fresh blueberries
⅔ cup firmly packed brown
  sugar, divided
2 teaspoons cornstarch
⅔ cup quick-cooking oats,
  uncooked
½ cup all-purpose flour
1 teaspoon grated lemon rind
⅓ cup butter or margarine,
  softened
Ice cream or whipped cream
  (optional)

Combine apple and lemon juice in a 1½-quart baking dish, tossing to coat apple. Add blueberries, stirring well. Combine ⅓ cup brown sugar and cornstarch; add to fruit mixture, tossing to coat fruit.

Combine remaining ⅓ cup brown sugar, oats, flour, and lemon rind in a medium bowl; stir well. Cut in butter with a pastry blender until mixture resembles coarse meal. Sprinkle crumb mixture over fruit mixture.

TO STORE: Cover and refrigerate up to 24 hours.

TO SERVE: Bake, uncovered, at 350° for 30 to 40 minutes or until lightly browned. Serve with ice cream or whipped cream, if desired. Yield: 4 to 6 servings.

Lemon Curd

2 cups sugar
1 cup butter or margarine
3 tablespoons grated lemon rind
⅔ cup fresh lemon juice
4 eggs, lightly beaten

Combine first 4 ingredients in top of a double boiler. Bring water to a boil. Reduce heat to low; cook over simmering water, stirring constantly, until butter melts. Gradually stir about one-fourth of hot mixture into eggs; add to remaining hot mixture, stirring constantly. Cook over simmering water, stirring constantly, until mixture thickens and coats a metal spoon (about 15 minutes). Remove from heat; cool.

TO STORE: Refrigerate in a tightly covered container up to 2 weeks.

TO SERVE: Serve over slices of pound cake or gingerbread. Yield: 2½ cups.

Praline-Pecan Sauce

¼ cup butter or margarine
1¼ cups firmly packed brown
  sugar
¾ cup light corn syrup
3 tablespoons all-purpose flour
1 (5-ounce) can evaporated milk
1½ cups chopped pecans,
  toasted

Melt butter in a heavy saucepan; add brown sugar, corn syrup, and flour, stirring until smooth. Bring mixture to a boil; reduce heat, and simmer 5 minutes, stirring constantly. Remove from heat, and cool 5 minutes. Gradually stir in evaporated milk and chopped pecans. Cool completely.

TO STORE: Refrigerate in a tightly covered container up to 2 weeks.

TO SERVE: Microwave at HIGH for 2 minutes, stirring after 1 minute. Serve warm over ice cream. Yield: 3 cups.

Strawberries with Custard Sauce

2 cups milk
5 egg yolks
⅔ cup sugar
⅛ teaspoon salt
1 teaspoon vanilla extract
4 cups strawberry halves

Place milk in top of a double boiler; bring water to a boil. Cook until milk is thoroughly heated, stirring frequently. Remove from heat, and set aside.

Beat egg yolks, sugar, and salt at medium speed of an electric mixer until thickened. Gradually stir about one-fourth of hot milk into egg mixture; add to remaining milk, stirring constantly. Cook custard mixture in double boiler over low heat, stirring occasionally, 30 minutes or until mixture thickens. Remove from heat; stir in vanilla. Cool completely, stirring occasionally.

TO STORE: Refrigerate in a tightly covered container up to 3 days.

TO SERVE: Spoon strawberries into individual dessert dishes. Drizzle custard sauce over strawberries. Yield: 8 servings.

Old-Fashioned Vanilla Ice Cream

4 cups milk
2¼ cups sugar
⅓ cup all-purpose flour
¼ teaspoon salt
5 eggs, beaten
5 cups half-and-half
1½ tablespoons vanilla extract

Heat milk in a 3-quart saucepan over low heat. Combine sugar, flour, and salt in a small bowl; gradually add sugar mixture to hot milk, stirring until blended. Cook over medium heat, stirring constantly, 8 to 10 minutes or until thickened.

Gradually stir about one-fourth of hot mixture into beaten eggs; add to remaining hot mixture, stirring constantly. Cook 1 minute; remove from heat, and let cool. Cover and refrigerate custard mixture at least 2 hours and up to 24 hours.

Add half-and-half and vanilla to chilled custard mixture; stir well. Pour mixture into freezer can of a 1-gallon hand-turned or electric freezer. Freeze according to manufacturer's instructions. Remove dasher; cover freezer can, and let ripen 1 hour.

TO STORE: Remove ice cream from freezer can. Freeze in a labeled airtight container up to 1 month.

TO SERVE: Scoop ice cream into individual dessert dishes. Serve immediately. Yield: 2½ quarts.

Raspberry and Champagne Sherbet

2 (10-ounce) packages frozen
   raspberries, thawed
1 cup whipping cream
½ cup sugar
1½ cups champagne
2 egg whites
¼ teaspoon cream of tartar
¼ cup sugar
Garnish: fresh mint sprigs

Press raspberries through a sieve or food mill; set puree aside, and discard seeds.

Combine whipping cream and ½ cup sugar in a medium saucepan; cook over low heat, stirring constantly, until sugar dissolves. Remove from heat; let cool. Stir in reserved puree and champagne. Pour mixture into a 13- x 9- x 2-inch pan; freeze 8 hours or until firm.

Beat egg whites (at room temperature) and cream of tartar at high speed of an electric mixer just until foamy. Gradually add ¼ cup sugar, 1 tablespoon at a time, beating until stiff peaks form and sugar dissolves (2 to 4 minutes). Set aside.

Position knife blade in food processor bowl. Break frozen mixture into large pieces, and place in processor bowl; process until fluffy but not thawed. Gently fold in egg white mixture. Return mixture to pan.

TO STORE: Cover tightly; freeze until sherbet is firm and up to 2 weeks.

TO SERVE: Scoop sherbet into individual dessert dishes. Garnish, if desired. Serve immediately. Yield: 5 cups.

Strawberry-Pineapple Sorbet

2 cups strawberries, halved
1 (8-ounce) can crushed
   pineapple, undrained
¼ cup sugar
1 tablespoon lemon juice
1 tablespoon chopped fresh
   mint leaves
Garnish: fresh mint sprigs

Combine strawberries and pineapple in container of an electric blender or food processor. Top with cover, and process until smooth. Add sugar, lemon juice, and chopped mint; process until smooth.

Spoon mixture into an 8½- x 4½- x 3-inch loafpan. Cover; freeze 4 hours or until firm. Break frozen mixture into small chunks, and place chunks in a mixing bowl. Beat at medium speed of an electric mixer until smooth but not melted. Return mixture to loafpan.

TO STORE: Cover tightly; freeze until sorbet is firm and up to 2 weeks.

TO SERVE: Scoop sorbet into dessert dishes. Garnish, if desired. Serve immediately. Yield: about 3 cups.

Coffee-Almond Tortoni

1 cup whipping cream
½ cup sugar, divided
1 teaspoon vanilla extract
¼ teaspoon almond extract
2 egg whites
¼ cup finely chopped almonds, toasted and divided
¼ cup flaked coconut, toasted and divided
1 teaspoon instant coffee granules

Combine whipping cream, ¼ cup sugar, and flavorings in a medium mixing bowl; beat at high speed of an electric mixer until soft peaks form.

Beat egg whites (at room temperature) at high speed of an electric mixer just until foamy. Gradually add remaining ¼ cup sugar, 1 tablespoon at a time, beating until soft peaks form. Fold in whipped cream mixture, 2 tablespoons almonds, and 2 tablespoons coconut; spoon half of mixture into 8 muffin cups lined with foil liners.

Stir coffee granules into remaining half of tortoni mixture; spoon over whipped cream mixture in muffin cups. Sprinkle with remaining 2 tablespoons almonds and 2 tablespoons coconut.

TO STORE: Cover tightly, and freeze 8 hours. Remove frozen tortoni from muffin pans, and place in a zip-top heavy-duty plastic bag. Freeze up to 1 month.

TO SERVE: Remove from freezer 15 minutes before serving. Yield: 8 servings.

Creamy Lemon Freeze in Lemon Shells

1 cup milk
1 cup whipping cream
1 cup sugar
3 tablespoons grated lemon rind
⅓ cup fresh lemon juice
Scalloped lemon shells (optional)
Garnish: fresh mint sprigs

Combine milk, whipping cream, and sugar in a medium bowl; stir until sugar dissolves. Cover and freeze 2 hours. Add rind and juice; beat at medium speed of an electric mixer 3 to 5 minutes or until thickened.

TO STORE: Cover tightly, and freeze at least 24 hours and up to 2 weeks.

TO SERVE: Scoop Creamy Lemon Freeze into scalloped lemon shells, if desired, or dessert dishes. Garnish, if desired. Serve immediately. Yield: about 4 cups.

Coffee, almonds, and coconut are combined in Coffee-Almond Tortoni for a dessert that will melt in your mouth.

Layered Ice Cream Dessert

¾ cup chocolate wafer crumbs,
  divided
1 cup butter or margarine
2 (1-ounce) squares
  unsweetened chocolate
2 cups sifted powdered sugar
3 eggs, separated
1 cup coarsely chopped pecans
1 quart vanilla ice cream,
  softened
Garnish: strawberry fans

Sprinkle ½ cup chocolate crumbs evenly in bottom of a 13- x 9- x 2-inch baking pan. Set aside.

Combine butter and chocolate in a large saucepan; cook over low heat until butter melts, stirring occasionally. Remove from heat; add powdered sugar, and beat at medium speed of an electric mixer 2 minutes. Add egg yolks, beating until smooth.

Beat egg whites (at room temperature) until stiff peaks form; fold into chocolate mixture. Carefully pour chocolate mixture over crumbs in pan, and sprinkle with pecans. Cover and freeze 4 hours or until firm.

Spread ice cream evenly over pecan layer; sprinkle with remaining ¼ cup chocolate crumbs.

TO STORE: Cover tightly; freeze until dessert is firm and up to 2 weeks.

TO SERVE: Cut into squares, and garnish, if desired. Serve immediately. Yield: 15 servings.

Blueberry and Ice Cream Crêpes

1½ cups all-purpose flour
1 tablespoon sugar
¼ teaspoon salt
2 cups milk
1 teaspoon vanilla extract
3 eggs
2 tablespoons butter or
  margarine, melted
Vegetable oil
2 cups fresh or frozen
  blueberries, thawed
⅓ cup sugar
1 quart vanilla ice cream
1½ cups whipping cream,
  whipped
Additional fresh blueberries
Garnish: edible flowers

Any occasion will be special when your menu includes elegant Blueberry and Ice Cream Crêpes.

Combine first 3 ingredients; stir well. Add milk and vanilla; beat at medium speed of an electric mixer until smooth. Add eggs, and beat well; stir in butter. Refrigerate at least 1 hour. (This allows flour particles to swell and soften so that crêpes will be light in texture.)

Brush the bottom of a 6-inch crêpe pan or heavy skillet with oil; place over medium heat just until hot, not smoking. Pour 2 tablespoons batter into pan; quickly tilt pan in all directions so that batter covers pan in a thin film. Cook about 1 minute or until lightly browned.

Lift edge of crêpe to test for doneness. Crêpe is ready for flipping when it can be shaken loose from pan. Flip crêpe, and cook about 30 seconds on other side. (This side is usually spotty brown and is the side on which the filling is placed.)

Place crêpe on a towel to cool. Repeat until all batter is used. Stack crêpes between layers of wax paper to prevent sticking.

TO STORE: Freeze crêpes in a labeled airtight container up to 2 weeks.

TO SERVE: Thaw crêpes at room temperature. Combine blueberries and ⅓ cup sugar; stir gently, and set aside. Fill each crêpe with about ¼ cup ice cream. Roll up, and place seam side up on a dessert plate. Top each crêpe with blueberry mixture, whipped cream, and additional fresh blueberries. Garnish, if desired. Serve immediately. Yield: 14 servings.

Coming Home to Supper

*F*ew thoughts are as comforting on busy days as knowing that supper is ready to heat and serve when you get home. You can forget weariness while visualizing a warming winter meal of Savory Meat Loaf with Old-Fashioned Macaroni and Cheese, or the summer refreshment of Grilled Swordfish with Lemon-Dill Butter and crisp Tangy Refrigerator Slaw.

Each of the menus in this chapter includes three do-ahead recipes. The recipes are as simple as possible, with most of the steps spread over a variety of time spans to let you choose the one that fits your schedule.

With a few minor changes, any one of these suppers can become a company dinner. The Summer Supper for Two menu suggests watermelon for dessert; you could enhance the meal by changing to Watermelon Sorbet from the Grilled Kabob Supper menu. Similarly, the Spinach Salad with Blue Cheese Dressing from the Neighborly Dinner would make the Put on a Pot of Chili menu perfect for a party, and something as simple as vanilla ice cream with Rich Caramel Sauce from the Mexican Fiesta menu would add a festive touch.

For added convenience, make an extra batch of meatballs or chili when ground beef is on sale. One meat loaf can be baked and frozen in slices for quick sandwich fixings.

When time is really at a premium, you can substitute a similar commercial item for a recipe in the menu. These may include salad ingredients from the supermarket salad bar, deli cole slaw, bakery bread, or a commercial dessert.

Three Pepper Pizza and Romaine Salad Italiano are ready in a flash to serve after a busy day. Menu begins on page 186.

Mexican Fiesta

Corn Salad Caliente

Burrito Supreme Casserole

Spanish rice

Vanilla ice cream with Rich Caramel Sauce

Serves 4

Bring the lively flavors and colors of Mexico to life with a menu guaranteed to rouse an olé from family members and friends.

Warm the casserole just before serving, and then add the finishing touch with a sprinkling of fresh lettuce, tomato, and avocado. A colorful marinated corn salad and commercial Spanish rice round out the menu.

Vanilla ice cream with a rich caramel sauce balances the spicy dishes from dinner, making it the perfect ending for this fiesta of flavor.

Corn Salad Caliente

2 (10-ounce) packages frozen corn, cooked and drained
1 (15½-ounce) can kidney beans, drained
¾ cup commercial oil and vinegar salad dressing
1 small purple onion, thinly sliced
1 small green pepper, cut into strips
½ cup (2 ounces) Monterey Jack cheese with jalapeño pepper, diced
½ cup sliced celery
½ cup sliced ripe olives
1 (2-ounce) jar diced pimiento, undrained
½ teaspoon salt
¼ teaspoon ground cumin
⅛ teaspoon ground red pepper

Combine all ingredients in a large bowl; toss gently.

TO STORE: Cover and refrigerate up to 24 hours.

TO SERVE: Serve with a slotted spoon. Yield: 4 to 6 servings.

Burrito Supreme Casserole

8 (8-inch) flour tortillas
1½ cups tomato juice
1 (1¼-ounce) envelope taco
   seasoning mix
1 tablespoon vegetable oil
½ pound ground beef
1 (16-ounce) can refried beans
3 cups (12 ounces) shredded
   Cheddar cheese, divided
1 small avocado
1 tablespoon lemon juice
1½ cups shredded lettuce
1 cup chopped tomato

Wrap tortillas securely in aluminum foil; bake at 350° for 15 minutes or until thoroughly heated.

Combine tomato juice, seasoning mix, and oil; stir well, and set aside.

Cook ground beef in a large skillet until browned, stirring to crumble; drain. Stir in beans and ½ cup tomato juice mixture. Bring to a boil; cover, reduce heat, and simmer 5 minutes or until mixture is thoroughly heated, stirring occasionally. Remove from heat.

Place ¼ cup beef mixture and 2½ tablespoons cheese down center of each tortilla. Roll up tortillas, and place seam side down in a lightly greased 13- x 9- x 2-inch baking dish.

TO STORE: Cover casserole, and refrigerate 8 hours. Refrigerate remaining tomato juice mixture in a tightly covered container.

TO SERVE: Pour remaining tomato juice mixture over casserole. Cover and bake, at 350° for 30 to 35 minutes. Uncover and sprinkle with remaining cheese; bake an additional 5 minutes or until cheese melts.

Peel and cube avocado; toss with lemon juice. Sprinkle avocado, lettuce, and tomato over casserole. Serve immediately. Yield: 4 servings.

Rich Caramel Sauce

½ cup plus 1 tablespoon
   sweetened condensed milk
¼ cup plus 2 tablespoons light
   corn syrup
¼ cup sugar
3 tablespoons brown sugar
3 tablespoons whipping cream
2 tablespoons butter or
   margarine
½ teaspoon vanilla extract
Vanilla ice cream

Combine first 4 ingredients in a heavy saucepan; stir well. Cook over medium heat, stirring constantly, until mixture reaches 220° on a candy thermometer. Remove from heat; stir in whipping cream, butter, and vanilla. Cool completely.

TO STORE: Refrigerate in a tightly covered container up to 4 days.

TO SERVE: Reheat in a saucepan over low heat, stirring occasionally, or microwave at HIGH for 2 to 4 minutes or until thoroughly heated, stirring occasionally. Serve warm over ice cream. Yield: 1½ cups.

Stir-Fry Delight

Chicken and Broccoli Stir-Fry

Sweet-and-Sour Slaw

Chinese fried noodles or rice

Orange-Coconut Crème

Serves 4

You don't need a wok to enjoy a tasty stir-fry. A large, heavy skillet works just as well.

Serve Chicken and Broccoli Stir-Fry over Chinese fried noodles or rice for a flavorful entrée. There's no time to prepare ingredients once you begin to stir-fry, so be sure to chop, measure, and assemble the ingredients before heating the skillet or wok.

A tangy slaw and a sweet orange dessert made the night before are easy additions to this quick supper.

Chicken and Broccoli Stir-Fry

¼ cup soy sauce
¼ cup dry sherry
2 tablespoons rice wine vinegar
2 tablespoons hoisin sauce
1 tablespoon brown sugar
½ cup chopped green onions
4 chicken breast halves, skinned and boned
2 tablespoons vegetable oil
3 cups broccoli flowerets
1 cup sliced fresh mushrooms
1 tablespoon cornstarch
¼ cup water
Chinese fried noodles or hot cooked rice

Combine first 6 ingredients in a medium bowl, stirring well; set aside. Cut chicken into 2-inch strips; add chicken to marinade, tossing to coat.

TO STORE: Refrigerate in a tightly covered container up to 24 hours.

TO SERVE: Pour oil around top of a preheated wok or skillet, coating sides; heat at medium high (325°) for 1 minute. Remove chicken from marinade. Place marinade in a small saucepan; bring to a boil, and cook 5 minutes. Set aside.

Add chicken to wok; stir-fry 2 to 3 minutes. Remove chicken, and set aside. Add broccoli to wok, and stir-fry 2 minutes. Add mushrooms; stir-fry 2 minutes or until vegetables are crisp-tender. Return chicken to wok; add marinade, stirring well. Combine cornstarch and water; add to wok. Cook, stirring constantly, until thickened. Serve chicken mixture over Chinese fried noodles or hot cooked rice. Yield: 4 servings.

Chicken and Broccoli Stir-Fry is a quick and colorful main dish. Serve it over a bed of Chinese fried noodles for a change from basic rice.

Sweet-and-Sour Slaw

2 cups shredded cabbage
2 cups shredded red cabbage
¾ cup shredded carrot
½ cup cider vinegar
¼ cup vegetable oil
3 tablespoons sugar
½ teaspoon ground ginger
¼ teaspoon ground red pepper

Combine cabbage and carrot in a large bowl; set aside. Combine vinegar and oil in a small saucepan; stir in sugar, ginger, and red pepper. Cook over low heat, stirring constantly, until sugar dissolves. Immediately pour hot vinegar mixture over vegetables; toss well.

TO STORE: Refrigerate in a tightly covered container at least 8 hours and up to 1 week. Yield: 4 servings.

Orange-Coconut Crème

1 (3-ounce) package
  orange-flavored gelatin
1 cup boiling water
Grated rind of 1 orange
¾ cup orange juice
2 teaspoons lemon juice
1 cup whipping cream
¼ cup sugar
¼ cup flaked coconut
Garnishes: whipped cream and
  mandarin orange slices

Dissolve gelatin in boiling water. Stir in orange rind, orange juice, and lemon juice. Chill until mixture is the consistency of unbeaten egg white.

Beat 1 cup whipping cream at high speed of an electric mixer until foamy; gradually add sugar, beating until stiff peaks form. Fold sweetened whipped cream and coconut into gelatin mixture; spoon into 4 stemmed glasses.

TO STORE: Cover and refrigerate up to 24 hours.

TO SERVE: Garnish, if desired. Yield: 4 servings.

Down-Home Supper

Savory Meat Loaf

Old-Fashioned Macaroni and Cheese

Green beans

Easy Apple Crunch with vanilla ice cream

Serves 6

After a busy day at work or school, the family will enjoy sitting down to a supper planned around some all-time favorite foods. This easy menu features a selection of "comfort foods" that is sure to please.

Bake the meat loaf and macaroni and cheese about 1 hour before serving. When they have completed cooking, bake Easy Apple Crunch. Serve the dessert piping hot from the oven with a big scoop of vanilla ice cream.

Savory Meat Loaf

1½ pounds ground beef
½ cup tomato sauce
2 eggs, lightly beaten
¾ cup soft breadcrumbs
¼ cup finely chopped onion
1 tablespoon Worcestershire
   sauce
2 teaspoons prepared mustard
1 teaspoon prepared horseradish
1 teaspoon salt
½ teaspoon poultry seasoning
¼ teaspoon pepper
⅓ cup catsup

Combine first 11 ingredients in a large bowl, mixing well. Shape mixture into an 8- x 4-inch loaf, and place in a 13- x 9- x 2-inch baking pan.

TO STORE: Cover and refrigerate up to 24 hours.

TO SERVE: Bake, uncovered, at 350° for 1 hour. Pour catsup over top of meat loaf, and bake an additional 15 minutes. Yield: 6 servings.

Old-Fashioned Macaroni and Cheese

1 (8-ounce) package elbow
  macaroni
¼ cup finely chopped onion
¼ cup butter or margarine,
  melted
¼ cup all-purpose flour
2 cups milk
2 cups (8 ounces) shredded
  sharp Cheddar cheese
½ teaspoon salt
1 egg, beaten
½ cup soft breadcrumbs
2 tablespoons butter or
  margarine, melted

Cook macaroni according to package directions; drain and set aside.

Sauté onion in ¼ cup butter in a medium saucepan over medium heat until tender; add flour, stirring until smooth. Cook 1 minute, stirring constantly. Gradually add milk; cook, stirring constantly, until mixture is thickened and bubbly. Remove from heat; add cheese and salt, stirring until cheese melts. Gradually stir about one-fourth of hot mixture into egg; add to remaining hot mixture, stirring constantly.

Stir cheese sauce into macaroni; pour into a lightly greased 2-quart baking dish.

TO STORE: Cover and refrigerate up to 2 days. Cover tightly, label, and freeze up to 1 month.

TO SERVE: Thaw in refrigerator. Combine breadcrumbs and 2 tablespoons butter; sprinkle over casserole. Bake at 350° for 50 to 55 minutes or until thoroughly heated. Yield: 6 servings.

Easy Apple Crunch

1 cup sugar
2 tablespoons all-purpose flour
¼ cup raisins
½ teaspoon ground cinnamon
2 (20-ounce) cans unsweetened
  apple slices, drained
¾ cup all-purpose flour
¾ cup quick-cooking oats,
  uncooked
¾ cup firmly packed brown
  sugar
½ cup butter or margarine,
  softened
½ cup chopped pecans
Vanilla ice cream

Combine 1 cup sugar, 2 tablespoons flour, raisins, and cinnamon in a large bowl; stir in apples. Spoon mixture into a lightly greased 8-inch square baking dish.

Combine ¾ cup flour, oats, and brown sugar; cut in butter with a pastry blender until mixture resembles coarse meal. Stir in pecans.

TO STORE: Cover apple mixture, and refrigerate up to 24 hours. Place crumb mixture in a zip-top plastic bag, and refrigerate up to 24 hours.

TO SERVE: Sprinkle crumb mixture over apple mixture. Bake, uncovered, at 350° for 40 to 45 minutes or until bubbly and topping is golden brown. Top each serving with ice cream. Yield: 6 servings.

Hurry-Up Curry

Asparagus and Sun-Dried Tomato Salad

Chicken Curry

Nut Rice

Frozen banana yogurt

Serves 4

Chicken in a spicy marinade laced with curry and onion adds a touch of the Far East to your supper. The chicken is chopped for faster cooking.

Just reheat the rice, pour the dressing over the salad, and you are ready to sit down and enjoy a quick supper with the family.

Asparagus and Sun-Dried Tomato Salad

½ pound fresh asparagus spears
2 cups torn red leaf lettuce
½ cup chopped purple onion
5 oil-packed sun-dried tomatoes, drained and chopped
⅓ cup olive oil
1 tablespoon balsamic vinegar
1 tablespoon Dijon mustard
½ teaspoon dried whole basil
½ teaspoon dried whole dillweed
½ teaspoon pepper
¼ teaspoon dried whole oregano
½ cup (2 ounces) shredded fontina cheese

Snap off tough ends of asparagus. Remove scales from stalks with a knife or vegetable peeler, if desired. Cut asparagus into 2-inch pieces. Cover and cook asparagus in a small amount of boiling water 5 to 6 minutes or until crisp-tender; drain. Rinse with cold water; drain again. Combine asparagus, lettuce, onion, and sun-dried tomatoes in a large bowl; set aside.

Combine olive oil and next 6 ingredients in a jar. Cover tightly, and shake vigorously.

TO STORE: Refrigerate dressing up to 3 days. Place salad ingredients in a large zip-top plastic bag, and refrigerate up to 24 hours.

TO SERVE: Place salad ingredients in a serving bowl; add cheese. Shake dressing vigorously. Pour dressing over salad, and toss well. Yield: 4 servings.

Asparagus and Sun-Dried Tomato Salad is a beautiful creation. Just toss with dressing, serve, and enjoy!

Chicken Curry

2 small onions, chopped
2 tablespoons butter or
  margarine, melted
½ teaspoon salt
½ teaspoon garlic powder
½ teaspoon ground allspice
½ teaspoon curry powder
¼ teaspoon ground turmeric
¼ teaspoon ground cardamom
¼ teaspoon ground cloves
¼ teaspoon ground red pepper
¼ teaspoon black pepper
¾ cup canned diluted chicken
  broth
Juice of 1 lime
3 cups chopped cooked chicken

Sauté onion in butter in a medium skillet 1 minute. Add salt and next 8 ingredients; cook 2 minutes. Stir in broth and lime juice; remove from heat. Cool.

TO STORE: Place chicken in a large zip-top heavy-duty plastic bag; pour onion mixture over chicken. Refrigerate up to 24 hours.

TO SERVE: Cook mixture in a medium saucepan over medium heat until thoroughly heated, stirring occasionally. Yield: 4 servings.

Nut Rice

2 cups water
2 tablespoons butter or
  margarine
½ teaspoon salt
1 cup long-grain rice, uncooked
1 cup finely chopped pecans,
  toasted
½ cup frozen English peas,
  thawed

Combine water, butter, and salt in a medium saucepan; bring to a boil. Add rice; cover, reduce heat, and simmer 20 minutes or until rice is tender and water is absorbed. Remove from heat. Gently stir in pecans and peas. Cool completely.

TO STORE: Refrigerate in a tightly covered container up to 2 days.

TO SERVE: Place rice in a 2-quart casserole. Cover tightly with heavy-duty plastic wrap; fold back a corner of wrap to allow steam to escape. Microwave at HIGH 3 to 4 minutes or until hot, stirring gently after 2 minutes. Serve immediately. Yield: 4 servings.

Tasty Spaghetti Supper

Italian Vegetable Salad

Spaghetti and Meatballs

Breadsticks

Frosty Spumoni Loaf

Serves 6

Food with an Italian flair tops the list of ethnic favorites. And what could be more Italian than spaghetti and meatballs?

The hearty meatballs and rich sauce are combined at serving time and spooned over hot spaghetti for an all-time favorite treat. It is accompanied by an Italian salad packed with fresh vegetables.

Frosty Spumoni Loaf is a variation of the classic Italian dessert and a fitting end to a delicious, colorful dinner. Bravo!

Italian Vegetable Salad

2 cups broccoli flowerets
1⅓ cups sliced fresh
 mushrooms
1 cup cherry tomatoes, halved
1 cup sliced celery
1 small purple onion, coarsely
 chopped
½ medium-size green pepper,
 thinly sliced
1 (2¼-ounce) can sliced ripe
 olives
¼ cup sliced water chestnuts,
 drained
⅓ cup commercial Italian salad
 dressing
1 teaspoon freshly ground
 pepper

Combine all ingredients in a large bowl, and toss gently to coat.

TO STORE: Refrigerate in a tightly covered container up to 2 days.

TO SERVE: Spoon salad into a serving bowl, using a slotted spoon. Yield: 6 servings.

Spaghetti and Meatballs

¾ pound ground beef
¾ pound ground pork
¾ cup soft breadcrumbs
½ cup chopped onion
1 egg, beaten
⅓ cup milk
¼ cup chopped fresh parsley
1 teaspoon dried Italian
 seasoning
½ teaspoon salt
¼ teaspoon garlic powder
¼ teaspoon pepper
Italian Sauce
Hot cooked spaghetti

Combine first 11 ingredients in a large bowl, mixing well; shape into 2-inch balls. Place balls ½ inch apart on lightly greased rack of a broiler pan. Bake at 350° for 35 minutes or until done. Drain on paper towels. Cool.

TO STORE: Refrigerate meatballs in a tightly covered container up to 2 days. Freeze meatballs in a labeled airtight container up to 1 month.

TO SERVE: Thaw meatballs and Italian sauce in refrigerator. Place meatballs and sauce in a large saucepan; cook over medium heat 10 minutes or until thoroughly heated, stirring occasionally. Serve over hot spaghetti. Yield: 6 servings.

Italian Sauce

¼ cup chopped onion
1 clove garlic, minced
2 tablespoons olive oil
1 (28-ounce) can whole
 tomatoes, undrained and
 chopped
1 (6-ounce) can tomato paste
1 tablespoon sugar
1 tablespoon grated Parmesan
 cheese
½ teaspoon salt
½ teaspoon dried whole basil
½ teaspoon dried whole
 oregano
¼ teaspoon crushed red pepper

Sauté onion and garlic in oil in a large saucepan over medium-low heat until tender. Stir in tomatoes and remaining ingredients; bring to a boil. Cover, reduce heat, and simmer 30 minutes. Cool.

TO STORE: Refrigerate sauce in a tightly covered container up to 1 week. Freeze in a labeled airtight container up to 1 month. Yield: 4 cups.

Frosty Spumoni Loaf

2 cups lime sherbet, softened
¼ cup finely chopped pecans,
 divided
1 (8-ounce) can crushed
 pineapple, drained
1 cup vanilla ice cream,
 softened
2 cups raspberry sherbet,
 softened

Line an 8½- x 4½- x 3-inch loafpan with plastic wrap; set aside.
 Combine lime sherbet and 2 tablespoons pecans; stir well. Spread sherbet mixture in bottom of prepared pan; freeze 30 minutes. Press pineapple between layers of paper towels to remove excess moisture. Combine pineapple and vanilla ice cream, stirring well. Spread evenly over lime sherbet; freeze 30 minutes. Combine raspberry sherbet and remaining 2 tablespoons pecans; stir well. Spread evenly over ice cream mixture.

TO STORE: Cover tightly, label, and freeze up to 1 week.

TO SERVE: Invert onto a serving platter. Let stand 5 to 10 minutes before slicing. Yield: 6 servings.

Easy Sunday Supper

Dijon Chicken

Crisp Carrot Marinade

Baked Cinnamon Apples

Chocolate ice cream with fudge sauce

Serves 4

Sunday evening is a time for relaxing before another busy week begins.

Relaxing is easy when you serve a supper on Sunday that was prepared on Saturday. All you have to do to complete the evening meal is bake the chicken and apples, and serve the marinated carrots on the side.

Something as simple as ice cream topped with a commercial fudge sauce is the perfect ending to this no-fuss meal.

Dijon Chicken

4 chicken breast halves, skinned and boned
¼ cup butter or margarine, softened
¼ cup chopped green onions
2 tablespoons Dijon mustard
2 tablespoons lemon juice
2 tablespoons brandy
½ teaspoon salt
¼ teaspoon pepper

Place each piece of chicken between 2 sheets of heavy-duty plastic wrap; flatten to ¼-inch thickness, using a meat mallet or rolling pin. Place chicken in a lightly greased 11- x 7- x 1½-inch baking dish.

Combine butter and remaining ingredients; stir well. Spread butter mixture evenly over chicken.

TO STORE: Cover and refrigerate up to 24 hours.

TO SERVE: Bake, uncovered, at 350° for 30 to 35 minutes or until tender. Yield: 4 servings.

This relaxing Sunday supper includes Dijon Chicken, Baked Cinnamon Apples, and Crisp Carrot Marinade, a simple but attractive combination.

Crisp Carrot Marinade

1 pound carrots, scraped and
thinly sliced
⅓ cup chopped onion
⅓ cup chopped green pepper
⅓ cup vinegar
⅓ cup sugar
3 tablespoons vegetable oil
1 teaspoon Worcestershire sauce
¼ teaspoon prepared mustard
Curly leaf lettuce

Cook carrot in boiling water to cover 5 minutes or until crisp-tender; drain.

Combine carrot, onion, and green pepper in a medium bowl. Combine vinegar and next 4 ingredients in a jar. Cover tightly, and shake vigorously. Pour dressing over vegetables; toss well.

TO STORE: Refrigerate in a tightly covered container up to 2 days.

TO SERVE: Serve on lettuce leaves, using a slotted spoon. Yield: 4 servings.

Baked Cinnamon Apples

4 large Rome apples
¼ cup firmly packed brown
sugar
2 teaspoons ground cinnamon
½ cup apple juice
2 tablespoons butter or
margarine, melted

Core apples to within ½ inch from bottom. Place apples in an 8-inch square baking dish. Combine brown sugar and cinnamon; spoon about 1 tablespoon sugar mixture into center of each apple.

TO STORE: Cover and refrigerate up to 24 hours.

TO SERVE: Pour apple juice into baking dish. Brush apples with melted butter. Cover and bake at 400° for 30 to 35 minutes. Yield: 4 servings.

Put on a Pot of Chili

Lettuce wedges with ranch dressing

Texas Chili

Southern Corn Sticks

Chocolate-Peppermint Parfaits

Serves 6

A favorite fall or winter food is chili. But not just any chili. Chili that's rich and meaty and full of spicy ingredients like onions, garlic, and jalapeño pepper will make more than one mouth water.

Add some homemade corn sticks and simple lettuce wedges, and you have a quick, satisfying dinner. Cap off the menu with a rich chocolate dessert bursting with mint flavor.

Texas Chili

1½ pounds ground beef
½ teaspoon chili powder
¼ teaspoon ground cumin
2 small onions, chopped
2 cloves garlic, minced
1 jalapeño pepper, seeded and chopped
1 tablespoon vegetable oil
2 (15-ounce) cans tomato sauce
1 (15½-ounce) can Mexican-style chili beans, undrained
1 cup water
1 (6-ounce) can tomato paste
¼ cup commercial green chile salsa or jalapeño salsa
2 tablespoons chili powder
1 (15½-ounce) can kidney beans, drained
½ (12-ounce) can beer
¼ teaspoon salt
¼ teaspoon pepper
Hot sauce to taste
Shredded Cheddar cheese
Corn chips

Combine ground beef, ½ teaspoon chili powder, and ¼ teaspoon cumin in a Dutch oven. Cook over medium heat until meat is browned, stirring to crumble meat. Drain well, and set aside.

Sauté onion, garlic, and jalapeño pepper in oil until tender. Add ground beef mixture, tomato sauce, and next 5 ingredients. Cover, reduce heat, and simmer 20 minutes. Add kidney beans, beer, salt, pepper, and hot sauce, stirring well. Cool.

TO STORE: Refrigerate chili in a tightly covered container up to 2 days. Freeze in a labeled airtight container up to 1 month.

TO SERVE: Thaw in refrigerator. Cook chili over medium heat until thoroughly heated, stirring occasionally. Serve with cheese and corn chips. Yield: 6 servings.

Southern Corn Sticks

1 cup yellow cornmeal
½ cup all-purpose flour
2¼ teaspoons baking powder
2 teaspoons sugar
½ teaspoon salt
1 egg, beaten
1 cup buttermilk
3 tablespoons vegetable oil

Combine first 5 ingredients in a medium bowl; stir well. Combine egg, buttermilk, and oil; add to dry ingredients, stirring just until moistened.

Place a well-greased cast-iron corn stick pan in a 450° oven for 3 minutes or until pan is hot. Remove pan from oven; spoon batter into pan, filling two-thirds full. Bake at 450° for 12 to 15 minutes or until lightly browned.

TO STORE: Freeze corn sticks in a labeled airtight container up to 1 month.

TO SERVE: Thaw at room temperature. Yield: 1 dozen.

Chocolate-Peppermint Parfaits

2⅓ cups whipping cream, divided
¼ cup sugar
2 eggs
2 egg yolks
6 (1-ounce) squares semisweet chocolate, melted
½ teaspoon peppermint extract
⅓ cup crushed peppermint candy
¾ cup cream-filled chocolate sandwich cookie crumbs
Garnish: peppermint sticks

Combine 1 cup whipping cream and sugar in a medium saucepan. Cook over medium-low heat, stirring constantly, until sugar dissolves. Remove from heat, and keep warm.

Beat eggs and egg yolks until thick and lemon colored. Gradually stir about one-fourth of hot mixture into eggs; add to remaining hot mixture, stirring constantly. Cook over medium heat, stirring constantly, until mixture thickens (do not boil). Remove from heat; stir in chocolate and peppermint extract. Set aside.

Beat remaining 1⅓ cups whipping cream at high speed of an electric mixer until soft peaks form; fold in crushed candy. Set aside.

Spoon about 1 tablespoon cookie crumbs into each of six 6-ounce parfait glasses; top with about 2½ tablespoons chocolate mixture and 3 tablespoons whipped cream mixture. Repeat layers, ending with whipped cream mixture.

TO STORE: Cover and refrigerate up to 24 hours.

TO SERVE: Garnish, if desired. Yield: 6 servings.

Summer Supper for Two

Grilled Swordfish with Lemon-Dill Butter

Grilled Zucchini and Squash

Tangy Refrigerator Slaw

French bread

Watermelon

Serves 2

You can keep the kitchen cool when you serve a summer patio supper from the grill. The swordfish and squash serve two, but the recipes can be doubled or tripled for a crowd.

The flavored butter for the fish is ready in the freezer, and any remaining slaw will keep nicely in the refrigerator for up to a week.

A refreshing dessert is made simply by serving a slice of ice cold watermelon; it's easy on the waistline and easy on the cook!

Grilled Swordfish with Lemon-Dill Butter

2 tablespoons butter or margarine, softened
1 teaspoon grated lemon rind
1 teaspoon lemon juice
1½ tablespoons minced fresh dillweed
1 small clove garlic, minced
2 (¾-inch-thick) swordfish steaks (about ¾ pound)

Combine first 5 ingredients; stir well. Freeze mixture until slightly firm; shape into a cube.

TO STORE: Cover and refrigerate up to 1 week. Cover tightly, and freeze up to 1 month.

TO SERVE: Grill swordfish steaks over hot coals 5 to 7 minutes on each side or until fish flakes easily when tested with a fork. Soften butter slightly, and cut into 4 pats. Top each steak with 2 pats of butter. Serve immediately. Yield: 2 servings.

Baste Grilled Zucchini and Squash with a flavorful marinade while it cooks. Sweet red peppers add a splash of color.

Grilled Zucchini and Squash

1 medium-size yellow squash
1 medium zucchini
1 small sweet red pepper
½ cup vegetable oil
2 teaspoons grated lemon rind
1 teaspoon white wine vinegar
¼ cup fresh lemon juice
2 cloves garlic, minced
2 teaspoons dried whole basil
1 teaspoon dried whole oregano
1 teaspoon dried whole savory
1 teaspoon pepper

Wash vegetables thoroughly; cut into 1-inch pieces. Place vegetables in an 11- x 7- x 1½-inch baking dish.

Combine oil and remaining ingredients in a jar. Cover tightly, and shake vigorously; pour over vegetables.

TO STORE: Cover and refrigerate up to 24 hours.

TO SERVE: Remove vegetables from marinade. Alternate vegetables on four 6-inch skewers. Grill vegetables over hot coals 8 to 10 minutes or until tender, turning once and basting frequently with marinade. Yield: 2 servings.

Tangy Refrigerator Slaw

3 cups shredded cabbage
½ cup finely chopped green
    pepper
⅓ cup finely chopped onion
6 pimiento-stuffed olives, sliced
⅛ teaspoon salt
3 tablespoons vinegar
3 tablespoons vegetable oil
2 tablespoons sugar
¼ teaspoon celery seeds
⅛ teaspoon mustard seeds

Combine first 5 ingredients in a medium bowl; toss well, and set aside.

Combine vinegar, oil, sugar, celery seeds, and mustard seeds in a small saucepan; bring to a boil. Pour dressing mixture over vegetables; toss gently.

TO STORE: Refrigerate in a tightly covered container at least 8 hours and up to 1 week.

TO SERVE: Serve with a slotted spoon. Yield: 2 to 4 servings.

Fireside Supper

Bibb Salad with Dijon Dressing

Chicken and Sausage Stew

Cottage Cheese-Dill Bread

Orange sherbet and chocolate wafers

Serves 4 to 6

For a casual family supper, this Chicken and Sausage Stew will bring comforting warmth to a cold winter evening spent gathered around the fireplace.

A pleasing accompaniment to the stew is a crisp salad with a tangy dressing that complements the flavor and texture of the entrée.

A snowy winter weekend is a good time for making wholesome homemade bread, a welcome addition to any meal.

Bibb Salad with Dijon Dressing

2 medium heads Bibb lettuce, torn into bite-size pieces
½ cup chopped celery
½ cup shredded carrot
½ cup olive oil
3 tablespoons balsamic vinegar
1 tablespoon chopped fresh chives
2 teaspoons dried whole basil
1½ teaspoons Dijon mustard
½ teaspoon pepper
¼ teaspoon garlic powder

Combine lettuce, celery, and carrot in a large bowl, and set aside.

Combine olive oil and remaining ingredients in a jar. Cover tightly, and shake vigorously.

TO STORE: Refrigerate dressing up to 1 week. Place salad ingredients in a large zip-top plastic bag, and refrigerate up to 2 days.

TO SERVE: Arrange salad on individual serving plates. Shake dressing vigorously, and pour over salad. Yield: 4 to 6 servings.

Chicken and Sausage Stew

4 chicken breast halves,
   skinned, boned, and cut into
   1-inch pieces
2 tablespoons vegetable oil
½ pound Italian sausage, sliced
1 (4-ounce) can chopped green
   chiles, drained
1 cup finely chopped onion
1 clove garlic, minced
2 (16-ounce) cans kidney beans,
   drained
1 (16-ounce) can stewed
   tomatoes, drained
1 (15-ounce) can tomato sauce
1 cup canned diluted chicken
   broth
1 (6-ounce) can tomato paste
2 teaspoons chili powder
1 teaspoon ground cumin
½ teaspoon salt
½ teaspoon crushed red pepper

Cook chicken in hot oil in a Dutch oven until browned on all sides. Remove chicken from Dutch oven; set aside. Add sausage to Dutch oven; cook until browned. Remove sausage with a slotted spoon, reserving drippings; drain sausage on paper towels.

Add green chiles, onion, and garlic to drippings in Dutch oven; sauté until tender. Add beans and remaining ingredients; bring to a boil. Return chicken and sausage to Dutch oven; reduce heat, and simmer, uncovered, 30 minutes or until thickened. Remove from heat; cool completely.

TO STORE: Refrigerate stew in a tightly covered container up to 2 days. Freeze in a labeled airtight container up to 1 month.

TO SERVE: Thaw in refrigerator. Place stew in a Dutch oven; cover and cook until thoroughly heated, stirring occasionally. Yield: 4 to 6 servings.

Cottage Cheese-Dill Bread

2 packages dry yeast
2 teaspoons sugar
½ cup warm water (105° to
   115°)
2 cups small-curd cottage cheese
2 eggs, beaten
2 tablespoons sugar
2 tablespoons dried whole
   dillweed
2 tablespoons finely chopped
   onion
1 teaspoon baking powder
1 teaspoon salt
4½ cups all-purpose flour
Butter or margarine, melted

Dissolve yeast and 2 teaspoons sugar in warm water; let stand 5 minutes. Combine cottage cheese and next 6 ingredients in a large mixing bowl; stir well. Gradually stir in enough flour to make a soft dough.

Turn dough out onto a well-floured surface, and knead 8 to 10 minutes or until smooth and elastic (dough will be sticky). Place in a well-greased bowl, turning to grease top. Cover and let rise in a warm place (85°), free from drafts, 1 hour or until doubled in bulk.

Punch dough down, and divide in half; shape each portion into a loaf. Place in 2 well-greased 8½- x 4½- x 3-inch loafpans. Cover and let rise in a warm place, free from drafts, 45 minutes or until doubled in bulk. Bake at 350° for 30 to 35 minutes or until loaves sound hollow when tapped. Remove loaves from pans; brush with melted butter. Cool completely on wire racks.

TO STORE: Wrap loaves tightly in freezer wrap, or place in zip-top heavy-duty plastic bags. Label and freeze up to 1 month.

TO SERVE: Thaw at room temperature. Yield: 2 loaves.

Pizza Tonight!

Romaine Salad Italiano

Three Pepper Pizza

Chocolate Chip Cupcakes

Serves 4

Ask any teenager what his or her favorite food is, and it is likely the answer will be "Pizza!" Make the dough for the crispy crust ahead of time, and store it in the freezer. (The dough recipe can be doubled if you have a group of *real* pizza lovers coming for supper!)

Just thaw and roll out the dough, add a flavorful pepper topping, and you'll have a homemade pizza in the time it takes to order out for one.

Complete the meal with a zesty salad and Chocolate Chip Cupcakes for a teen-pleasing supper.

Romaine Salad Italiano

½ cup olive oil
2 tablespoons red wine vinegar
1 tablespoon lemon juice
1 clove garlic, crushed
1 teaspoon dried whole oregano
1 teaspoon dried whole basil
½ teaspoon salt
¼ teaspoon crushed red pepper
½ head romaine lettuce, torn into bite-size pieces
1 medium tomato, cut into thin wedges
1 small cucumber, peeled and sliced
½ small onion, thinly sliced
2 tablespoons grated Parmesan cheese

Combine first 8 ingredients in a jar; cover tightly, and shake vigorously.

TO STORE: Refrigerate dressing up to 1 week.

TO SERVE: Combine romaine, tomato, cucumber, and onion in a large salad bowl. Toss with dressing, and sprinkle with Parmesan cheese. Yield: 4 to 6 servings.

Three Pepper Pizza

1 cup warm water (105° to
 115°)
2 tablespoons olive oil
2 teaspoons sugar
1 teaspoon salt
1 package dry yeast
3¼ cups all-purpose flour,
 divided
1 teaspoon yellow cornmeal
2 (8-ounce) cans tomato sauce
2 cloves garlic, minced
1 teaspoon dried whole oregano
1 teaspoon dried whole basil
½ teaspoon crushed red pepper
½ sweet red pepper, cut into
 thin strips
½ sweet yellow pepper, cut into
 thin strips
½ green pepper, cut into thin
 strips
1 small onion, thinly sliced
2 tablespoons sliced ripe olives
1 cup (4 ounces) shredded
 Monterey Jack cheese
1 cup (4 ounces) shredded
 Cheddar cheese

Combine water, oil, sugar, and salt in a large bowl; add yeast, stirring to dissolve. Add 1½ cups flour; beat at medium speed of an electric mixer until blended. Gradually add enough flour to make a soft dough.

Turn dough out onto a well-floured surface; knead until smooth and elastic (about 5 minutes). Place in a well-greased bowl, turning to grease top. Cover and let rise in a warm place (85°), free from drafts, 1 hour or until doubled in bulk.

TO STORE: Punch dough down, and divide in half. Grease each half of dough on all sides. Wrap dough tightly in plastic wrap, and place in a large zip-top heavy-duty plastic bag. Refrigerate up to 3 days, punching dough down daily. Label and freeze up to 1 month.

TO SERVE: Thaw dough in refrigerator or at room temperature. Roll half of dough to a 12-inch circle on a floured surface. Transfer dough to an ungreased pizza brick or 12-inch pizza pan sprinkled with cornmeal. Fold over edges of dough, and pinch to form crust. Prick bottom and sides of crust with a fork. Repeat procedure with remaining dough. Bake at 450° for 10 minutes.

Combine tomato sauce and next 4 ingredients; spread over crusts, leaving a ½-inch border. Top with peppers, onion, and olives. Bake at 450° for 15 minutes; sprinkle with cheeses, and bake an additional 5 minutes or until cheese melts. Yield: two 12-inch pizzas.

Chocolate Chip Cupcakes

2 (3-ounce) packages cream
 cheese, softened
1⅓ cups sugar, divided
1 egg, lightly beaten
⅛ teaspoon salt
1 (6-ounce) package semisweet
 chocolate morsels
1½ cups all-purpose flour
1 teaspoon baking soda
½ teaspoon salt
¼ cup cocoa
1 cup water
½ cup vegetable oil
1 tablespoon vinegar
1 teaspoon vanilla extract

Combine cream cheese, ⅓ cup sugar, egg, and ⅛ teaspoon salt; beat at medium speed of an electric mixer until smooth. Stir in chocolate morsels; set aside.

Combine flour, remaining 1 cup sugar, soda, ½ teaspoon salt, and cocoa; stir well. Combine water, oil, vinegar, and vanilla; add to flour mixture. Beat until well blended.

Spoon batter into paper-lined muffin pans, filling half full. Spoon 1 tablespoon cream cheese mixture into center of each cupcake. Bake at 350° for 25 to 30 minutes or until a wooden pick inserted in center comes out clean. Remove from pans; cool on wire racks.

TO STORE: Refrigerate cupcakes in a tightly covered container up to 3 days. Freeze cupcakes in a labeled airtight container up to 1 month.

TO SERVE: Thaw cupcakes at room temperature. Yield: 1½ dozen.

Grilled Kabob Supper

Marinated Pork Kabobs

New Potato Casserole

Wheat rolls

Watermelon Sorbet

Serves 4

Today's lean and tender pork is a perfect choice for grilled kabobs. The spicy marinade makes the naturally delicious flavors of the pork and vegetables come alive.

Serve new potatoes in a casserole rich in cream cheese, sour cream, and lots of fresh chives and Romano cheese. And for a dessert that satisfies the sweet tooth but isn't too rich, serve cool, frosty Watermelon Sorbet.

Marinated Pork Kabobs

½ cup soy sauce
¼ cup dry sherry
¼ cup apple juice
½ cup minced onion
2 cloves garlic, minced
½ teaspoon ground ginger
¼ teaspoon pepper
1 pound pork tenderloin, cut into 1-inch cubes
4 small boiling onions
2 small zucchini, cut into 1-inch slices
8 large fresh mushrooms

Combine first 7 ingredients in a small bowl; stir well. Place pork in a zip-top heavy-duty plastic bag; pour marinade over pork.

TO STORE: Refrigerate pork up to 24 hours, turning occasionally.

TO SERVE: Parboil onions 10 minutes; drain well, and set aside. Remove pork from marinade, reserving marinade. Place marinade in a small saucepan; bring to a boil, and cook 5 minutes. Alternate meat and vegetables on four 12-inch skewers. Grill kabobs over medium-hot coals 20 minutes or until done, turning and basting frequently with marinade. Yield: 4 servings.

Savor the flavor of your favorite melon by turning it into Watermelon Sorbet, a frosty, sweet treat.

New Potato Casserole

1½ pounds new potatoes
2 to 4 tablespoons milk
1 (8-ounce) package cream
  cheese, softened
½ cup sour cream
½ cup chopped fresh chives
¼ cup grated Romano cheese
½ teaspoon salt
¼ teaspoon ground white
  pepper
Paprika

Cook potatoes in boiling water to cover 20 minutes or until tender; drain. Combine potatoes and milk; mash potatoes. Combine cream cheese and next 5 ingredients, stirring well; fold into potato mixture. Spoon mixture into a lightly greased 1½-quart casserole. Sprinkle with paprika.

TO STORE: Cover and refrigerate up to 2 days.

TO SERVE: Bake, uncovered, at 350° for 30 minutes or until thoroughly heated. Yield: 4 servings.

Watermelon Sorbet

½ cup water
½ cup sugar
6 cups cubed, seeded
  watermelon
2 tablespoons lemon juice

Combine water and sugar in a saucepan; bring to a boil, and cook, stirring until sugar dissolves. Cool.

Place watermelon, in batches, in container of an electric blender or food processor; process until smooth. Combine sugar mixture, pureed watermelon, and lemon juice. Pour into an 8-inch square pan; freeze until firm. Break mixture into large pieces, and place in batches in container of electric blender or food processor; process until fluffy, not melted. Return mixture to pan.

TO STORE: Cover tightly, and freeze until firm and up to 1 week.

TO SERVE: Spoon sorbet into individual dessert dishes. Yield: 4 servings.

Neighborly Dinner

Spinach Salad with Blue Cheese Dressing

Chicken and Pasta Bake

Garlic bread

Banana Split Pie

Serves 6

Pasta comes in all shapes, sizes, and colors. The pasta featured in this entrée is shell pasta, which resembles tiny seashells. This hearty pasta entrée and a dressed-up green salad are the perfect dishes to cook up when the neighbors come for a casual dinner. And you will have nothing to do but take the casserole out of the oven, dish up the salad, and set out the luscious pie.

Spinach Salad with Blue Cheese Dressing

8 cups torn fresh spinach
¼ cup shredded carrot
¼ cup chopped purple onion
¼ cup chopped cucumber
½ cup sour cream
½ cup mayonnaise
½ cup small-curd cottage cheese
½ cup crumbled blue cheese
1 clove garlic, minced
1 tablespoon lemon juice
Dash of hot sauce
⅛ teaspoon salt
Dash of pepper
4 slices bacon, cooked and
    crumbled

Combine spinach, carrot, onion, and cucumber in a large bowl; set aside.

Combine sour cream and next 8 ingredients in a small bowl; stir well.

TO STORE: Place dressing in a tightly covered container. Place salad ingredients in a large zip-top plastic bag. Refrigerate dressing and salad ingredients up to 2 days.

TO SERVE: Arrange salad on individual serving plates. Spoon dressing over salad, and sprinkle with crumbled bacon. Yield: 6 servings.

Chicken and Pasta Bake

1 cup chopped onion
1 cup sliced fresh mushrooms
1 cup sliced zucchini
½ cup chopped celery
1 clove garlic, minced
3 tablespoons butter or
　margarine, melted
1 (14½-ounce) can whole
　tomatoes, drained and
　chopped
1 teaspoon dried whole basil
½ teaspoon salt
¼ teaspoon crushed red pepper
8 ounces shell macaroni,
　uncooked
3 cups chopped cooked chicken
1½ cups whipping cream
2 cups (8 ounces) shredded
　Monterey Jack cheese
½ cup grated Parmesan cheese

Sauté first 5 ingredients in butter until vegetables are crisp-tender. Stir in tomatoes, basil, salt, and crushed red pepper; set aside.

Cook pasta according to package directions; drain. Combine pasta, vegetable mixture, and chicken in a large bowl; spoon mixture into an 11- x 7- x 1½-inch baking dish. Combine whipping cream and cheeses in a medium saucepan; cook over low heat until cheese melts, stirring frequently. Pour sauce over pasta mixture.

TO STORE: Cover and refrigerate up to 24 hours.

TO SERVE: Bake, covered, at 350° for 40 to 45 minutes or until thoroughly heated. Yield: 6 to 8 servings.

Banana Split Pie

1 pint vanilla ice cream,
　softened
1 (9-inch) graham cracker crust
Chocolate sauce (recipe follows)
1 cup chopped pecans, divided
½ pint chocolate ice cream,
　softened
1 (8-ounce) can crushed
　pineapple, drained
2 small bananas, sliced
1 cup whipping cream
¼ cup sifted powdered sugar
1 tablespoon grated
　unsweetened chocolate
　(optional)

Spread half of vanilla ice cream over graham cracker crust; cover and freeze until firm. Spread one-third of chocolate sauce over ice cream layer; sprinkle with ½ cup pecans; cover and freeze until firm.

Spread chocolate ice cream over pie; cover and freeze until firm. Spoon half of remaining chocolate sauce over ice cream; top with pineapple. Cover; freeze until firm. Spread remaining vanilla ice cream over pie. Cover; freeze until firm. Spread remaining chocolate sauce over ice cream; top with remaining ½ cup pecans and banana.

Beat whipping cream at high speed of an electric mixer until foamy; gradually add powdered sugar, beating until soft peaks form. Spread whipped cream over pie; sprinkle with grated chocolate, if desired.

TO STORE: Cover tightly, and freeze up to 2 weeks.

TO SERVE: Let stand at room temperature 5 to 10 minutes before serving. Yield: one 9-inch pie.

Chocolate Sauce

½ cup semisweet chocolate
　morsels
1 (5-ounce) can evaporated milk
1 cup sifted powdered sugar
¼ cup butter or margarine

Combine all ingredients in top of a double boiler; bring water to a boil. Reduce heat to low; cook 15 minutes or until slightly thickened, stirring occasionally. Cool.

TO STORE: Refrigerate in a tightly covered container up to 1 week. Yield: about 1¼ cups.

Pasta, Please

Green Salad with Raspberry Vinaigrette

Ham and Spaghetti Casserole

Pesto-Parmesan Toasts

Fresh fruit and cheese

Serves 6

Ham makes the flavor difference in this pasta casserole. And a fresh salad topped with a tangy vinaigrette makes the perfect companion.

Crusty slices of French bread spread with pesto sauce and Parmesan cheese add a pleasant contrast to this hearty menu.

With everything prepared ahead, you're ready when the kids rush through the door yelling, "We're hungry! What time is supper?"

Green Salad with Raspberry Vinaigrette

2 heads Boston lettuce, torn into bite-size pieces
1 medium leek, cut into julienne strips
1 small green pepper, sliced lengthwise
½ small cucumber, sliced
⅓ cup vegetable oil
1 tablespoon plus 1 teaspoon balsamic vinegar
2 teaspoons mayonnaise
2 teaspoons raspberry preserves
1½ teaspoons sugar
1 teaspoon garlic powder
1 teaspoon Dijon mustard
½ teaspoon dried whole basil
½ teaspoon pepper

Combine lettuce, leek, green pepper, and cucumber in a large bowl; set aside.

Combine vegetable oil and remaining ingredients in a jar; cover tightly, and shake vigorously.

TO STORE: Refrigerate dressing up to 2 days. Place salad ingredients in a large zip-top plastic bag; refrigerate up to 24 hours.

TO SERVE: Pour dressing over salad; toss gently. Yield: 6 servings.

Serve crisp Green Salad with Raspberry Vinaigrette and Pesto-Parmesan Toasts as nice additions to this pasta menu.

Ham and Spaghetti Casserole

1 small onion, chopped
¼ cup butter or margarine, melted
¼ cup all-purpose flour
½ teaspoon dry mustard
2¼ cups milk
1 teaspoon chicken-flavored bouillon granules
1 teaspoon Worcestershire sauce
1 (8-ounce) package spaghetti, cooked
2 cups diced cooked ham
1 (6-ounce) jar sliced mushrooms, drained
1 cup (4 ounces) shredded Cheddar cheese

Sauté onion in butter in a saucepan over medium heat until tender; add flour and mustard, stirring until smooth. Cook 1 minute, stirring constantly. Combine milk, bouillon granules, and Worcestershire sauce. Gradually add milk mixture to flour mixture; cook, stirring constantly, until mixture is thickened and bubbly.

Combine spaghetti, sauce, ham, and mushrooms; spoon into a greased 11- x 7- x 1½-inch baking dish.

TO STORE: Cover and refrigerate up to 24 hours.

TO SERVE: Bake, covered, at 350° for 30 minutes. Uncover and bake 5 minutes; sprinkle with cheese, and bake 10 minutes or until cheese melts. Yield: 6 servings.

Pesto-Parmesan Toasts

1 (1-pound) loaf French bread, cut into ½-inch-thick slices
¼ cup commercial pesto sauce
¼ cup grated Parmesan cheese

Place bread slices in a single layer on a baking sheet; broil 6 inches from heat until toasted on one side. Combine pesto and Parmesan cheese. Spread 1 teaspoon pesto mixture on untoasted side of bread slices.

TO STORE: Refrigerate bread in a tightly covered container up to 2 days. Freeze in a labeled airtight container up to 2 weeks.

TO SERVE: Place bread in a single layer on an ungreased baking sheet. Broil 6 inches from heat until browned. Yield: 2 dozen.

Ready for Entertaining

A good party starts in the imagination; picture a warm, lively scene, and then make it happen. Decide whom to invite, what day and time to have the party, and what to serve. Then set the stage with festive or elegant tableware, linens, and flowers. Do the planning in small steps over a period of time, leading up to "opening night." You'll find timing suggestions with each of the following menus. Study these suggestions; then adapt them to your own schedule.

The menus in this chapter highlight year-round occasions for entertaining. For springtime there is a Lunch for the Ladies and a Race-Day Brunch; for summer, a Cookout on the Patio and a Picnic in the Park; for winter, a Supper After the Theater and a Cocktail Buffet for Forty. Whichever menu you choose, remember that careful planning puts you in a better position to enjoy your own party.

To make your party go smoothly, imagine it happening, and write down the details that will need your attention. Start with the doorbell ringing. Where will guests put their coats? What beverages, alcoholic and non-alcoholic, will you offer? What appetizers will you offer? Will the food be placed in the living room, den, or out on the patio? Anticipating the answers to these "party production" questions goes hand-in-hand with do-ahead cooking to ensure starring roles for you and your food.

For a memorable cookout, include Two Bean and Cheese Salad, Grilled Corn on the Cob, Herbed Tomato Wedges, and Marinated Flank Steak. Menu begins on page 212.

Picnic in the Park

Chilled Zucchini Soup

Sesame Breadsticks

Herbed Cheese Spread

Assorted fresh fruit

Beef and Cucumber-Stuffed Pitas

Cherry Tomatoes in Basil Vinaigrette

Orange Brownies

Serves 8

Picnics are one of summer's most pleasurable occasions. But a picnic need not always be a casual affair. Why not break away from the "fried chicken and potato salad" routine with this elegant, yet manageable, picnic menu?

These foods can be eaten with few utensils. And though most of the foods should be kept cool, those that will spoil easily have been avoided.

Chilled Zucchini Soup

1 cup chopped onion
3 tablespoons vegetable oil
1½ pounds zucchini, cut into ½-inch pieces
3 cups chicken broth
2 cups half-and-half
2 tablespoons chopped fresh parsley
1 tablespoon lemon juice
½ teaspoon salt
½ teaspoon ground white pepper

Sauté onion in oil in a large saucepan until tender. Add zucchini; cover and cook 5 minutes, stirring occasionally. Stir in chicken broth and remaining ingredients; cover, reduce heat, and simmer 15 minutes or until zucchini is tender. Remove from heat; cool.

Pour about one-third of mixture into container of an electric blender or food processor; process until smooth. Repeat procedure twice with remaining mixture.

TO STORE: Refrigerate in a tightly covered container up to 2 days.

TO SERVE: Pour chilled soup into a large thermal container. Serve cold. Yield: 8 cups.

Sesame Breadsticks

1 package dry yeast
1 cup warm water (105° to 115°)
2 cups all-purpose flour, divided
1½ teaspoons sugar
1 teaspoon salt
¼ teaspoon garlic powder
¼ cup shortening
1 egg
1 tablespoon water
Sesame seeds
Grated Parmesan cheese

Dissolve yeast in 1 cup warm water in a large mixing bowl; let stand 5 minutes. Add 1 cup flour, sugar, salt, garlic powder, and shortening, beating at low speed of an electric mixer 2 minutes or until smooth. Gradually stir in enough remaining 1 cup flour to make a moderately stiff dough.

Turn dough out onto a lightly floured surface, and knead until smooth and elastic (5 to 8 minutes). Place dough in a well-greased bowl, turning to grease top. Cover and let rise in a warm place (85°), free from drafts, 1 hour or until dough is doubled in bulk.

Punch dough down; turn out onto a lightly floured surface. Divide dough in half; divide each half into 12 equal pieces. Shape each piece into a 4-inch rope. (Cover remaining dough with a damp towel to prevent drying.) Place ropes 1 inch apart on greased baking sheets.

Combine egg and 1 tablespoon water in a small bowl, stirring well. Brush mixture gently over ropes; sprinkle with sesame seeds and Parmesan cheese. Bake at 375° for 20 minutes or until lightly browned. Cool.

TO STORE: Refrigerate breadsticks in a tightly covered container up to 3 days. Freeze breadsticks in a labeled airtight container up to 1 month.

TO SERVE: Thaw at room temperature. Yield: 2 dozen.

Herbed Cheese Spread

1 (8-ounce) package cream cheese, softened
1 cup (4 ounces) shredded Monterey Jack cheese
¼ cup grated Parmesan cheese
¼ cup Chablis or other dry white wine
2 tablespoons butter or margarine, softened
1 teaspoon Dijon mustard
1 teaspoon white wine Worcestershire sauce
½ teaspoon grated lemon rind
½ teaspoon dried whole marjoram
½ teaspoon dried whole tarragon

Combine all ingredients in a large mixing bowl. Beat at medium speed of an electric mixer until smooth.

TO STORE: Refrigerate in a tightly covered container up to 3 days.

TO SERVE: Serve spread with assorted fresh fruit. Yield: 1¾ cups.

Beef and Cucumber-Stuffed Pitas

2 (1-pound) flank steaks
1 medium cucumber, thinly sliced
1 cup chopped purple onion
¼ cup vegetable oil, divided
3 tablespoons red wine vinegar, divided
2 teaspoons Dijon mustard
1 teaspoon salt
½ teaspoon dried whole thyme
¼ teaspoon pepper
4 (6-inch) whole wheat pita bread rounds, halved
Curly leaf lettuce

Trim fat from steaks; score on both sides in 1½-inch squares. Place steaks on a greased rack in a roasting pan. Broil 4 inches from heat 4 to 5 minutes on each side or to desired degree of doneness. Slice steaks diagonally across grain into thin slices. Cut slices into thin strips.

Combine cucumber, onion, 2 tablespoons oil, and 1 tablespoon vinegar; stir well. Combine remaining 2 tablespoons oil and 2 tablespoons vinegar, meat, mustard, and next 3 ingredients; toss well.

TO STORE: Refrigerate both mixtures separately in tightly covered containers up to 24 hours.

TO SERVE: Drain cucumber mixture. Line pita halves with lettuce leaves. Divide meat mixture evenly among pita halves, and top with cucumber mixture. Yield: 8 sandwiches.

Cherry Tomatoes in Basil Vinaigrette

24 large cherry tomatoes, halved
¼ cup plus 2 tablespoons chopped fresh basil
¼ cup plus 2 tablespoons olive oil
3 tablespoons red wine vinegar
½ teaspoon salt
⅛ teaspoon freshly ground pepper

Place tomatoes in a large zip-top heavy-duty plastic bag; sprinkle with basil. Combine oil and remaining ingredients in a jar. Cover tightly, and shake vigorously; pour over tomatoes. Turn plastic bag to coat tomatoes.

TO STORE: Refrigerate up to 24 hours, turning bag occasionally.

TO SERVE: Serve with a slotted spoon. Yield: 8 servings.

Orange Brownies

½ cup butter or margarine
¾ cup sugar
2 tablespoons orange juice
1 (6-ounce) package semisweet chocolate morsels
½ teaspoon grated orange rind
½ teaspoon vanilla extract
½ teaspoon orange extract
2 eggs
¾ cup all-purpose flour
¼ teaspoon baking soda
¼ teaspoon salt
½ cup finely chopped walnuts

Combine butter, sugar, and orange juice in a medium saucepan; cook over medium heat, stirring frequently, until mixture comes to a boil. Remove from heat. Add chocolate morsels, orange rind, and flavorings, stirring until chocolate melts. Add eggs, one at a time, beating well after each addition. Combine flour, soda, and salt; stir flour mixture and walnuts into chocolate mixture.

Pour batter into a greased and floured 9-inch square pan. Bake at 325° for 30 minutes. Cool completely on a wire rack. Cut into squares. Yield: 9 servings.

Celebrate springtime with a picnic that includes Beef and Cucumber-Stuffed Pitas and Cherry Tomatoes in Basil Vinaigrette.

Lunch for the Ladies

Crab Quiche

Spicy Tomato Aspic

Green Bean Bundles

Rolls

Almond Wafers

Pineapple sorbet

Bellinis

Serves 4

On a beautiful spring afternoon have the ladies over for lunch. Show your guests to the patio where you have set out your lacy linens and delicate china. With a setting like this, no one will ever guess that you didn't spend hours in the kitchen preparing lunch. Visit with your guests while the quiche bakes; put the rolls in the oven just before sitting down to lunch.

Crab Quiche

Pastry for 9-inch pie
2 tablespoons minced green onions
1 tablespoon butter or margarine, melted
4 eggs, beaten
1½ cups whipping cream
2 (6-ounce) packages frozen crabmeat, thawed and drained
1 cup (4 ounces) shredded Swiss cheese
2 tablespoons sherry
¾ teaspoon salt
⅛ teaspoon ground red pepper
Garnish: fresh parsley sprigs

Roll dough to ⅛-inch thickness on a lightly floured surface. Place in a 9-inch quiche dish; trim excess pastry along edges. Prick bottom and sides of pastry with a fork. Bake at 400° for 3 minutes; remove from oven, and gently prick with a fork. Bake pastry shell an additional 5 minutes; set aside.

Sauté onions in butter until tender; set aside. Combine eggs and cream in a large bowl, stirring well. Stir in onions, crabmeat, cheese, sherry, salt, and pepper.

TO STORE: Cover pastry shell, and refrigerate up to 24 hours. Refrigerate filling in a tightly covered container up to 24 hours.

TO SERVE: Pour filling into pastry shell. Bake at 425° for 15 minutes. Reduce heat to 325°, and bake 25 to 30 minutes or until set. Let stand 10 minutes before serving. Garnish, if desired. Yield: one 9-inch quiche.

Spicy Tomato Aspic

2 envelopes unflavored gelatin
3 cups spicy vegetable juice
   cocktail, divided
1 tablespoon grated onion
¼ teaspoon salt
¾ cup chopped green pepper
¾ cup chopped celery
Curly leaf lettuce

Sprinkle gelatin over 1 cup juice; let stand 1 minute. Cook over medium heat, stirring until gelatin dissolves. Stir in onion, salt, and remaining 2 cups juice. Chill until the consistency of unbeaten egg white. Fold in green pepper and celery; pour into an oiled 4-cup ring mold.

TO STORE: Cover and refrigerate up to 24 hours.

TO SERVE: Unmold onto a lettuce-lined serving plate. Yield: 4 servings.

For a menu the ladies will rave about, serve Crab Quiche, Green Bean Bundles, and Spicy Tomato Aspic.

Guests will enjoy sparkling Bellinis, a refreshing blend of peaches and champagne.

Green Bean Bundles

1 pound fresh green beans
⅓ cup olive oil
2 tablespoons lemon juice
¼ teaspoon salt
Dash of pepper
1 small sweet red pepper, cut
   into 4 rings

Wash beans; trim ends, and remove strings. Cook beans in a small amount of boiling water 15 minutes or until crisp-tender. Drain beans, and plunge into cold water; drain again. Place beans in a large bowl.

Combine oil, lemon juice, salt, and pepper. Pour mixture over beans; toss gently.

TO STORE: Refrigerate beans in a tightly covered container up to 24 hours.

TO SERVE: Divide beans into 4 bundles; place each bundle through a red pepper ring. Arrange on a serving platter. Yield: 4 servings.

Almond Wafers

½ cup butter or margarine,
   softened
¾ cup firmly packed brown
   sugar
1 egg
1 teaspoon almond extract
1¾ cups all-purpose flour
½ teaspoon baking soda
¼ teaspoon salt
½ cup finely chopped almonds
Whole blanched almonds

Cream butter; gradually add sugar, beating well at medium speed of an electric mixer. Add egg and almond extract, mixing well.

Combine flour, soda, and salt in a small bowl; add to creamed mixture, mixing well. Stir in chopped almonds. Divide dough in half. Spoon each half of dough onto a large piece of wax paper, and shape into a 12-inch log. Wrap rolls in wax paper.

TO STORE: Refrigerate at least 2 hours and up to 2 days. Freeze wrapped rolls in a labeled airtight container up to 1 month.

TO SERVE: Cut frozen rolls into ¼-inch slices (an electric knife works well), and place on ungreased cookie sheets. Press a whole almond into center of each slice. Bake at 350° for 10 to 12 minutes or until lightly browned. Cool slightly on cookie sheets; remove cookies to wire racks to cool completely. Yield: 6½ dozen.

Bellinis

2 cups sliced fresh or frozen
  peaches, thawed
⅔ cup peach or apricot nectar
2½ cups champagne

Combine peaches and nectar in container of an electric blender or food processor. Top with cover, and process until smooth.

TO STORE: Freeze peach mixture in a labeled airtight container up to 1 week.

TO SERVE: Remove peach mixture from freezer 30 minutes before serving. Spoon about ⅔ cup peach mixture into each of 4 stemmed glasses, and add about ⅔ cup champagne to each glass. Yield: 4 servings.

Race-Day Brunch

Apricot-Almond Fruit Dip

Assorted fresh fruit

Strawberry-Romaine Salad

Country Ham Links

Cheese and Asparagus Strata

Sweet Potato Biscuits

Orange marmalade   Butter

Sweepstakes Tassies

Mint juleps

Serves 12

One of the premier racing events of the year is the Kentucky Derby, held every year on the first Saturday in May. Parties abound, but none is more eagerly anticipated than a pre-race brunch.

A traditional Derby brunch includes country ham, asparagus, and strawberries. A wise choice of make-ahead dishes will free the hostess so that she can enjoy her guests and the races.

Apricot-Almond Fruit Dip

2 (8-ounce) cartons sour cream
¾ cup apricot preserves
1 teaspoon almond extract
Garnishes: edible flower and
   fresh mint sprig

Combine first 3 ingredients; stir well.

TO STORE: Refrigerate in a tightly covered container up to 24 hours.

TO SERVE: Garnish, if desired. Serve with fresh fruit. Yield: 2½ cups.

Before the races begin, treat guests to Apricot-Almond Fruit Dip, served with fresh fruit, and Strawberry-Romaine Salad.

Strawberry-Romaine Salad

1 cup vegetable oil
¾ cup sugar
½ cup red wine vinegar
2 cloves garlic, minced
½ teaspoon salt
½ teaspoon paprika
¼ teaspoon ground white
  pepper
1 large head romaine lettuce
1 head Boston lettuce
1 pint strawberries, sliced
1 cup (4 ounces) shredded
  Monterey Jack cheese
½ cup chopped walnuts, toasted

Combine first 7 ingredients in a large jar. Cover tightly, and shake vigorously.

TO STORE: Refrigerate up to 1 week.

TO SERVE: Tear lettuce into bite-size pieces. Combine torn lettuce, strawberries, cheese, and walnuts in a large salad bowl. Shake dressing vigorously; pour over salad, and toss gently. Yield: 12 servings.

Country Ham Links

2 pounds ground cooked
  country ham
1 pound ground pork
1 cup fine, dry breadcrumbs
¼ cup firmly packed brown
  sugar
¼ cup finely chopped onion
2 eggs, lightly beaten
2 tablespoons vinegar
1½ teaspoons dry mustard
¼ teaspoon pepper

Combine all ingredients in a large bowl, mixing well. Shape mixture into 40 links. Cook links in a large skillet over medium heat 10 to 12 minutes or until browned, turning frequently; drain on paper towels. Cool.

TO STORE: Freeze ham links in a labeled airtight container up to 2 weeks.

TO SERVE: Place frozen links on a 15- x 10- x 1-inch jellyroll pan. Bake at 325° for 30 to 35 minutes or until hot. Yield: 40 links.

Cheese and Asparagus Strata

24 slices white bread
2 (10-ounce) packages frozen
  asparagus spears, thawed
4 cups (16 ounces) shredded
  Cheddar cheese
1 (4-ounce) jar diced pimiento,
  drained
10 eggs, beaten
6 cups milk
½ cup finely chopped onion
2 tablespoons prepared mustard
1 teaspoon salt
½ teaspoon pepper

Trim crust from bread. Line the bottoms of 2 lightly greased 13- x 9- x 2-inch baking dishes with 6 bread slices each. Cut asparagus spears into 1-inch pieces. Sprinkle asparagus, shredded cheese, and pimiento evenly over bread in both dishes; top each with remaining bread slices. Combine eggs and remaining ingredients; stir well. Pour mixture evenly over casseroles.

TO STORE: Cover and refrigerate up to 24 hours.

TO SERVE: Bake, uncovered, at 325° for 1 hour or until thoroughly heated. Yield: 12 servings.

Sweet Potato Biscuits, a Southern favorite, are served with butter, orange marmalade, and strawberries.

Sweet Potato Biscuits

2 cups self-rising flour
¼ cup sugar
¼ teaspoon ground cinnamon
3 tablespoons shortening
2 tablespoons butter or
  margarine, softened
1 cup cooked, mashed sweet
  potato
⅓ cup milk
1 tablespoon butter or
  margarine, melted

Combine first 3 ingredients; cut in shortening and butter with a pastry blender until mixture resembles coarse meal. Add potato and milk; stir until dry ingredients are moistened. Turn dough out onto a floured surface; knead 3 or 4 times. Roll dough to ½-inch thickness; cut with a 2-inch biscuit cutter. Place on greased baking sheets.

TO STORE: Cover tightly, and freeze up to 1 week.

TO SERVE: Bake frozen biscuits, uncovered, at 425° for 18 to 20 minutes or until golden brown. Brush with melted butter. Yield: 2 dozen.

Sweepstakes Tassies

½ cup butter or margarine,
  softened
1 (3-ounce) package cream
  cheese, softened
1½ cups all-purpose flour
¼ cup plus 2 tablespoons sugar
3 tablespoons cocoa
1 cup firmly packed brown
  sugar
2 tablespoons butter or
  margarine, softened
2 eggs
¾ cup chopped pecans
½ cup semisweet chocolate
  morsels, coarsely chopped
2 teaspoons vanilla extract

Combine ½ cup butter and cream cheese; stir well. Combine flour, sugar, and cocoa; add to butter mixture, stirring well. Cover; refrigerate 1 hour. Shape dough into 36 (1-inch) balls. Place in ungreased miniature (1¾-inch) muffin pans, shaping each ball into a shell.

Combine brown sugar and 2 tablespoons butter; beat until creamy. Add eggs, mixing well. Stir in pecans, chocolate morsels, and vanilla. Spoon mixture into pastry shells, filling three-fourths full. Bake at 325° for 25 to 30 minutes, or until lightly browned. Cool in pans 10 minutes. Remove from pans, and cool on wire racks.

TO STORE: Refrigerate in a tightly covered container up to 2 days. Freeze in an airtight container up to 2 weeks.

TO SERVE: Thaw at room temperature. Yield: 3 dozen.

The Pleasures of Afternoon Tea

Creamy Cucumber Rolls

Curried Chicken Salad Puffs

Miniature Shrimp Quiches

Spiced Pineapple Scones

Butter   *Jam*

Fresh strawberries with powdered sugar

Favorite Tea Cakes

Tea

Cream   *Lemon wedges*   *Sugar cubes*

Serves 12

Guests will delight in the relaxed yet elegant atmosphere of an afternoon tea party. Most of the finger foods featured in this menu can be made in advance, and then frozen or refrigerated. So sit back, relax, and enjoy a spot of tea with special friends.

Creamy Cucumber Rolls

1 large cucumber, peeled and seeded
1 (8-ounce) package cream cheese, softened
⅓ cup minced green onions
1 tablespoon minced fresh parsley
1 tablespoon mayonnaise
¼ teaspoon salt
⅛ teaspoon ground white pepper
6 slices white bread
6 slices whole wheat bread

Shred and thoroughly drain cucumber; press between paper towels to remove excess moisture. Combine cucumber and next 6 ingredients in a medium bowl, and stir well.

TO STORE: Refrigerate cucumber mixture in a tightly covered container up to 2 days.

TO SERVE: Remove crust from bread. Flatten bread slices, using a rolling pin. Spread each slice with approximately 2 tablespoons cucumber filling, and roll up jellyroll fashion. Cut each roll in half. Yield: 2 dozen.

Curried Chicken Salad Puffs

1 cup water
½ cup butter or margarine
1 cup all-purpose flour
¼ teaspoon salt
4 eggs
2 cups finely chopped cooked chicken
1 (8-ounce) can pineapple tidbits, drained
1 (8-ounce) can sliced water chestnuts, drained and finely chopped
½ cup finely chopped celery
½ cup mayonnaise
1½ teaspoons curry powder
1 teaspoon lemon juice
1 teaspoon soy sauce
¼ teaspoon salt

Combine water and butter in a saucepan; bring to a boil. Add flour and salt, all at once, stirring vigorously over low heat until mixture leaves sides of pan and forms a smooth ball. Cool 10 minutes. Add eggs, one at a time, beating well after each. (Mixture may separate as each egg is added; beat until smooth.) Drop dough by heaping teaspoonfuls 2 inches apart on ungreased baking sheets. Bake at 400° for 15 minutes. Reduce heat to 350°, bake 10 minutes or until puffed and golden. Cool on wire racks.

Combine chicken and remaining ingredients in a medium bowl; stir well.

TO STORE: Freeze cream puffs in a labeled airtight container up to 1 month. Refrigerate chicken salad mixture in a tightly covered container up to 24 hours.

TO SERVE: Thaw cream puffs at room temperature. Bake at 250° for 5 minutes. Cut tops off cream puffs; pull out and discard soft dough inside. Fill bottoms with 1 tablespoon chicken salad mixture; cover with tops. Yield: 5 dozen.

Dainty finger foods such as Curried Chicken Salad Puffs are ideal for an afternoon tea.

Miniature Shrimp Quiches

1 cup (4 ounces) shredded
  Swiss cheese
½ cup finely chopped cooked
  shrimp
2 tablespoons chopped fresh
  chives
½ teaspoon dried whole thyme
Pastry shells (recipe follows)
2 eggs, beaten
½ cup half-and-half
¼ teaspoon salt
¼ teaspoon ground nutmeg
¼ teaspoon pepper
Dash of hot sauce

Combine cheese, shrimp, chives, and thyme; spoon mixture evenly into pastry shells. Combine eggs and remaining ingredients, stirring well. Pour mixture into pastry shells, filling three-fourths full. Bake at 350° for 30 to 35 minutes or until set. Cool.

TO STORE: Refrigerate quiches in a tightly covered container up to 24 hours. Freeze quiches in a labeled airtight container up to 2 weeks.

TO SERVE: Thaw in refrigerator. Place quiches on baking sheets. Bake at 300° for 10 minutes or until hot. Yield: 3 dozen.

Pastry Shells

½ cup butter or margarine,
  softened
½ (8-ounce) package cream
  cheese, softened
1½ cups all-purpose flour
¼ teaspoon salt

Beat butter and cream cheese at medium speed of an electric mixer until well blended. Stir in flour and salt. Cover dough, and refrigerate 1 hour.

Shape chilled dough into 36 (1-inch) balls. Place in ungreased miniature (1¾-inch) muffin pans, shaping each ball into a shell. Yield: 3 dozen.

Spiced Pineapple Scones

2 cups all-purpose flour
2 teaspoons baking powder
½ teaspoon baking soda
¼ teaspoon salt
¼ cup sugar
½ teaspoon ground cinnamon
¼ teaspoon ground nutmeg
⅓ cup butter or margarine, softened
1 (8¼-ounce) can crushed pineapple, undrained
1 egg, beaten
¼ cup finely chopped almonds
1 tablespoon milk
1 tablespoon sugar

Combine first 7 ingredients in a medium bowl, stirring well; cut in butter with a pastry blender until mixture resembles coarse meal. Add pineapple, egg, and almonds, stirring just until dry ingredients are moistened (dough will be sticky). Turn dough out onto a floured surface, and knead lightly 4 or 5 times.

Pat dough to ½-inch thickness; cut with a floured 1½-inch cutter. Place on ungreased baking sheets. Brush tops lightly with milk, and sprinkle with 1 tablespoon sugar. Bake at 400° for 12 to 15 minutes or until golden brown. Cool.

TO STORE: Store scones at room temperature in a tightly covered container up to 24 hours. Freeze scones in a labeled airtight container up to 2 weeks.

TO SERVE: Thaw at room temperature. Place scones on baking sheets. Bake at 300° for 10 minutes or until hot. Yield: 2½ dozen.

Favorite Tea Cakes

½ cup butter or margarine, softened
1 cup sugar
1 egg
1 teaspoon vanilla extract
1 teaspoon grated lemon rind
2¾ cups all-purpose flour
½ teaspoon baking soda
½ teaspoon salt
¼ cup buttermilk
Sugar

Cream butter; gradually add 1 cup sugar, beating well at medium speed of an electric mixer. Add egg, vanilla, and lemon rind; beat well.

Combine flour, soda, and salt in a medium bowl; add to creamed mixture alternately with buttermilk, beginning and ending with flour mixture. Cover dough, and refrigerate at least 2 hours.

Roll dough to ¼-inch thickness on a lightly floured surface. Cut with a 2-inch cookie cutter, and place on lightly greased baking sheets; sprinkle with sugar. Bake at 375° for 6 to 8 minutes or until edges are lightly browned. Cool on wire racks.

TO STORE: Store cookies at room temperature in a tightly covered container up to 2 days. Freeze in a labeled airtight container up to 1 month.

TO SERVE: Thaw cookies at room temperature. Yield: 3½ dozen.

This menu wouldn't be complete without Favorite Tea Cakes. These light and crispy cakes are as good as the ones your grandmother used to make.

Cookout on the Patio

Two Bean and Cheese Salad

Marinated Flank Steaks

Grilled Corn on the Cob

Herbed Tomato Wedges

Garlic bread

Melon wedges

Serves 6

A cookout is the perfect choice for casual summertime entertaining. While guests gather on the patio to chat, they are treated to the mouth-watering aromas of dinner cooking on the grill. With a little attention to timing, the steak and corn can be grilled together. When ready to serve, bring accompaniments from the kitchen to take their place on the patio buffet.

Two Bean and Cheese Salad

1 (10-ounce) package frozen lima beans, cooked and drained
1 (15-ounce) can kidney beans, rinsed and drained
¼ cup chopped onion
2 tablespoons vegetable oil
2 tablespoons olive oil
2 tablespoons vinegar
1 tablespoon Dijon mustard
1 teaspoon sugar
½ teaspoon salt
¼ teaspoon dried Italian seasoning
¼ teaspoon pepper
⅛ teaspoon garlic powder
1 cup (4 ounces) cubed sharp Cheddar cheese
Bibb lettuce leaves

Combine lima beans, kidney beans, and onion in a medium bowl; set aside.

Combine vegetable oil and next 8 ingredients in a jar. Cover tightly, and shake vigorously. Pour over vegetable mixture, stirring gently.

TO STORE: Refrigerate in a tightly covered container up to 2 days.

TO SERVE: Add cheese to bean mixture, tossing well. Spoon bean mixture into individual lettuce-lined bowls, using a slotted spoon. Yield: 6 servings.

Marinated Flank Steaks

2 (1-pound) flank steaks
1 cup Chablis or other dry
  white wine
½ cup vegetable oil
¼ cup soy sauce
1 teaspoon Worcestershire sauce
2 cloves garlic, crushed
½ teaspoon dry mustard
½ teaspoon pepper

Trim excess fat from steaks; score on both sides in 1½-inch squares. Place steaks in a large shallow dish, and set aside.

Combine wine and remaining ingredients; pour over steaks, turning to coat.

TO STORE: Cover and refrigerate up to 2 days, turning occasionally.

TO SERVE: Remove steaks from marinade, reserving marinade. Place marinade in a small saucepan. Bring to a boil; reduce heat, and simmer 5 minutes. Grill steaks over hot coals 6 to 8 minutes on each side or to desired degree of doneness, basting often with marinade. Cut steaks diagonally across grain into thin slices. Yield: 6 servings.

Grilled Corn on the Cob

6 ears fresh corn
½ cup butter or margarine,
  softened
1 teaspoon chopped fresh chives
1 teaspoon chopped fresh
  parsley
1 teaspoon chopped fresh basil
¼ teaspoon salt
¼ teaspoon pepper

Remove husks and silks from corn just before grilling. Combine butter and remaining ingredients; spread on corn, and place each ear on a piece of a heavy-duty aluminum foil. Roll foil lengthwise around each ear; twist at each end to seal.

TO STORE: Refrigerate up to 24 hours.

TO SERVE: Grill wrapped corn over hot coals 25 to 30 minutes, turning occasionally. Yield: 6 servings.

Herbed Tomato Wedges

3 medium tomatoes
½ cup vegetable oil
¼ cup white wine vinegar
¼ cup thinly sliced green
  onions
2 tablespoons chopped fresh
  parsley
1 tablespoon chopped fresh
  basil
¾ teaspoon chopped fresh
  thyme
½ teaspoon salt
¼ teaspoon pepper
⅛ teaspoon garlic powder

Cut each tomato into 6 wedges. Place wedges in a medium bowl. Combine oil and next 8 ingredients in a jar. Cover tightly, and shake vigorously. Pour over tomatoes, tossing gently to coat.

TO STORE: Refrigerate in a tightly covered container up to 24 hours, stirring occasionally.

TO SERVE: Serve with a slotted spoon. Serve marinade separately, if desired. Yield: 6 servings.

After-Work Dinner
for Company

Dill Dip

Assorted fresh vegetables

Spicy Baked Chicken Breasts

Wheat-Vegetable Pilaf

Marinated Asparagus

Cool Mocha Pie in Pecan Crust

Serves 6

Two-career couples can entertain friends during a busy week, but entertaining on a week night takes some planning. For a hassle-free weekday company dinner, choose do-ahead dishes that are ready, or ready to assemble, as soon as you walk into the kitchen. Bring the meal to a close with a coffee-laced chocolate pie in a pecan crust.

Dill Dip

1 cup mayonnaise
1 (8-ounce) carton sour cream
1½ tablespoons minced fresh
    parsley
1½ tablespoons grated onion
1 tablespoon dried whole
    dillweed
½ teaspoon seasoned salt
Garnish: fresh dillweed sprigs

Combine first 6 ingredients; stir well.

TO STORE: Refrigerate in a tightly covered container up to 1 week.

TO SERVE: Stir well. Garnish, if desired. Serve with assorted fresh vegetables. Yield: 2 cups.

Entertain on a week night by serving Spicy Baked Chicken Breasts, Marinated Asparagus, and Wheat-Vegetable Pilaf.

Spicy Baked Chicken Breasts

¼ cup orange juice
¼ cup pineapple juice
¼ cup lime juice
2 tablespoons vegetable oil
1 teaspoon grated lime rind
6 chicken breast halves, skinned
1 cup round buttery cracker crumbs
¼ teaspoon ground white pepper
¼ teaspoon ground ginger
⅛ teaspoon ground cumin
Garnish: fresh flat leaf parsley sprigs

Combine first 5 ingredients in a small bowl, stirring well. Place chicken in a shallow dish. Pour orange juice mixture over chicken.

TO STORE: Cover and refrigerate up to 24 hours.

TO SERVE: Combine cracker crumbs, pepper, ginger, and cumin in a plastic bag; shake to mix. Remove chicken from marinade; discard marinade. Place 2 pieces of chicken in bag, and shake to coat. Repeat procedure with remaining chicken. Place chicken in a lightly greased 13- x 9- x 2-inch baking dish. Cover and bake at 350° for 20 minutes; uncover and bake an additional 30 minutes or until tender. Garnish, if desired. Yield: 6 servings.

End the evening on an elegant note with Cool Mocha Pie in Pecan Crust. This luscious frozen dessert needs only a few minutes to thaw before serving.

Wheat-Vegetable Pilaf

1 small zucchini, thinly sliced
½ cup sliced green onions
½ cup chopped sweet red pepper
½ cup diced carrot
3 tablespoons butter or margarine, melted
1 cup bulgur wheat
2 cups chicken broth
½ teaspoon onion powder
¼ teaspoon salt
¼ teaspoon pepper
3 large tomatoes
¾ teaspoon salt

Sauté first 4 ingredients in butter in a large skillet 5 minutes or until vegetables are crisp-tender. Add bulgur wheat; sauté 5 minutes, stirring well. Stir in broth, onion powder, ¼ teaspoon salt, and pepper. Bring to a boil; cover, reduce heat, and simmer 20 minutes or until all liquid is absorbed.

Cut tomatoes in half. Scoop out pulp, leaving shells intact; reserve tomato pulp for other uses. Sprinkle inside of each tomato half with ⅛ teaspoon salt, and invert on paper towels to drain. Spoon bulgur mixture into tomato shells.

TO STORE: Refrigerate in a tightly covered container up to 24 hours.

TO SERVE: Place on ungreased baking sheets. Bake at 350° for 10 minutes. Yield: 6 servings.

Marinated Asparagus

1½ pounds fresh asparagus
½ cup sugar
½ cup cider vinegar
1½ tablespoons lemon juice
1 teaspoon salt
⅛ teaspoon seasoned pepper
Garnish: lemon rind curls

Snap off tough ends of asparagus. Remove scales with a knife or vegetable peeler, if desired. Cook asparagus, covered, in a small amount of boiling water 6 to 8 minutes or until crisp-tender; drain, reserving ½ cup liquid. Place asparagus in a large shallow container, and set aside.

Combine reserved liquid, sugar, and next 4 ingredients in a small saucepan; bring to a boil, stirring constantly. Pour mixture over asparagus.

TO STORE: Cover and refrigerate 8 hours.

TO SERVE: Arrange asparagus on a serving platter. Garnish, if desired. Yield: 6 servings.

Cool Mocha Pie in Pecan Crust

6 (1-ounce) squares semisweet
  chocolate
½ teaspoon instant coffee
  granules
2 eggs, beaten
3 tablespoons Kahlúa or other
  coffee-flavored liqueur
¼ cup sifted powdered sugar
¾ cup whipping cream,
  whipped
1 teaspoon vanilla extract
Pecan Crust
¾ cup whipping cream
1 tablespoon Kahlúa or other
  coffee-flavored liqueur
Grated chocolate

Place chocolate squares and coffee granules in top of a double boiler; bring water to a boil. Reduce heat to low; cook until chocolate melts. Gradually stir about one-fourth of hot mixture into eggs; add to remaining hot mixture, stirring constantly. Gradually stir in 3 tablespoons Kahlúa and powdered sugar. Cook, stirring constantly, until mixture reaches 165° on a candy thermometer. Cool to room temperature.

Fold whipped cream into chocolate mixture. Stir in vanilla. Spoon mixture into Pecan Crust.

TO STORE: Cover tightly, and freeze at least 8 hours and up to 3 weeks.

TO SERVE: Place frozen pie in refrigerator 1 hour before serving. Beat ¾ cup whipping cream at high speed of an electric mixer until foamy; gradually add 1 tablespoon Kahlúa, beating until stiff peaks form. Pipe or dollop whipped cream around edge of pie. Sprinkle with grated chocolate. Yield: one 9-inch pie.

Pecan Crust

1¾ cups finely chopped pecans
⅓ cup firmly packed brown
  sugar
3 tablespoons butter or
  margarine, melted
2 teaspoons Kahlúa or other
  coffee-flavored liqueur

Combine all ingredients, stirring well. Firmly press mixture evenly over bottom and up sides of a 9-inch pieplate. Bake at 350° for 10 to 12 minutes. Press sides of crust with the back of a spoon to flatten. Cool. Yield: one 9-inch crust.

The Boss Comes to Dinner

Overnight Chicken Divan

Wild Rice Salad

Tangy Marinated Carrots

French bread

Chocolate Dream Dessert

Serves 8

On that important night when the boss comes to dinner even the calmest host or hostess can feel nervous.

When you serve an array of enticing do-ahead food, the last thing you will have to worry about is the menu. There's no reason to panic at the last minute because everything will be done except baking the chicken and heating the bread. Offer a glass of wine, and relax with your guests instead of worrying about last-minute preparations.

Overnight Chicken Divan

8 chicken breast halves
1 teaspoon salt
2 (10-ounce) packages frozen
  broccoli spears
1 (10½-ounce) can cream of
  chicken soup, undiluted
½ cup sour cream
½ cup mayonnaise
2 tablespoons dry sherry
1 teaspoon paprika
1 teaspoon prepared mustard
¼ teaspoon curry powder
⅓ cup grated Parmesan cheese
Paprika

Combine chicken and salt in a Dutch oven; add enough water to cover chicken. Bring to a boil; cover, reduce heat, and simmer 1 hour or until tender. Remove chicken, and cool slightly. (Reserve broth for other uses.) Bone chicken, and coarsely chop meat; set aside.

Cook broccoli according to package directions; drain well. Arrange broccoli in a lightly greased 13- x 9- x 2-inch baking dish. Combine soup and next 6 ingredients; spoon half of sauce over broccoli. Arrange chicken over sauce; top with remaining sauce.

TO STORE: Cover and refrigerate up to 24 hours.

TO SERVE: Bake, uncovered, at 350° for 30 to 35 minutes or until thoroughly heated. Sprinkle with cheese and paprika; bake an additional 5 minutes. Yield: 8 servings.

Wild Rice Salad

1 (6-ounce) package long-grain and wild rice mix
3 green onions, cut into ½-inch pieces
1 (8-ounce) can sliced water chestnuts, drained
½ cup chopped walnuts, toasted
⅓ cup mayonnaise
Dash of pepper
Raddichio leaves

Cook rice according to package directions; cool slightly. Combine rice and next 5 ingredients; stir well.

TO STORE: Refrigerate in a tightly covered container up to 8 hours.

TO SERVE: Serve on raddichio leaves. Yield: 8 servings.

Tangy Marinated Carrots

5 cups scraped and thinly sliced carrots
¼ cup olive oil
¼ cup white wine vinegar
1 teaspoon dried whole basil
¼ teaspoon finely chopped garlic
½ teaspoon salt
Dash of freshly ground pepper

Cook carrots in boiling water to cover about 7 minutes or until crisp-tender; drain. Combine carrots and remaining ingredients in a medium bowl; toss gently.

TO STORE: Refrigerate in a tightly covered container up to 24 hours.

TO SERVE: Toss gently before serving. Serve with a slotted spoon. Yield: 8 servings.

Chocolate Dream Dessert

2 dozen ladyfingers, split lengthwise
¼ cup Kahlúa or other coffee-flavored liqueur
12 (1-ounce) squares semisweet chocolate
2 (8-ounce) packages cream cheese, softened
½ cup sugar
3 eggs, separated
2 teaspoons vanilla extract
2 cups whipping cream, whipped
Garnishes: sweetened whipped cream, chocolate curls, and maraschino cherries

Brush cut side of ladyfingers with Kahlúa. Line bottom and sides of a 9-inch springform pan with ladyfingers, placing rounded sides of ladyfingers toward pan. Set prepared pan aside.

Place chocolate squares in top of a double boiler; bring water to a boil over medium heat. Reduce heat to low; cook until chocolate melts. Cool.

Beat cream cheese and sugar at high speed of an electric mixer until light and fluffy. Add egg yolks, one at a time, beating well after each addition. Add melted chocolate and vanilla, stirring until smooth.

Beat egg whites (at room temperature) at high speed of electric mixer until stiff peaks form. Fold egg whites and whipped cream into chocolate mixture; pour into prepared pan.

TO STORE: Cover and refrigerate at least 8 hours and up to 24 hours.

TO SERVE: Carefully remove sides from pan. Garnish, if desired. Yield: 8 servings.

Supper After the Theater

Royal Seafood Casserole

Colorful Squash Marinade

Pinwheel Wheat Rolls

Orange Crème Cups

Celebrity Champagne Cocktail

Serves 6

For a fitting encore to an evening at the theater, invite friends over for an elegant late-night supper. The stars of the menu can be prepared ahead and served 30 to 45 minutes after guests arrive.

Royal Seafood Casserole

6 cups water
1½ pounds unpeeled
  medium-size fresh shrimp
½ (7-ounce) package vermicelli
  or thin spaghetti
⅓ cup butter or margarine
⅓ cup all-purpose flour
⅔ cup chicken broth
⅔ cup whipping cream
¾ cup (3 ounces) shredded
  Swiss cheese
2½ tablespoons dry sherry
½ teaspoon salt
⅛ teaspoon ground white
  pepper
1 (4-ounce) jar diced pimiento,
  drained
2 tablespoons grated Parmesan
  cheese
2 tablespoons slivered almonds
Garnish: chopped fresh parsley

Bring water to a boil; add shrimp, and cook 3 to 5 minutes. Drain well; rinse shrimp with cold water. Peel and devein shrimp; set aside.

Cook vermicelli according to package directions; drain well, and set aside.

Melt butter in a heavy saucepan over low heat; add flour, stirring until smooth. Cook 1 minute, stirring constantly. Gradually add broth and cream; cook over medium heat, stirring constantly, until mixture is thickened and bubbly. Add Swiss cheese, sherry, salt, and pepper, stirring until cheese melts. Remove from heat; add shrimp, vermicelli, and pimiento, stirring gently.

Spoon mixture into a lightly greased 2-quart casserole. Sprinkle with Parmesan cheese and almonds.

TO STORE: Cover and refrigerate up to 24 hours.

TO SERVE: Bake, uncovered, at 350° for 20 minutes or until thoroughly heated. Broil 6 inches from heat 6 minutes or until lightly browned. Garnish, if desired. Yield: 6 servings.

Entertaining friends after the show is easy with rich Royal Seafood Casserole and Pinwheel Wheat Rolls.

Give squash an updated flavor and appearance when you serve Colorful Squash Marinade.

Colorful Squash Marinade

3 small yellow squash, thinly sliced
3 small zucchini, thinly sliced
1 large sweet red pepper, cut into thin strips
¼ cup chopped green onions
¼ cup vegetable oil
3 tablespoons vinegar
½ teaspoon salt
½ teaspoon pepper
⅛ teaspoon garlic powder
Curly leaf lettuce

Combine squash, zucchini, red pepper, and green onions; toss gently. Combine oil and next 4 ingredients; mix well, and pour over vegetables.

TO STORE: Refrigerate in a tightly covered container at least 8 hours and up to 2 days, stirring occasionally.

TO SERVE: Spoon mixture into a lettuce-lined bowl, using a slotted spoon. Yield: 6 servings.

Pinwheel Wheat Rolls

2 packages dry yeast
1¾ cups warm water (105° to 115°)
½ cup sugar
1 teaspoon salt
¼ cup butter or margarine, melted
1 egg, lightly beaten
2¼ cups whole wheat flour
2½ to 3 cups all-purpose flour
Melted butter

Dissolve yeast in warm water in a large bowl; let stand 5 minutes. Add sugar and next 4 ingredients; beat at medium speed of an electric mixer 2 minutes. Gradually stir in enough all-purpose flour to make a soft dough.

Turn dough out onto a well-floured surface, and knead until smooth and elastic (about 5 minutes). Place dough in a well-greased bowl, turning to grease top. Cover and let rise in a warm place (85°), free from drafts, 1 hour or until dough is doubled in bulk.

Punch dough down; cover and let rise in a warm place, free from drafts, 45 minutes or until doubled in bulk.

Punch dough down; turn out onto a lightly floured surface, and knead lightly 4 or 5 times. Divide dough in half; roll each portion to a 14- x 6-inch rectangle. Cut each rectangle into 12 (7- x 1-inch) strips. Roll each strip into a spiral, and place in well-greased muffin pans.

Brush rolls with melted butter. Let rise, uncovered, in a warm place, free from drafts, 40 minutes or until doubled in bulk. Bake at 400° for 8 minutes; remove from pans, and cool on wire racks.

TO STORE: Freeze partially baked rolls in a labeled airtight container up to 1 month.

TO SERVE: Thaw at room temperature 20 minutes. Place rolls on ungreased baking sheets, and bake at 400° for 7 minutes or until golden brown. Brush with melted butter. Yield: 2 dozen.

Orange Crème Cups

1 cup milk
1 cup whipping cream
1 cup sugar
2 tablespoons grated orange rind
¼ cup orange juice
6 small oranges

Combine milk, whipping cream, and sugar in a medium bowl; stir until sugar dissolves. Cover and freeze 2 hours. Add orange rind and juice; beat at medium speed of an electric mixer 3 to 5 minutes or until thickened.

TO STORE: Cover tightly, and freeze at least 24 hours and up to 2 weeks.

TO SERVE: Cut off top one-fourth of each orange; discard tops. Carefully scoop out pulp. (Reserve pulp for other uses.) Scoop orange crème into orange cups. Serve immediately. Yield: 6 servings.

Celebrity Champagne Cocktail

¾ cup lemon juice
3 tablespoons Grand Marnier or
  other orange-flavored liqueur
3 tablespoons vodka
3 tablespoons sugar
Crushed ice
Champagne
Garnish: lemon rind curls

Combine lemon juice, liqueur, vodka, and sugar; stir until sugar dissolves.

TO STORE: Refrigerate in a tightly covered container up to 2 weeks.

TO SERVE: Place 3 tablespoons lemon juice mixture into each of six 6-ounce stemmed cocktail glasses. Add crushed ice, and fill with champagne. Garnish, if desired. Yield: 6 servings.

Cocktail Buffet for Forty

Beef Tenderloin with Horseradish Spread

Cocktail rolls

Salmon Mousse

Assorted crackers

Marinated Mushrooms and Artichokes

Fruit and Cheese Logs

Double Cheese Wafers

Rosy Herb Dip

Assorted crudités

Mixed nuts

Cocktails   Beer   Wine

Serves 40

A large cocktail party is the perfect "entertaining opportunity" for the busy host or hostess to resolve any overdue social obligations. Assemble a lively group of friends and acquaintances, and set out an impressive spread of tempting finger foods. Efficient planning and these make-ahead foods will leave you relaxed and ready to join the party.

Beef Tenderloin with Horseradish Spread makes hearty yet elegant little sandwiches when served on cocktail rolls.

Beef Tenderloin with Horseradish Spread

¾ cup vegetable oil
½ cup soy sauce
⅓ cup firmly packed brown
    sugar
¼ cup red wine vinegar
2 cloves garlic, crushed
2 teaspoons ground ginger
½ teaspoon ground coriander
1 (5- to 6-pound) beef
    tenderloin, trimmed
2 teaspoons pepper
Commercial cocktail rolls
Horseradish Spread
Garnishes: fluted mushrooms
    and fresh watercress sprigs

Combine first 7 ingredients; stir well. Place tenderloin in a large shallow dish; add marinade. Cover; refrigerate up to 8 hours, turning tenderloin occasionally.

Remove tenderloin from marinade, reserving marinade. Place marinade in a saucepan. Bring to a boil; reduce heat, and simmer 5 minutes. Place tenderloin on a rack in a roasting pan; sprinkle with pepper. Insert meat thermometer into thickest portion of tenderloin. Bake at 425° for 30 minutes. Reduce heat to 375°; bake 25 minutes or until thermometer registers 140° (rare) or 160° (medium), basting frequently with marinade. Cool.

TO STORE: Refrigerate in a tightly covered container up to 24 hours.

TO SERVE: Thinly slice tenderloin across grain. Serve warm or cold with cocktail rolls and Horseradish Spread. Garnish, if desired. Yield: 40 appetizer servings.

Horseradish Spread

1 (3-ounce) package
    lemon-flavored gelatin
½ cup boiling water
1 tablespoon vinegar
¼ teaspoon salt
¾ cup prepared horseradish
⅛ teaspoon hot sauce
1 cup whipping cream, whipped

Dissolve gelatin in boiling water; stir in vinegar and salt. Chill until consistency of unbeaten egg white. Stir in horseradish and hot sauce; fold in whipped cream. Pour mixture into a lightly oiled 3-cup mold.

TO STORE: Cover spread, and refrigerate until set and up to 2 days.

TO SERVE: Unmold onto a serving plate. Yield: 3 cups.

Salmon Mousse

2 envelopes unflavored gelatin
½ cup cold water
1 (15½-ounce) can red salmon, drained
1 cup mayonnaise
2 tablespoons vinegar
2 tablespoons catsup
Dash of ground red pepper
Dash of pepper
15 pimiento-stuffed olives, sliced
2 hard-cooked eggs, chopped
2 tablespoons sweet pickle relish
1 cup whipping cream, whipped
Flowering cabbage
Garnishes: lemon slices and chopped fresh parsley

Sprinkle gelatin over cold water in a small saucepan; let stand 1 minute. Cook over low heat, stirring until gelatin dissolves. Remove from heat, and set aside.

Remove skin and bones from salmon, if desired; flake salmon with a fork. Combine salmon and next 5 ingredients; stir well. Add reserved gelatin mixture, olives, egg, and relish; stir well. Gently fold in whipped cream. Spoon mixture into a well-greased 5½-cup mold.

TO STORE: Cover and refrigerate up to 2 days.

TO SERVE: Unmold onto a serving plate lined with flowering cabbage. Garnish, if desired. Serve with assorted crackers. Yield: 5½ cups.

Marinated Mushrooms and Artichokes

2 pounds small fresh mushrooms
2 (14-ounce) cans artichoke hearts, drained and quartered
½ cup olive oil
¼ cup vegetable oil
½ cup white wine vinegar
½ cup lemon juice
3 cloves garlic, minced
1 tablespoon chopped fresh parsley
1 teaspoon salt
1 teaspoon crushed red pepper
1 teaspoon dried whole basil
1 teaspoon dried whole oregano
½ teaspoon dried whole thyme
Garnish: fresh basil sprig

Combine mushrooms and artichokes in a large bowl. Combine olive oil and next 10 ingredients; stir well. Pour marinade over mushrooms and artichokes, tossing gently to coat.

TO STORE: Refrigerate in a tightly covered container up to 3 days, stirring occasionally.

TO SERVE: Spoon mixture into a serving bowl, using a slotted spoon. Garnish, if desired. Yield: about 8½ cups.

Salmon Mousse and Marinated Mushrooms and Artichokes are eye-catching additions to your cocktail buffet table.

Fruit and Cheese Logs

2 (8-ounce) packages cream
  cheese, softened
½ cup finely chopped dried
  apricots
½ cup chopped dates
2 tablespoons Grand Marnier or
  other orange-flavored liqueur
2 teaspoons grated orange rind
1½ cups finely chopped
  hazelnuts, toasted

Combine first 5 ingredients; stir well. Divide mixture in half. Spoon each half of mixture onto a large piece of wax paper, and shape into an 8-inch log. Roll each log in hazelnuts; wrap in wax paper.

TO STORE: Refrigerate up to 2 days.

TO SERVE: Slice logs, and serve with assorted crackers. Yield: two 8-inch logs.

Double Cheese Wafers

¾ cup butter or margarine,
  softened
⅔ cup shredded Cheddar cheese
⅔ cup crumbled Roquefort
  cheese
2 cups all-purpose flour
2 teaspoons minced fresh chives
1 teaspoon minced fresh parsley
½ teaspoon Worcestershire
  sauce
¼ teaspoon ground red pepper
⅛ teaspoon garlic powder
1 cup sesame seeds, toasted

Cream butter; add cheeses, and beat at medium speed of an electric mixer until well blended. Add flour and next 5 ingredients; mix well. Shape dough into a ball; cover and refrigerate at least 2 hours.

Shape dough into ¾-inch balls; roll in sesame seeds. Place on lightly greased baking sheets, and flatten to ¼-inch thickness with a fork, making a crisscross pattern. Bake at 350° for 12 to 14 minutes or until edges are golden brown. Cool on wire racks.

TO STORE: Refrigerate wafers in a tightly covered container up to 3 days. Freeze in a labeled airtight container up to 1 month.

TO SERVE: Thaw wafers at room temperature. Yield: about 7 dozen.

Rosy Herb Dip

2 cups sour cream
1 (3-ounce) package cream
  cheese, softened
3 tablespoons tomato paste
3 tablespoons finely chopped
  onion
2 tablespoons chopped fresh
  parsley
1 clove garlic, minced
1 teaspoon sugar
1 teaspoon dried whole basil
1 teaspoon dried whole dillweed
¼ teaspoon salt
¼ teaspoon ground white
  pepper

Combine all ingredients in a medium bowl; stir well.

TO STORE: Refrigerate dip in a tightly covered container up to 2 days.

TO SERVE: Spoon dip into a serving bowl. Serve with assorted crudités. Yield: about 2⅔ cups.

Serve Rosy Herb Dip with a large platter of colorful fresh vegetables.

Freezer Guide

The storage times stated in this chart are for optimum taste and quality. Some items may be stored longer, but the quality will not be as superior.

Breads

Brown-and-serve rolls

TO FREEZE: Prepare rolls as directed. Bake at 325° for 10 to 15 minutes (do not let brown); cool. Wrap in moisture/vapor-proof material, or place in an airtight container. Seal and label. *Storage time: up to 2 months.*

TO SERVE: Unwrap and thaw at room temperature 15 minutes. Bake at 350° for 15 to 20 minutes or until golden brown.

Coffee cakes, sweet rolls, baked

TO FREEZE: Wrap in moisture/vapor-proof material, or place in an airtight container. Seal and label. *Storage time: up to 1 month.*

TO SERVE: Thaw at room temperature. Wrap in aluminum foil. Bake at 325° for 15 to 20 minutes or until warm.

Crêpes

TO FREEZE: Stack crêpes, separating each with wax paper to prevent sticking. Wrap in moisture/vapor-proof material, or place in an airtight container. Seal and label. *Storage time: up to 1 month.*

TO SERVE: Thaw, wrapped, at room temperature.

Muffins, baked

TO FREEZE: Wrap in moisture/vapor-proof material, or place in an airtight container. Seal and label. *Storage time: up to 1 month.*

TO SERVE: Wrap frozen muffins in aluminum foil. Bake at 350° for 20 to 25 minutes or until warm.

Quick breads, baked

TO FREEZE: Wrap in moisture/vapor-proof material, or place in an airtight container. Seal and label. *Storage time: up to 1 month.*

TO SERVE: Unwrap and thaw at room temperature 2 hours before serving.

Yeast bread loaves, baked

TO FREEZE: Wrap in moisture/vapor-proof material, or place in an airtight container. Seal and label. *Storage time: up to 1 month.*

TO SERVE: Unwrap and thaw at room temperature 3 hours before serving.

Yeast rolls, baked

TO FREEZE: Wrap in moisture/vapor-proof material, or place in an airtight container. Seal and label. *Storage time: up to 1 month.*

TO SERVE: Wrap frozen rolls in aluminum foil. Bake at 350° for 15 to 20 minutes or until warm.

Cakes

Frosted cakes

TO FREEZE: Chill frosted cake in freezer until frosting is firm. Wrap cake in moisture/vapor-proof material, or place in an airtight container. Seal and label. *Storage time: up to 2 months.*

TO SERVE: Unwrap immediately, and thaw at room temperature.

Layer cakes

TO FREEZE: Remove cake layers from pans. Wrap each layer separately in moisture/vapor-proof material, or place in an airtight container. Seal and label. *Storage time: up to 1 month.*

TO SERVE: Thaw, wrapped, at room temperature.

Pound cakes

TO FREEZE: Wrap cooled pound cake in moisture/vapor-proof material, or place in an airtight container. Seal and label. *Storage time: up to 1 month.*

TO SERVE: Thaw, wrapped, at room temperature.

Candies, Cookies, and Nuts

Candy, fondant, fudge

TO FREEZE: Place candy in an airtight container. Seal and label. *Storage time: up to 6 months.*

TO SERVE: Thaw at room temperature.

Cookies, baked

TO FREEZE: Place cookies in a rigid airtight container or zip-top plastic bag, separating layers with wax paper. Place the plastic bag in a box or tin to prevent breakage. Seal and label. *Storage time: up to 1 month.*

TO SERVE: Thaw at room temperature.

Cookies, unbaked

TO FREEZE: Dough for slice-and-bake cookies can be shaped into rolls. Wrap rolls in wax paper, then wrap in moisture/vapor-proof material, or place in an airtight container. Seal and label. *Storage time: up to 1 month.*

TO SERVE: Cut rolls into slices, and bake as directed.

Nuts

TO FREEZE: Place nuts in an airtight container. Seal and label. *Storage time: up to 8 months.*

TO SERVE: Remove from freezer as needed.

Dairy Products

Egg whites

TO FREEZE: Place 1 egg white in each section of an ice cube tray. Cover tightly and label. *Storage time: up to 1 month.*

TO SERVE: Thaw in refrigerator.

Dairy Products (*continued*) _____

Egg yolks

TO FREEZE: For dessert recipes, add 1 teaspoon sugar to each yolk. For sauces and egg dishes, add ½ teaspoon salt to each yolk. Place in an airtight container; seal and label. *Storage time: up to 3 weeks.*

TO SERVE: Thaw in refrigerator.

Whipped cream

TO FREEZE: Drop spoonfuls of whipped cream onto an aluminum foil-lined baking sheet; place in freezer. When frozen, store in a rigid airtight container, separating layers with wax paper. Seal and label. *Storage time: up to 1 month.*

TO SERVE: Place frozen spoonfuls of whipped cream on dessert, and allow to thaw until serving time.

Main-Dish Casseroles _____

Meat casseroles with pasta, vegetables

TO FREEZE: Prepare dish as directed, undercooking slightly. Cool quickly. Cover with moisture/vapor-proof material, or place in an airtight container. Seal and label. *Storage time: up to 1 month.*

TO SERVE: Thaw in refrigerator. Bake as directed.

Meats _____

Beef, veal, lamb, pork, cooked

TO FREEZE: Large cuts of meat dry out the least. Cover sliced meats with gravy or sauces, if possible, to retain moisture. Wrap meat in moisture/vapor-proof material, or place in an airtight container. Seal and label. *Storage time: up to 3 months.*

TO SERVE: Thaw in refrigerator. Defrost time will depend on size and amount of meat.

Country ham

TO FREEZE: An unsliced ham will keep longer than sliced ham. Wrap meat in moisture/vapor-proof material, or place in an airtight container. Seal and label. *Storage time: up to 3 months.*

TO SERVE: Thaw in refrigerator. Defrost time will depend on size and amount of meat.

Meatballs, meat loaf, cooked

TO FREEZE: Freeze meatballs in sauce to retain moisture. Wrap cooled meat in moisture/vapor-proof material, or place in an airtight container. Seal and label. *Storage time: up to 1 month.*

TO SERVE: Thaw in refrigerator. Wrap meat loaf in aluminum foil, and bake at 325° for 40 minutes or until thoroughly heated. Cook meatballs and sauce in a saucepan over medium heat 10 minutes or until thoroughly heated.

Meat pies

TO FREEZE: Cook meat and vegetables; cool quickly. Place in dish(es), and top with pastry. Cut slits in crust to allow steam to escape. Wrap pie(s) in moisture/vapor-proof material, or place in an airtight container. Seal and label. *Storage time: up to 1 month.*

TO SERVE: Bake at 400° for 45 minutes or until crust is golden.

Pies

Fruit, unbaked

TO FREEZE: Toss fruit with ascorbic acid or lemon juice to prevent darkening. Wrap prepared pie in heavy-duty aluminum foil; label. *Storage time: up to 1 month.*

TO SERVE: Bake as directed, shielding edges of pie with aluminum foil as necessary to prevent browning.

Ice cream with crumb crust

TO FREEZE: Wrap prepared pie in moisture/vapor-proof material, or place pie in an airtight container. Seal and label. *Storage time: up to 1 week.*

TO SERVE: Thaw, uncovered, at room temperature 20 to 30 minutes or until easy to cut, but slightly frozen.

Pastry shells, baked

TO FREEZE: Place dish containing baked pastry shell in freezer. When frozen, remove and stack shells in a rigid covered container, or store, covered, in disposable foil pans. *Storage time: up to 1 month.*

TO SERVE: Thaw, uncovered, at room temperature. Fill and serve as directed.

Pastry shells, unbaked

TO FREEZE: Prepare pastry as directed, and place in pieplate. Wrap in moisture/vapor-proof material, or place in an airtight container. Seal and label. *Storage time: up to 2 months.*

TO SERVE: Thaw slightly, uncovered, at room temperature. Follow specific baking instructions for the type of pie being baked.

Poultry

Chicken, turkey, cooked

TO FREEZE: Remove stuffing from cooked poultry before freezing. Wrap poultry in moisture/vapor-proof material, or place in an airtight container. Seal and label. *Storage time: up to 3 months.*

TO SERVE: Thaw in refrigerator. Defrost time will depend on size and amount of poultry.

Sandwiches

Cheese, meat, peanut butter

TO FREEZE: Wrap sandwiches in moisture/vapor-proof material, or place sandwiches in an airtight container. Seal and label. *Storage time: up to 2 weeks.*

TO SERVE: Thaw before serving. Some meat and cheese sandwiches may need to be thawed in the refrigerator.

Soups and Stews

Vegetable soups and stews

TO FREEZE: Select vegetables that freeze well; omit potatoes. Place cooled soup or stew in a labeled airtight container. Seal and label. *Storage time: up to 1 month.*

TO SERVE: Thaw in refrigerator. Heat in a large pan over medium-high heat until thoroughly heated, stirring occasionally.

Recipe Index

Photographers and Stylists

Photography by Ralph Anderson; styling by Kay E.
Clarke.

Additional photography by Jim Bathie, pages 18, 22,
25, 28, 30, 33, 38, 41, 194, 201, 203, 225, 226, 229;
additional styling by Virginia R. Cravens, pages 194,
201, 203, 225, 226, 229.